An introduction to working with children

An introduction to working with children

A guide for social workers

Matthew Colton,
Robert Sanders and
Margaret Williams

palgrave

First published 2001 by
PALGRAVE
Houndmills, Basingstoke, Hampshire RG21 6XS and
175 Fifth Avenue, New York, N.Y. 10010
Companies and representatives throughout the world

PALGRAVE is the new global academic imprint of
St. Martin's Press LLC Scholarly and Reference Division and
Palgrave Publishers Ltd (formerly Macmillan Press Ltd).

ISBN 0–333–69308–6

This book is printed on paper suitable for recycling and made from fully managed and sustained forest sources.

A catalogue record for this book is available from the British Library.

10 9 8 7 6 5 4
10 09 08 07 06 05 04

Printed in Great Britain by
Creative Print and Design, Ebbw Vale (Wales)

Table of Contents

List of Tables

List of Figures

Exercises and Case Examples

CHAPTER 1

The origins and contexts of contemporary child welfare

To understand the forces that drive child welfare today, it is necessary to look at the forces that have shaped it in the past. You may groan at the thought of beginning your study of child welfare with a history lesson. You may secretly believe that it doesn't matter what the Victorians did: the world has changed so much that the issues of the nineteenth century are totally irrelevant to us today. In some fields, you may be right, but in the field of child welfare the same issues reoccur generation after generation because they are not matters of fact to be discovered and resolved but matters of judgement, perspective and belief. What rights should a child have, for example? (*answer*: none, if you regard a child as property.) What rights should a parent have? What rights should society have? Whose rights take precedence in the case of conflict? Who decides whose rights take precedence? Through what process? Based on what criteria?

We need to know how these questions were answered in the past and why they were answered that way and what the consequences were of answering them like that. Then, we might be able to avoid making the same mistakes again. Then, we might be able to recognise that there are fashions in child welfare as there are in everything else: the pendulum swings from removing children (to save them from bad parents) to keeping children in their homes (to avoid the traumatic psychological effects of separation), back to removal (often following a tragedy to a child at home) and back again to an emphasis on speedy reunification with the birth family. With each new swing, the knowledge and wisdom so painfully acquired in the previous swing are lost. With each new swing, we start again, more in a spirit of revolutionary fervour than in a balanced effort to improve what went before.

Accordingly, in this chapter, we will begin by tracing the history of child welfare from Victorian times through to the most recent major piece of child-care legislation: the Children Act 1989. We will continue with a discussion of the social and economic context of child welfare today, and conclude with an overview of the ways that child-welfare workers interact with children, families and organisations.

Objectives

It is always a good idea to know what you are reading a chapter for. You were told to read it – very good – but what exactly is it supposed to teach you? This chapter should help you to understand the origins and key elements of the Children Act 1989. It should enable you to explore the vital balance between promoting children's rights, protecting children and respecting parents' rights. It should give you a beginning understanding of the social worker's role in relation to children and families.

The development of child-welfare services

Victorian child welfare

An issue that confronts people today as it did in Victorian times is the treatment of the able-bodied unemployed. Will giving them money for their keep while they stay at home encourage them in idleness? The Victorians thought so. In 1834, they passed the Poor Law Amendment Act, which stated that the able bodied would receive their keep only if they entered the workhouse. The aim of the Act was to force the unemployed to seek employment, to eradicate 'out-relief' (benefits provided to people living at home), and to generally deter applications for social assistance. To this end, conditions in the workhouse were made as harsh as possible. Husbands and wives were separated; inmates lost the right to vote; and compulsory work routines were boring, unpleasant and physically hard. This calculated use of cruelty caused much misery, but failed in its central purpose: to deter applications for social support. Holman (1988) notes that the number of workhouse inmates rose from 78,000 in 1838 to 306,000 by 1848. Nevertheless, many preferred literally to starve rather than enter the work-house, and the Poor Law was detested and feared by working-class people until it was abolished in 1948.

The notable philanthropist Dr Barnardo identified two failings in the pro-vision of child care under the Poor Law. First, its deterrent nature resulted in hundreds of destitute children struggling to survive on the streets. (Preferring to starve meant preferring to have your children starve with you.) Secondly, for those who were compelled to go there, the regimes in the large barracks-like workhouses deprived children of their individuality and rights, and completely failed to prepare them for life in the outside world.

The obvious need to provide more humane forms of care led to the foun-dation of a number of voluntary child-care societies in the second half of the nineteenth century, many of them started by individual philanthropists. These voluntary societies believed that their task was to rescue children from bad environments, including 'bad parents', and provide them with a fresh start. Often, the fresh start involved a placement overseas. Between 1867 and 1906, Barnardo's alone sent 18,645 children abroad (Holman, 1988). All the large child-care societies shipped children overseas to desti-nations such as Canada, Australia and New Zealand. The boys usually became farm labourers and most of the girls were placed in domestic ser-vice. Despite the suffering caused to families and the evident unhappiness of many of the children concerned, the practice of child emigration contin-ued until after the Second World War.

Although the voluntary societies were established as a direct response to perceived flaws in the Poor Law, the state and voluntary sectors had much in common. Both sectors stigmatised the receipt of help. Both held that children in need, who were always the children of the poor, should be removed from the unfortunate influence of idle and evil parents. Neither sector was concerned with maintaining contact between children and par-ents. Neither entertained the notion that help provided in their own homes might prevent children from entering institutions in the first place. Of course, from the state's perspective, such help would have constituted the very out-relief that the Poor Law was designed to abolish.

Postwar children's departments

The hostile attitude towards birth parents which characterised the child-care system during the Victorian era changed little until the arrival of the

Children Act 1948. This Act created Children's Departments, and adopted an altogether more humane approach to the care of separated children, including provision for reuniting children with their birth parents.

Although the Act itself did not mention the concept of prevention, the new staff responsible for the Children's Departments (a Children's Officer and Child-Care Officers in each department) formed professional associations that campaigned for powers to intervene with families to prevent their children being taken into care. The case for prevention was fuelled by the comprehensive social-welfare legislation introduced in the 1940s by the Labour government. This provided the more favourable socio-economic context needed for preventive work. Concern about the high costs of residential care and the high rates of fostering breakdown, together with Bowlby's (1952) theories about the deleterious effects of maternal deprivation (which we will discuss in more detail in Chapter 2), provided a further impetus. In addition, The Children and Young Persons (Amendment) Act 1952 required Children's Departments to act on any information indicating that a child was in need of care and protection, whether or not the neglect was 'wilful'. Thus, by the mid-1950s, most Children's Departments were actively working to prevent the admission of children into care (Packman, 1975).

At the same time, concern centred on another facet of preventive work: preventing delinquency. The Ingleby Report viewed delinquency as a consequence of family problems, to be considered by the courts in the context of the family (*Report of the Committee on Children and Young Persons*, 1960). One of the recommendations of the Ingleby Report became Section 1 of the Children and Young Persons Act 1963. This Section placed a duty on social workers to help any family whose children were in need but were not in the care of the local authority. The Children's Departments thus moved from providing a rescue service to promoting the welfare of children by working with the family as a whole. This role was supported by the later Children and Young Persons Act 1969. Though never fully implemented, the 1969 Act attempted to do three things: integrate methods for dealing with deprived and with delinquent youngsters (since delinquency was now viewed as a consequence of deprivation); reduce the role of criminal proceedings in dealing with young people; and assign responsibility for both the prevention and treatment of delinquency to the Children's Departments.

Reorganisation of the personal social services

Respected though the Children's Departments appear to have been, they were relatively short-lived. On 1 April 1971, the Local Authority Social Services Act came into operation, and the Children's Departments were incorporated into single, generic, social services departments (SSDs), together with other previously separate local authority departments such as those for welfare and mental health. This amalgamation had been recommended by the Seebohm Committee (*Report of the Committee on Local Authority and Allied Services*, 1968). In fact, this was perhaps the only recommendation of note from the Committee's visionary report that reached the statute book. The Seebohm Report urged much more than the mere reorganisation of the personal social services. It included a whole chapter on the prevention of social distress; it wanted services to be accessible to communities; it argued that communities should participate in the running of services, and that services should be directed toward the well-being of whole communities and not only to social casualties.

None of this came to pass. Moreover, many soon came to believe that the reorganisation of the personal social services had led to a deterioration in the quality of children's services. For example, it was felt that insufficient attention was devoted to prevention and rehabilitation, and that social workers had lost the skills required to place children with good quality substitute parents. These failings were attributed to the negative impact of the generic approach to social work, staff changes, pressure of work, and the large size and complexity of the new SSDs (Parker, 1980).

Greater demands were also placed on social workers by rising poverty and deprivation in the 1970s (Townsend, 1979). SSDs were obliged to ration services, focusing on providing protection to children who had already been neglected or abused rather than undertaking preventive work. Increasingly, social workers came to be perceived by service users as withholders rather than distributors of resources (National Institute of Social Work, 1982).

The permanency movement

The standing of social workers and the case for prevention were further undermined by other significant events that took place in the 1970s. These included the tragic death of six-year-old Maria Colwell, who was killed by her stepfather after being removed from foster care and reunited with her birth mother. Maria's death sparked a media onslaught against social workers, who were accused of worshipping the 'blood tie' between children and birth parents, to the point where the rights of the birth parents were put before the rights of the foster parents or the child (Parton, 1985). The publication in 1973 of Rowe and Lambert's book *Children Who Wait* was also influential. These authors reported that large numbers of children were allowed to 'drift in care' without decisions being taken to ensure their permanent futures (Rowe and Lambert, 1973). Holman (1988) considers that the book was unfairly used as ammunition by the growing adoption lobby, who saw adoption as an answer to drift and as an ultimate form of permanency. Nevertheless, Maria's appalling death after removal from a stable foster home, combined with Rowe and Lambert's book, did seem to suggest that children were at risk from inadequate birth parents and could and should be placed with substitute parents.

The thrust towards permanent removal of children from their birth parents was supported by those who believed that children need a single set of parents in order to be emotionally stable (Goldstein et al., 1973, 1979). It was further fuelled by the 'cycle of deprivation' theory that was much favoured by Sir Keith Joseph, the then Minister of State for Social Services. This theory identified child abuse as primarily a problem of the lower social classes, and claimed that inadequate parents pass on their weaknesses to their children, who reproduce them in the next generation. You might note an echo here of the 'idle and evil' parents from whom children were being saved the century before.

However, there were a number of organisations which opposed the government's intention to make permanence a central part of child-care policy. These included the Family Rights Group, the Child Poverty Action Group, the National Council of One Parent Families, Gingerbread, MIND and the British Association of Social Workers. Despite the efforts of these bodies, the Children Act 1975 clearly reflected the philosophies of the permanency movement. The 1975 Act gave SSDs much greater control over the lives of children in their care, facilitated an easier severance of parental links, and gave greater security to children in their substitute homes (Parton, 1985).

The permanency doctrine, coupled with further child-abuse inquiries throughout the 1970s, changed social-work practice. Most SSDs set up child-abuse registers, area review committees, and special training for practitioners. A large number of SSDs formulated policies designed to operationalise permanency. For example, specialist fostering and adoption units were created to find permanent homes for 'children who wait'. The Departments were also more willing to assume 'parental rights'. According to Holman (1988), a higher proportion of parents had lost their say in their children's lives by the end of the 1970s than at any other time, including the reign of the Poor Law.

Immediate origins of the Children Act 1989

Those who opposed the permanency movement continued to campaign for a more preventive approach to vulnerable families, and against injustices suffered by birth parents. In the early 1980s, the Family Rights Group demonstrated a need for a change in the law by compiling a dossier of cases in which birth parents had unjustly been deprived of their parental rights. In 1984, a High Court judge argued that the law was being manipulated against birth parents and in favour of adoptive parents (Hill and Aldgate, 1996, p. 5).

The Social Services Committee of the House of Commons, chaired by Renée Short MP, launched an inquiry. The Short Report (House of Commons, 1984) argued that the emphasis on permanency had inhibited the development of policies and practices that would enable parents either to look after their own children permanently or to maintain links with them in long-term care. It recommended a range of measures to support and protect parents and to reunite children in care with their families. It also supported the concept of a family court as the most suitable environment for making decisions about children's lives. Logically enough, given the emphasis on the family court, the report called for a major review of the legal framework of child care.

At roughly the same time as the Short Report was published, an influential series of nine research projects commissioned by the Department of Health came to fruition. An anthology was published, entitled *Social Work Decisions in Child Care*, which drew together the findings from these studies (Department of Health and Social Security (DHSS), 1985a). In a praiseworthy effort to communicate research findings to policy-makers and practitioners, the anthology was widely circulated and became known as the 'Pink Book'. The Pink Book showed that it was becoming more difficult for vulnerable families to receive help and support, while, at the same time, local authorities were showing an increasing readiness to take compulsory action in relation to children (Hill and Aldgate, 1996). One of the studies revealed that children in foster and residential care often quickly lost contact with their birth parents, although maintenance of such contact was associated with an early return home (Millham et al., 1986). Another study showed that the majority of parents whose children were placed away from home were willing and able to care for their own children, once given the opportunity (Fisher et al., 1986).

Together, these studies highlighted the need for partnership with parents and provided examples of successful partnerships between parents and social workers. In some cases, social workers were able to help parents retain their role as responsible authority figures in relation to their children. If short-term care were necessary, it need not be viewed negatively in terms of failure, but should rather be regarded as a positive way to prevent the permanent break-up of families by providing temporary relief (DHSS, 1985a, p. 16). Given such a positive viewpoint, social workers were able to facilitate parental involvement in the processes, negotiations and family dynamics related to admission and discharge (DHSS, 1985a, p. 20).

Drawing on examples of successful partnership efforts, the Pink Book emphasised the concepts of respite care, shared care and reunification.

In response to the Short Report and the Pink Book, the government established an interdepartmental committee whose findings led, in 1985, to the publication of a *Review of Child Care Law* (DHSS, 1985b). While the *Review* failed to consider the introduction of family courts and did not emphasise the role of primary prevention, it did follow the Short Report in emphasising the need to enable parents to keep or receive back their children. For example, the *Review* supported the notions of 'respite' and 'shared care'. It also recommended that local authority power to assume parental rights should be annulled, and that compulsory removals should need court approval. In addition, it recommended changes aimed at reducing the number of children in care. These included restricting the use of Place of Safety Orders and Interim Care Orders, and abolishing school non-attendance as a sole ground for making a care order. The *Review* also argued that, unless it was contrary to the interests of the children concerned, local authorities should have a duty to return separated children to their parents. Following from the *Review of Child Care Law*, the government produced a White Paper entitled *The Law on Child Care and Family Services*, which was published in January 1987 (House of Commons, 1987).

This move towards protecting the rights of parents was countered by the resurgence of widespread concern about the child-abuse deaths that occurred in the mid-1980s. Such tragedies drew attention to inadequate levels of protection for vulnerable children. The most publicised cases were those of Jasmine Beckford, Tyra Henry and Kimberley Carlile (see respectively, London Borough of Brent, 1985; London Borough of Lambeth, 1987; and London Borough of Greenwich, 1987). The deaths of these children underscored many of the issues highlighted in the case of Maria Colwell: the child's good relationship with her foster parents; the weak or non-existent bond with the natural mother; the problems surrounding the stepfather figure; the failure of welfare agencies to respond adequately to signs of abuse; and the failure to take notice of the child's wishes (Hendrick, 1994).

Jasmine Beckford and Tyra Henry were both in local authority care and both were killed after being returned to their natural families. The social workers in each case were perceived as 'being too naive and sentimental with parents, and failing to concentrate on the interests of the children and to use the statutory authority invested in them' (Parton, 1991, p. 75). By contrast, Kimberley Carlile was not in care and the report indicated that 'both the child care system and the law had failed the social worker(s) in their primary task. Both law and system were therefore seen as in need of major reform' (Parton, 1991, pp. 75–6). The report also recognised the difficulties and contradictions inherent in child-protection work in a liberal state. Nevertheless, in the final analysis, the primary blame and responsibility for Kimberley's death was felt to lie with the senior social worker carrying the case. This conclusion may be viewed as the inevitable outcome of the quasi-judicial way that child-abuse inquiries operate. Parton (1991, p. 77) argues that 'when an inquiry sets about its task in such individualistic and legalistic ways it will always find an individual – usually the frontline social worker – to hold responsible'.

In the wake of such inquiries, social-work policy and practice in relation to child abuse became rather conservative and defensive. Not surprisingly, it sought to minimise risk and avert the public furore associated with child deaths. Such a restricted and guarded approach to children and families contrasted sharply with the approach promoted by the Short Report, the research on decision-making in child care, and the *Review of Child Care Law* (Parton, 1991, p. 78).

This clash of perspectives was one of the factors that fed into the Cleveland controversy about child sexual abuse that occurred in mid-1987 (Parton, 1991, p. 78). In June 1987, prior to the publication of the Kimberley Carlile and Tyra Henry reports in December of that year, the media reported that an unusually large number of children, around 200, had been removed from their parents and placed into care. The social workers concerned had acted on the recommendation of two paediatricians who, using a newly developed physical test, had diagnosed the majority of the children as having been anally abused (La Fontaine, 1990). The local MP supported the distraught parents and raised the matter in Parliament. This led to the establishment of a public inquiry chaired by Mrs Justice Butler-Sloss (Butler-Sloss, 1988; Corby, 1993). Parton (1991, p. 79) observes that:

> if previous inquiries demonstrated that welfare professionals, particularly social workers, failed to protect the lives and interest of children and intervened too little too late into the private, the concerns focused around Cleveland seemed to demonstrate that professionals, this time paediatricians as well as social workers, failed to recognise the rights of parents and intervened too soon and in a too heavy-handed way into the family.

The Cleveland Report lent support to the legal framework set out in the White Paper, with modifications to reinforce the rights of parents and make more explicit the shift towards 'identifying the law itself as the crucial mechanism for both informing decision-making and resolving disputes' (Parton, 1991, p. 114).

This anguished push–pull between the right of children to be protected and the right of parents to autonomy was a major factor in the shaping of the Children Act 1989. One of the most important objectives of the Act was to strike a balance between the protection of children and the autonomy of the family. However, there were also other factors to be considered: for example, the previously separated and fragmented public and private laws regarding children. In this chapter so far, we have considered the influences associated with public law. With regard to private law, Hill and Aldgate (1996, pp. 4 and 5) note that throughout the 1980s there had been growing concern in the courts that children in divorce cases were victims of an adversarial approach which frequently severed their links with the non-custodial parent. Moreover, research had shown the adverse consequences that protracted court cases could have on the welfare of such children. The Act brought together public and private law.

A third factor concerned children with disabilities. Child abuse scandals and research on the variable quality of services for children with disabilities had highlighted the need for improved services for such children. The 1989 Act unified services caring for all children, including children with disabilities, those with special educational needs, those in boarding schools and those living in hospital on a long-term basis.

Key elements of the 1989 Act

The Children Act 1989 is widely seen as the most important piece of child-care law passed by the British Parliament for England and Wales in the twentieth century. The over-arching aims of the Act are to make the law concerning children easier to understand and use, more consistent across different situations, and more flexible. The Act is also intended to make the law more appropriate to the needs of children by promoting services for, and decisions about, children, young people and their families that are more child-centred (Open University, 1990).

The Department of Health (1989a, p. 1) states that the 'Act rests on the belief that children are best looked after within the family with both parents playing a full part and without resort to legal proceedings'. That belief is reflected in:

- the new concept of parental responsibility;
- the ability of unmarried fathers to share that responsibility by agreement with the mother;
- the local authorities' duty to give support for children and their families;
- the local authorities' duty to return a child looked after by them to the family unless this is against his or her interest;
- the local authorities' duty to ensure contact with the parents whenever possible for a child looked after by them away from home.

The new concept of parental responsibility replaces the notion of 'parental rights' and is intended to emphasise the obligations of parents towards their children. Parents are only given rights if they exercise responsibility. Additionally, the rights that parents have in relation to their children are for the purpose of enabling the parents to fulfil their parental responsibility in relation to their children (and not for their own benefit). Parental responsibility can be shared, thus allowing the inclusion of absent parents and other close relatives. For example, unmarried fathers may obtain parental responsibility, either by agreement with the mother or by court order (see Eekelaar and Dingwall, 1990).

The Act also acknowledges that parents may need support in fulfilling their responsibilities. Therefore, previously restricted notions of prevention are supplanted by 'family support' and local authorities are given a new duty to facilitate the upbringing of children by their parents. Moreover, the Act promotes partnership between parents and local authorities. Under the Act, local authorities can no longer assume parental rights or demand notice of a child's removal from 'accommodation'. Instead, they must work on the basis of negotiation and voluntary agreements. Where this fails and children are removed, parents must be kept fully informed and can only be denied access to their children in exceptional circumstances.

The Act also introduces new principles for court proceedings. The child's welfare is paramount and must be considered in the context of his or her physical, emotional and educational needs, age, gender, background and the capacity of caregivers to perform their task adequately. Further, when legal process becomes necessary, delay must be avoided: emergency protection orders must be of short duration and courts must work to timetables to prevent children suffering the adverse consequences of delay. In addition, no order should be made unless an order is considered preferable to no order at all. Finally, the child's voice must be heard: children's wishes and feelings must be taken into account when decisions are made.

The Act seeks a balance between children and parents, the state and families, courts and local authorities. Where power is unequal, the Act attempts to safeguard the weak. Thus, the needs of children are placed first because of their dependence and vulnerability, but parents and other significant adults are accorded increased respect and consideration (Packman and Jordan, 1991).

The Act makes specific reference to race, culture, language and religion as factors that must be considered in relation to the welfare of children. The Act confers a new duty on local authorities to take account of the different racial groups to which children in need belong when providing day care or accommodation. The Department of Health (1989b), *The Care of Children, Principles and Practice in Regulations and Guidance*, emphasises the special issues that arise for black children and young people and those from ethnic minority groups. It states that such children need to develop a positive self image that includes their cultural and ethnic origins, and that this must be taken into account by services planners and caregivers.

It should be noted that the law on the adoption of children (see Chapter 6) is little affected by the 1989 Act. In addition, more recent legislation in England and Wales has addressed youth justice (Criminal Justice Acts 1991 and 1993) and education (Education Act 1993). Nevertheless, the 1989 Children Act does represent the main legal context for social work with children in England and Wales, and deals with most areas of child care, including residential care, disability, day care, child abuse, and family support.

Scotland and, to some degree, Northern Ireland, have separate legal systems (Ruxton, 1996). Until recently, the central legislation concerning child care in Scotland was the Social Work (Scotland) Act 1968. This provided the legislative foundation for local authority social-work departments, and introduced a system of children's hearings (Tisdall, 1996). The Children (Scotland) Act 1995 has introduced new arrangements for protecting children at risk and caring for children and families in need. This was necessary as only part of the Children Act 1989 – that concerned with day care – applied to Scotland. A Children (Northern Ireland) Order has also been introduced. This is closely modelled on the Children Act 1989 for England and Wales (Kelly and Pinkerton, 1996).

Social work with children and families

Now that we have looked at the key elements of the 1989 Act, we come to the application of these key elements in working with children and families. Families perform the primary role in the socialisation of children. However, the nature of family life has undergone considerable change over recent decades (Allan, 1997). Knowledge of changing family forms and of the diverse nature of childhood experience is essential for effective social work. This is in part because there is an ideology about ideal family types and ideal childhoods of which workers need to be aware so that they do not attempt, consciously or implicitly, to impose these ideal types on the families they are working with.

Family trends

Ruxton (1996, p. 65) identifies the following major demographic and socio-economic changes that have influenced families throughout the European

Union (EU) over the past 20–30 years:

- a decline in the birth rate so that deaths outnumber births;
- a decline in the number of marriages, an increase in the period of time between marriage and the birth of the first child, and a rise in the number of divorces;
- an increase in cohabitation, especially in northern countries in the Community;
- an increase in life expectancy, and an ageing population;
- a diversification of family types, including a growth in stepfamilies and lone-parent families;
- a fall in the number of large families;
- an increase in women's employment, in particular on a part-time basis.

Ruxton (1996, p. 65) attributes these changes to a number of factors, including: economic restructuring and increasing labour-market flexibility; shifts in personal attitudes – particularly towards women's roles – resulting from the rise of feminism; increased control over fertility; the growth of multi-racial societies; increasing debate over gay and lesbian lifestyles; and the effects of government policies.

Most people in Europe live in private households. Households with a family can be classified as childless couples, couples with children, and lone parents with children. Lone parents can be grouped into four main categories: single, divorced, separated and widowed. Over the last 30 years there has been a dramatic rise in the number of lone-parent family households as a consequence of the rise in divorce rates, and the number of births outside marriage. Ireland has the highest proportion of lone-parent households in the EU (10.6 per cent), followed by Belgium (9.2 per cent) and the UK (9.0 per cent), while Finland (4.1 per cent) and Sweden (3.9 per cent) have the lowest proportions (Ruxton, 1996, p. 71).

In the UK, the increasing number of one-parent families has caused concern about the future of the family and, indeed, society. The number of divorces and one-parent families have more than doubled in the UK since 1971 (Dennis and Erdos, 1992). By 1993 the UK had by far the highest divorce rate in the EU at 3.1 per thousand of the population; Denmark and Sweden were second highest (Ruxton, 1996). Around 28 per cent of births in the UK now take place outside marriage, and each year the parents of an estimated 150,000 additional children under 16 are divorced (Dennis and Erdos, 1992).

For both left and right of the political spectrum the family is seen as the foundation stone of a free society; as the place where children learn voluntary restraint, respect for others and a sense of personal responsibility (Dennis and Erdos, 1992). From this perspective, the decline of the 'traditional family' and the rise in the numbers of single mothers is seen as having resulted in increased crime, violence and degradation (see Davies, Berger and Carlson, 1993).

Charles Murray (1990) has linked the growth in numbers of single unmarried mothers to what he regards as a developing British underclass comprised of persons who live outside the norms of social life, whose family ties are broken, who rely on welfare benefits rather than work, and who resort to crime and drugs. However, Brown (1990) has challenged Murray's assertion that single unmarried mothers constitute a special problem, arguing that divorced mothers as a group spend longer on benefit than unmarried mothers and that never-married mothers remain lone parents for a shorter average period than divorced mothers. Further, Walker (1990) contends that Murray's underclass thesis 'blames the victim' and, therefore, diverts attention from the true cause of the problem: the mechanisms through which resources are distributed.

The social construction of childhood

It may seem that it is quite easy to define childhood. Childhood is that period of time during which one is a child. Since being a child is a matter of biology, it would follow that childhood is a biological category and should vary little either culturally or historically (Stainton Rogers and Stainton Rogers, 1992). This easy assumption has been increasingly challenged over recent decades. In a seminal work entitled *Centuries of Childhood*, Ariès (1962) contended that in medieval society the idea of childhood did not exist.

> This is not to suggest that children were neglected, forsaken or despised. The idea of childhood is not to be confused with affection for children; it corresponds to an awareness of the particular nature of childhood, that particular nature which distinguishes the child from the adult, even the young adult. In medieval society, this awareness was lacking.
>
> (Ariès, 1962)

Whilst his methodology and conclusions have been challenged (Pollock, 1993; Cunningham, 1995), his material has strongly contributed to the developing notion of childhood as a social construct. Jenks (1982) as well notes that childhood is not a natural phenomenon, but rather a social construct: that is, we view children and relate to them differently depending on our theories about what children are like and what their role ought to be in society; and these theories change across cultures and over time. Jenks (1982) says:

> Children have always been with us. However, the manner of their recognition by adults and thus the form of their relationship with adults has

altered from epoch to epoch. They cannot be treated as invariant features of the social landscape. Their location emerges from a set of social relations of control, operating through a hierarchy and based on age. As a social category the child has come to us through time and this passage has accompanied changes in the economy, alterations in the structure of the family, the transition to industrialization and urbanization.

Hendrick (1994) begins his historical account of child welfare in England from 1872 to 1989 by surveying important social constructions of British childhood during the nineteenth century. In approximate chronological order, these were: the natural child, the Romantic child, the evangelical child, the factory child, the delinquent child, the schooled child and the psycho-medical child. Whilst not denying that these constructions are devoid of a biological dimension, or denying the effects of physical being, Hendrick (1994) considers that 'childhood' was, and is, composed by adults – mainly from the professional middle class.

To guide his analysis of child welfare, Hendrick employs two dualisms – mind/body and victim/threat. Much of the history of child-welfare policy has involved the imposition of adult will over children's bodies and minds. Equally, children have been variously presented as victims or threats throughout the course of the last two centuries. These dualisms were not ends in themselves but rather served as ordering categories by which child welfare could be justified or organised. According to Hendrick, their task was to transform children into investments of a racial, educational, familial, medical, social or political nature. Put another way, 'the health, welfare and rearing of children have been linked in thought and practice to the destiny of the nation and the responsibilities of the state' (Hendrick, 1994, p. 14).

Certainly, contemporary child-welfare policy and practice continue to reflect the concerns of the state. Fox Harding (1991) considers that in the UK, 'despite disputes, there seems to be a broad consensus about the *importance* of children and of the safeguarding of their welfare' (p. 4). However, there is a big difference between consensus around safeguarding children and allocation of resources to enhance their welfare. This may also be illustrated by the apparent difference in policy between enhancing the welfare of children *in their own right* (for example, in child protection) and enhancing their welfare within their family context (in family support).

Fox Harding (1991) has proposed a model of four possible ways of looking at child-care policy. She developed the following classification (p. 10), which also reflects a chronological development in our thinking about children and childhood.

1. *Laissez-faire and patriarchy*
People holding this perspective believe that power in the family should not be disturbed except in very extreme circumstances, and the role of the state should be a minimal one.

2. *State paternalism and child protection*
Here, there is a belief in the legitimacy of state intervention to protect children from their families; intervention may undervalue the biological family connections and be authoritarian in approach. In this perspective children are seen as essentially vulnerable and dependent.

3. *The modern defence of the birth family and parents' rights*
Intervention of the state is for the purpose of supporting families, helping to defend and preserve birth families. This perspective is critical of the lack of emphasis on prevention and reuniting children separated from their families; having entered care, children should be kept in contact with their families and helped to return to them.

4. *Children's rights and child liberation*
People holding this perspective view the child as an actor in his or her own situation, an independent person with rights. In the extreme positions, children should be allowed the same rights as adults (e.g., driving, drinking, engaging in sexual relations). In the more moderate positions, children have rights to express their views and to have those views taken into consideration in decisions about them. It incorporates a greater emphasis on the self-determination of the child.

Theoretical classifications may not, on the face of it, seem particularly relevant to practice; but all social workers have personal views about how far the state should interfere with the family and they tend to practise in such a way that what they do fits as far as possible with what they believe to be right. If you are a 'defender of the birth family', for example (category 3 above), you will work hard to reunite children with even the least promising of birth parents, and a higher percentage of children on your caseload will go home than would have been the case had you believed differently. Conversely, if you are a 'child-protection' person (category 2), you may believe that abused children should be automatically apprehended and their parents, who were to blame for the abuse in the first place, should have no further say in the matter. You will be less likely to pursue reunification and more likely to make active efforts to find the child a permanent living situation outside the birth family.

In a broader sense, you behave in practice according to what you believe your purpose as a social worker to be – which brings us to a consideration of the purpose of social work.

The purpose of social work

There is no doubt that the nature of professional social work places it firmly among the most challenging occupations. Jordan (1997) argues that social work exists in tension between its principles of care, compassion and harmony, and its tasks of assessment, rationing and enforcement. Social workers serve the most vulnerable and disadvantaged in our society – people who may be viewed, on the one hand, as victims of society, deserving care and compassion, or on the other hand, as threats to society, needing to be controlled through the machinery of state. Most social workers would incline to the former view. Like Davies (1997, p. 2) they see their primary task as 'making life more bearable for those whom others might prefer to forget – or choose to condemn' and they would agree with the Central Council for Education and Training in Social Work (CCETSW, 1996, p. 16) when it states that 'the purpose of social work is to enable children, adults, families, groups and communities to function, participate and develop in society'.

Nevertheless, most social workers will find themselves, at various points in their careers, in positions where the controlling function seems to be paramount. They will be 'employed by a range of statutory, voluntary, and private organisations, and work in collaboration with colleagues from allied professions and departments, as part of a network of welfare, health, housing, education and criminal justice provision' (CCETSW, 1996, p. 16). In other words, they will work as representatives of the very systems with which the people they are trying to help are most often in conflict.

In addition, professional social workers practise within legislative frameworks and organisational policies and procedures. They are hedged in by paperwork, bound by procedures and principles with which they might not agree. The art then is to find a balance. In the words of CCETSW (1996, p. 16), social workers must 'balance the needs, rights, responsibilities and resources of people with those of the wider community, and provide appropriate levels of support, advocacy, care, protection and control'. This is obviously easier said than done. Jordan (1997, p. 10) likens social workers to:

> blue-helmeted UN troops serving as peace-keepers in a civil war, their role is ambiguous, and they are often denounced, and sometimes attacked by both sides. They are open to manipulation and exploitation by the combatants, and their work is always morally compromised. Their

future is as uncertain as they search for bargains and compromises amid escalating antagonism.

Given that a social worker's role, while so worthwhile, is yet so challenging and demanding, it is apparent that social workers need a high level of professional competence.

Professional competence

Evans (1997, pp. 357–8) offers a model of social-work professional competence that comprises four components:

1. *A repertoire upon which the worker draws*, which contains: (a) the requisite knowledge, skills and values set out in the relevant literature (e.g. CCETSW, 1996); (b) attributes relevant to the professional worker as a whole person, including warmth, empathy, emotional maturity, commitment, integrity and creativity.

2. *Effective practice*, which comprises all the activities undertaken by the professional worker. This includes direct work with services users, indirect work, internal judgement and decision-making, and observable behaviours.

3. *Higher order learning skills*, which include: (a) skills for employing the repertoire of knowledge, skills and values in practice, such as relating theory and research to practice; (b) transfer of learning; (c) skills for developing the repertoire, such as critical reflection on practice; evaluating practice outcomes; effective use of supervision, consultancy and other dialogue; and study skills.

4. *Development through time*, which takes account of the way that professionals can adapt their higher-order learning skills through time as they gain experience.

To qualify for the award of the Diploma in Social Work, CCETSW (1996) stipulates that students in the UK must provide evidence of their competence to:

1. *Communicate and engage*
Communicate and engage with organisations and people within communities to promote opportunities for children, adults, families and groups at risk or in need to function, participate and develop in society.

2. *Promote and enable*
Promote opportunities for people to use their own strengths and expertise to enable them to meet responsibilities, secure rights and achieve change.

3. *Assess and plan*
Work in partnership to assess and review people's circumstances and plan responses to need and risk.

4. *Intervene and provide services*
Intervene and provide services to achieve change, through provision or purchase of appropriate levels of support, care, protection and control.

5. *Work in organizations*
Contribute to the work of organizations.

6. *Develop professional competence*
Manage and evaluate their own capacity to develop professional competence.

CCETSW (1996, p. 17) holds that 'competence in social work is the product of knowledge, skills and values. It is only practice which is founded on values, carried out in a skilled manner and informed by knowledge, critical analysis and reflection which is competent practice.'

Throughout the rest of the book, we will be looking at ways in which social workers can apply these competencies to the challenging situations which arise in the field of child welfare. In this first chapter, we have discussed where the Children Act 1989 came from in terms of its history and what its key elements are. We have looked briefly at the way that ideas about 'family' and 'childhood' change over time; and we have touched on issues around the different and often conflicting rights of children, parents and the state. In the next chapter, we will explore theories of child development.

Some exercises

- Do you think that delinquent youngsters are delinquent because they have been deprived? What might be other factors contributing to delinquency? Relate your discussion to the two dualisms employed by Hendrick (1994) – mind/body and victim/threat.
- What do you think needs to be in place before efforts at prevention can be expected to be successful? Discuss attitudes, resources and policies that you think would be necessary.
- Do these attitudes, resources and policies also apply to family support?

CHAPTER 2

Child development theory

Objectives

It is essential for anyone undertaking work with a child to understand how children develop. Such knowledge enables the social worker to understand how the child has reached his or her current stage of development. Just as importantly, it provides an understanding of which factors, among many in the child's social environment, are most likely to influence how the child develops in the future. This then provides a focus for intervention as the worker will want to target those factors that are most significant. Like most things in social work, this is easier said than done. Four centuries of thinking about how children develop have not yielded easy answers, but have rather revealed the complexity of various influences on children's lives.

In this chapter, we will describe the nature–nurture debate – the fundamental dualism underlying knowledge of how children develop – and then we will explore a number of theories of child development to see where they fit within that debate. Throughout, there is an emphasis on understanding cultural variations in how children develop in order to avoid ethnocentrism in practice. Two particular models are discussed in some depth: attachment theory (Bowlby and successors) and social-ecological theory (Bronfenbrenner). At the end of the chapter the reader should have an overview of a broad typology of child development theories and an awareness of more recent thinking on the significant influences on children's lives.

The nature–nurture divide

One of the earliest fundamental divisions between groups of child-development theorists stemmed from the belief among some that children are the way they are because they are born that way, and the belief among others that the environment is the main (if not the exclusive) influence on how children develop. As Burman (1994, p. 49) asks, 'Do children grow or are they made?' This question, now applied to children, is essentially the same question that Western philosophers have been asking over 2000 years about ways of acquiring knowledge. Does true knowledge come from within (is it inborn) or can it only be acquired through the scientific method of empirical research? It is thus no coincidence that the first child-developmental theorists, John Locke and Jean-Jacques Rousseau, are considered to be philosophers in their own right. Let us look more closely at what they thought, keeping in mind that contemporary thinking on the nature–nurture division accepts that both genetic and environmental influences have a part to play.

John Locke (1632–1704)

John Locke was the earlier of the two theorists (he died eight years before Rousseau was born) and he emphasised the importance of environmental influences. Locke did not believe that children are born sinful (as religious thinking of the time suggested) but thought rather that the way they develop is determined by their early experiences. He used the metaphor of the blank slate [*tabula rasa*] to describe a child's development. At birth there is nothing, and life writes the child's story on the slate. He refuted the concept of innate ideas (as put forward by philosophers such as Descartes and Plato), in which there are certain fundamentals (for example, the existence of God) which the child is born knowing. Experience is everything. Through his or her interactions with people the child's unique personality (character and abilities) is formed. Temperament may vary from child to child, but this is largely irrelevant to the method through which the child's mind is developed. It may seem strange to us now that 'development' should be considered solely in terms of the intellect, ignoring the social and emotional self, but we must remember the philosophical roots of the argument: the debate about how children developed sprang from and reflected the earlier debate about how knowledge was acquired.

Applying philosophy to practice, Locke acknowledged the importance of early experiences in ensuring optimum child development. Parents were advised to encourage their children's curiosity, and answer questions to the best of their ability. They should strive to make learning an enjoyable experience for the child by transforming it into recreation and play. They should also allow the child to be free and unrestrained as far as possible while still respecting the rights and needs of others. Locke's work, and particularly his book on child guidance, was extremely influential. According to Cunningham (1995),

> Locke became the guide for innumerable middle-class families. There had been more than a dozen English editions by the mid-eighteenth century, and several editions in French, German, Italian, Dutch, and Swedish in the course of the eighteenth century... the premier child-guidance book of the eighteenth century ... (p. 65)

How does the environment shape the mind of the child? Locke suggested four specific mechanisms: association (ideas become linked); repetition; imitation; and reward and punishment. He was opposed to the use of physical punishment because he believed that it created undesirable associations, generally it was ineffective, and when it was not ineffective it tended to 'break the mind'. It is interesting to relate these points to the modern debate on the physical punishment of children. In terms of rewards he tended to favour social reinforcement (praise and flattery) rather than sweets or money.

There were some inconsistencies, though, between Locke's blank-slate theory and his ideas about how children learn. For example, he contended that children have innate curiosity (so much for the blank slate!) and will learn for learning's sake. In some of his later thinking, he also seemed to be moving towards an appreciation of the inherent nature underlying at least some of children's readiness to learn (i.e., benefit from the environment). For example, he thought that children have difficulty remembering rules in the abstract and therefore he favoured a modelling approach to teaching children. The notion that very young children are not capable of abstract thinking was later developed by Piaget.

Jean-Jacques Rousseau (1712–78)

In contrast to Locke, Rousseau emphasised the importance of nature, or internal forces. At birth, children have their own individual natures, and adults are advised not to damage this individuality by trying to impose adult notions of reason or social order. Children grow in accordance with Nature's plan, and it is important to allow Nature to guide the child's growth and development. Rousseau, although also a political philosopher addressing the nature of human relations, had little faith in society's ability to guide children's development. Individuals who are well socialised are too dependent upon how others see them and have forgotten how to see with their own eyes and think with their own minds. Rousseau's thinking here might usefully be compared with some of the thinking on conformity, anti-conformity, and non-conformity in the middle of the twentieth century. From some points of view, conformity is a social value in itself, and helping children to take a role in society in which they conform to social expectations is considered to be a good thing. From other points of view, actualisation of the self (e.g., Maslow, 1943) is not necessarily, or even probably, achieved by conforming to the expectations of others.

Rousseau believed that we should be helping children to develop their capacity to think rather than teaching them *how* to think. Nature is described as being like a 'hidden tutor' helping children to develop different capacities at different stages of their lives. Young children are little experimenters, and if given a chance (and an environment that encourages it), they will explore and learn. Knowledge is not something that should be passed from adult to child like a parcel. Rather, children will arrive at a point where they can think logically through the progressive unfolding of inherent abilities. It is only when they are older, in late childhood, that adults should begin to think about actively trying to teach them; doing it too early can be unhelpful.

Rousseau was the first of the 'stage' theorists. For him, the gradual unfolding of the child's inherent capacities came in four main stages of development.

1. *Infancy* (birth to about 2 years)
In this stage, children experience the world through the senses and know nothing of ideas or reason. They experience pleasure and pain. It is the stage of language acquisition.

2. *Childhood* (about 2 to 12 years)
In this stage, children acquire a new independence; they learn to walk, talk and feed themselves. There is also the beginning of a type of reasoning (intuitive), but abstract reasoning does not come until later.

3. *Late childhood* (about 12 to 15 years)
This is a transitional stage during which there are tremendous gains in physical strength. The child's cognitive functions develop, but are still very concrete.

4. *Adolescence*
Children have little interest in others during the first three stages, but in this final stage their social development advances. It is like a 'second birth', and the body changes considerably. It is also a time of transition, when children are neither child nor adult. They are no longer self-sufficient, and are attracted to and need the company of others.

Rousseau's stages give rise to three important considerations: the time frame of the stages; the invariant sequence of stages; and the international influence of both Locke and Rousseau.

The timeframe of the stages. When you look at these four stages, you will probably say, 'But children do that before that age.' For example, by 7/8 months most babies can move forward on their stomachs, by 9 months they can crawl on all fours, and by 12 months many can walk. This is at variance with Rousseau's suggestion that physical independence does not begin until the second stage. Likewise, the emphasis on social relations beginning in adolescence is at variance with the work of Parten (1932) and Dunn (1988, 1993). Parten looked very closely at young children's social (play) behaviour and described a number of stages: unoccupied behaviour, solitary play, onlooking play, parallel play and cooperative play. Dunn, in her work on understanding sibling relationships as the child's first peer relationships, concluded that children's understanding of, and participation in, social relationships begins much earlier than previously thought, when we use certain methods to appraise this (for example, observation techniques). As another example, we might consider that starting adolescence at 15 is very late in light of how most people would experience it today. What might account for these differences? One possibility is that children do in fact develop earlier today than they did several hundred years ago. Another is that research methodologies have improved so that we can now identify achievements of young children which may have escaped us earlier.

The invariant sequence of the stages. The second consideration in Rousseau's work is the sequence of the stages. It is common parlance to say, 'You have to walk before you can run.' In effect, this colloquial expression, applied to the physical development of the child, means that there are certain skills that cannot be acquired until the child has successfully passed through a previous stage. This seems perfectly self-evident and we have been so happy with the idea that we have applied it to concepts other than physical development. For example, Maslow's hierarchy of needs begins with the satisfaction of physical needs and moves on through various stages (safety, belongingness, self-esteem) to the achievement of self-actualisation. We have only recently begun to question Maslow's assertion that higher needs cannot be reached until lower needs have been satisfied. To be fair, Maslow himself believed that everyone was capable of self-actualisation provided they did not conform too closely to a society which stressed the importance of the lower needs. But we have tended to ignore that part and have concentrated instead on the sequence of the stages, thereby doing grave damage to our understanding of the complexities of human motivation.

The international influence of Locke and Rousseau. The third consideration is the international differences which have resulted from the separate influences of Locke and Rousseau. We have already mentioned that Locke's book on child guidance was translated into many languages. Rousseau's work was also extremely influential. Let us compare the influence of Locke and Rousseau with respect to the notion of children's readiness to be educated. It is widely known that children in the UK begin formal schooling earlier than children in other European countries. In the UK it can be as early as 3 years old. In most European countries, although there is widespread provision for pre-school children, formal schooling does not begin until they are 6 or 7 years of age. This is consistent with the influence of Locke in the UK (children learn from the time of birth), and the influence of Rousseau in other European countries (before a certain age, formal education is unhelpful). This highlights perhaps just how strongly the influence of these two pioneers continues into present-day dialogues about how to promote the development of children.

There has been no shortage of child-development theories following on from Locke and Rousseau. Some are quite global; some address very specific aspects of how children develop. Frequently, consideration of how children develop is divided into physical, intellectual (or cognitive), emotional and social development. Sometimes a further category is added, spiritual or moral development. Most, but not all, are chronological (i.e., dealing with how children change over time).

There is insufficient space here to allow for a detailed consideration of the models put forward by subsequent theorists – and anyway, you are probably familiar with them through courses in psychology. We will just look very briefly at how some of their theories are linked with the work of

Locke and Rousseau. The important word here is 'linked'. We are not say-ing that subsequent theorists were followers or members of a 'school of thought' as put forward by Locke or Rousseau, just that it is interesting to consider the links.

Locke and the environmentalists	Rousseau and the developmentalists
Pavlov (1849–1936)	Freud (1856–1939) (and followers)
Watson (1878–1958)	Erikson (1902–94)
Skinner (1905–1990)	Piaget (1896–1980) and Kohlberg
Bandura (1925–)	(1927–87)
	Gesell (1880–1961)
	Maslow (1908–70)

Locke and the environmentalists

Pavlov and Watson

As previously mentioned, Locke suggested that children learn from the environment through an association of ideas. Pavlov used the association ideas with dogs, conditioning them to salivate to the sound of a bell by associating the bell with food. Watson adapted Pavlov's conditioning exper-iments to a young child, 'little Albert'. Watson induced a fear of white furry objects in little Albert by making a very loud, startling noise whenever a rabbit was produced. In time Albert came to fear the presentation of the rabbit. Hopefully, you are horrified that a researcher was allowed to do such a thing to a child and you are relieved that our ethical standards in research are now very much more stringent. Nevertheless, the experiment did provide evidence that children learn by associating ideas.

Skinner

It was Skinner who took the rather restricted concept of learning by association, and extended it to learning by reinforcement. In extensive experiments with rats, pigeons and other animals, he monitored the impact of reinforcing a particular behaviour. He discovered that a behaviour could be increased by positive reinforcement (reward) and decreased by negative reinforcement (punishment) or lack of reinforcement (ignoring the behaviour). This behavioural model has gained a very strong position in the repertory of methods of helping troubled children. The methods can be linked to Locke's understanding of learning through rewards and punishments.

Bandura

Through his experiments on aggressive behaviour towards a toy doll ('Bobo'), Bandura showed that children can learn not just by association and by the direct consequences of their behaviour (being rewarded, or ignored, or punished), but also by indirect consequences. If a child sees another individual being rewarded (e.g., praised) or punished (e.g., scolded) for a particular behaviour, then it has an impact on the extent to which the child will behave in that way Bandura concluded that children learn behaviour from having it modelled and by imitating behaviour. His maxim was: 'Children are more likely to do what we do than what we tell them to do.' This fits with Locke, who talked of imitation as being a way that children learn from the environment.

Rousseau and the developmentalists

Freud (and followers)

The Freudian theory of psychoanalysis rests on several basic principles which are closely related to Rousseau's concepts. First, Freud placed a great emphasis on the biological. His early notions of drives (*Das Trieb*) were refined to notions of basic life forces (Eros and Thanatos) driving human behaviour towards life and death. This biological basis of the personality is rooted in the 'nature' side of the nature/nurture dichotomy. Additionally, Freud believed that the human expression of drives (described as 'sexuality') developed through psychosexual stages:

Oral (birth to the 2nd year)
Anal (coincides with period of toilet training)
Phallic (around the 4th year)
Latency (5th to 12th year)
Genital (onset of puberty)

These stages are seen as invariant in sequence. Problems experienced at one stage can lead to specific types of psychological difficulties which are distinct from the difficulties resulting from problems at a different stage.

Erikson

Erikson was one of many followers of Freud who broke with the psychoanalytic tradition to develop thinking in a different direction. Erikson took the emphasis away from the biological and psychosexual and looked at the development of the individual of psycho*social* development over the entire lifespan. The stages he proposed are as follows:

1. Basic trust *vs.* Basic mistrust (birth to 1 year)
2. Autonomy *vs.* Shame and doubt (1–3 years)
3. Initiative *vs.* Guilt (3–6 years)
4. Industry *vs.* Inferiority (7–11 years)
5. Identity *vs.* Role confusion (adolescence)
6. Intimacy *vs.* Isolation (early adulthood)
7. Generativity *vs.* Stagnation (middle adulthood)
8. Ego integrity *vs.* Despair (late adulthood)

His debt to Rousseau is seen in terms of the unfolding of an inherent plan of development.

Piaget and Kohlberg

If one is familiar with the work of Piaget when reading Rousseau, the extent of the harmony between the two becomes apparent. Piaget's focus was primarily on the cognitive development of children, although he did theorise as well about their emotional development (but not so much about their social development). He put forward a model of cognitive development in which the mental apparatus of the individual becomes increasingly complex and capable of dealing with the comprehension of complex concepts through two processes called *assimilation* and *accommodation*. Both of these processes deal with how the young child integrates experiences which do not fit into his or her view of the world. In the first (assimilation), the child modifies the experience so that it fits. In accommodation, a more radical transformation occurs: the child adapts his or her way of understanding the world in order to be able to integrate the new experience.

Piaget developed a four-stage theory of child development:

- *Period of sensorimotor intelligence* (from birth to the appearance of language, i.e., around 18 months)
- *Pre-operational period* (18 months–7 years)
    pre-conceptual stage (18 months–4 years)
    intuitive stage (4 years–7 years)
- *Period of concrete operations* (7 years to adolescence)
- *Period of formal operations* (around 12 years and peaking about three years later)

Again, the stages are invariant sequentially: one must come after the other and the individual cannot operate at a later stage until the earlier stage has been mastered. However, individuals progress through the stages at different rates, and some may not get to the most advanced stage (formal operations) at all.

Piaget also developed a two-stage theory of moral development. At the first stage, called 'moral realism', children judge the morality of an act in terms of its consequences and are incapable of weighing intentions. For example, someone who breaks twelve plates by accident is much guiltier than someone who breaks two plates on purpose by throwing them at her sister. At the second stage, called 'moral realism', children realise that there is no absolute right and wrong, and that morality depends not on consequences but on intentions (those things that the road to hell is paved with).

Lawrence Kohlberg (1981) extended Piaget's two stages of moral development to three levels, each level containing two stages so that there are six stages altogether. These stages represent the growth of moral concepts or ways of judging, not moral behaviour. Kohlberg's three levels are: (1) preconventional (based on punishments and rewards); (2) conventional (based on social conformity); and (3) postconventional (based on moral principles). Again, the levels and stages are sequential and one cannot progress to a higher stage until one has passed through the stage before.

Gesell

Gesell's approach is considered to be maturationist; that is, human traits are determined primarily by genetics. Children simply mature with age, and environment plays a minor role. This can be seen most clearly through the metaphor of the growing plant. As long as the plant is given an environment that does not hold back its development (water, sun, soil, protection from severe elements) it will develop in a way that is pre-programmed. A poor environment may produce a poor rose and a rich environment a richer, more beautiful rose, but a rose it will be and not a carnation. It is clear that this model is allied to Rousseau's concept of the innate unfolding of the child's character.

Maslow

Abraham Maslow represents an interesting example because he began by believing in nurture and changed to the nature perspective. He writes:

> Our first baby changed me as a psychologist. It made the behaviourism I had been so enthusiastic about look so foolish that I could not stomach it any more. It was impossible. Having a second baby, and learning how profoundly different people are even before birth, made it impossible for me to think in terms of the kind of learning psychology in which one can teach anybody anything. (Maslow, 1973, p. 176)

As we have already mentioned, Maslow developed a model of a hierarchy of human needs, with physical needs at the base of the pyramid of needs and self-actualisation at the top. The drive for self-actualisation is seen as inherent: one needs to fulfil one's intrinsic nature and become all that one can be in the same way as an acorn needs to grow into an oak. However, this drive is usually suppressed in early childhood by the needs of adults to have children conform to expectations. In adulthood, the drive is suppressed by the willingness of adults to conform to society's expectations.

Crain (1992, p. 322), in his consideration of Maslow, notes:

> If Maslow's ideas sound familiar, they are. Maslow and the modern humanist psychologists have ... drawn heavily upon the developmental tradition. Since Rousseau, developmentalists have been preoccupied with the same basic problem as Maslow: Children, as they become socialized, quit relying on their own experience and judgements; they become too dependent on conventions and the opinions of others.

Now that we have looked at some of the ideas of theorists in child development, let us turn our attention to cultural issues.

Cultural issues in child development

Conceptions of how children do develop, how they should develop, and how parents should act in relation to them are not power-neutral concepts based on dispassionate findings from science. Rather, such notions, reflect a balance between those with power and those without. It would be reasonable to suggest, therefore, that theories of child development, like concepts of 'childhood' and 'child abuse', can be viewed as being socially constructed (Stainton Rogers, 1989; Parton, 1985; Burman, 1994). Social construction means that a socio-political phenomenon (for example, child abuse, childhood, elder abuse, mental disorder, 'whiteness', etc.) is not an objective entity but something which arises out of the process of people defining issues (i.e., 'discourse'). Thus, the process of defining the phenomenon becomes part of what is being defined. Since power differentials are part of any discourse, power differentials influence (and indeed become an inherent part of) how a concept comes to be defined. Consider the following metaphor from Pence (1992, pp. 2, 4) in relation to quality in the provision of services for children:

> I am interested in not only the small 'r' *ruler* we use in attempting to measure quality, but also the capital 'R' *Ruler* who defines what it is that will be measured. ... 'Who is the Ruler?' appears to be *the* question one

must address before the questions of 'What is the ruler and what is to be measured?' can be considered.

One way of understanding this is by noting that conceptions of how children do, and should develop vary over time within a culture and at the same time between different cultures.

Martin Woodhead (1998, p. 8) observes, 'With few exceptions, "textbook" child development originates mainly in Europe and North America, and mainly within a fairly narrow socio-economic band within these continents.' Likewise, Burman (1994, p. 6) notes, 'developmental psychology ... is usually conducted and written by researchers from Western societies'. Let us look at some examples of researchers and the countries they come from:

Albert Bandura (Canada, then USA)   Maria Montessori (Italy)
Erik Erikson (Germany, then USA)   Ivan Pavlov (Russia)
Sigmund Freud (Austria, then UK)   Jean Piaget (Switzerland)
Arnold Gesell (USA)   Jean Jacques Rousseau (France)
Lawrence Kohlberg (USA)   B. F. Skinner (USA)
John Locke (England)   Lev Vygotsky (Russia)
Abraham Maslow (USA)   John B. Watson (USA)

The countries from which these theorists originate, and in which they worked, represent a relatively small population of children compared with the total population of children in the entire world. Moreover, it is a population that contains for the most part only Western children. Yet theories drawn from work with this population (or samples of it) have been generalised to explain how all children develop the world over. To make matters worse, child-development theorists develop their models with a view to understanding not only how children do develop, but also how they *should* develop, and what actions adults should take in relation to those children. Thus, there is a real potential that Western theorists will dictate to the non-Western world how children should develop and how they should be brought up.

Sanders (1999) looks at this issue in his consideration of the role of ethnocentrism and cultural relativism in child abuse internationally. He considers the extent to which children's needs are the same all over the world, and in particular the need for autonomy and/or responsibility as described by a number of Western child-development theorists (Maslow, 1943; Kellmer Pringle, 1975; Erikson, 1963). He concludes that we can get into serious difficulties if we assume that Western notions of child development have a normative application outside Western cultures.

The very concept of 'needs' presents difficulties if we try to answer the question: 'To what extent do children all over the world have the same needs?' or (the opposite side of the same coin) 'To what extent do children of different cultures have different needs?' These questions are particularly important in relation to international attempts to meet the common needs of all children: for example, the UN Convention on the Rights of Children. On the surface, it would appear that biological and physiological needs are more likely to be common to all children than psychological, emotional and social needs. Woodhead (1990) considers that an understanding of children's needs is so culture specific that it should be banned from discourses about children. He says:

> My conclusion, provocatively, is that our understanding and respect for childhood might be better served if 'children's needs' were outlawed from future professional discourse, policy recommendations, and popular psychology. (Woodhead, 1990, p. 60)

While this may be a rather extreme position, it certainly reminds practitioners and students to be very cautious about generalising notions of children's needs outside the cultural context. The following is also from Woodhead (1998, p. 14):

> While a mother from Boston might view the Gusii [Kenya] practice of demand feeding as 'spoiling' the child, the demand for obedience as 'repressive' and the use of young children as caregivers as 'abusive', the traditional Gusii mother might view the Western practice of leaving infants to cry as 'abusive', tolerating a toddler's challenging behaviour as 'spoiling' and encouraging playful fun as 'over indulgent'.

Trawick-Smith (1997) considers five major theories of child development: the maturationists (Gesell); the behaviourists (Skinner, Watson, Bandura); the psychoanalytic school (Freud, Erikson); the cognitive/developmental school (Piaget, Vygotsky); and ecological systems theory (Bronfenbrenner). For each of these, in relation to a particular case study (Adam), he describes the general principles of the theory, how it would apply to Adam's story, general criticisms of the theory, and the multicultural criticisms of the theory. For brevity, we will only consider his multicultural criticisms. We will also only consider the first four major theories, leaving ecological systems theory to be described afterwards.

The work of the *maturationists* (Gesell) is seen as leading to, or at least supporting, cultural bias. The work of Jensen is cited as an example; Jensen suggested that African American children have lower IQs than white children because of genetically derived intellectual deficiencies. The danger is that the argument of genetic determinism can be used, as it has been for centuries, to advance a belief that some races are inferior. It is important to remember that genetic differences are just that, differences, not deficits.

In relation to *behavioural theory*, one might ask how it is that in some families or cultural groups in which positive reinforcement is virtually never used, children still manage to grow and learn. An equally important question, arising in part from the effectiveness of behavioural approaches, is the issue of which behaviours are to be reinforced? Who should make the decision as to which behaviours are undesirable and which are to be encouraged? There is a danger of behaviourism being used to promote Anglo-Saxon ideals, i.e. behaviour designed to conform to standards of white, middle-class culture. Trawick-Smith notes, for example, that in some cultures eye contact is an indicator of disrespect, and quietness of children is a quality which is highly valued. In others, eye contact is seen as something to be promoted, and children's verbal participation is viewed as a good thing. These kinds of conflicts can lead to 'mixed socialisation messages'.

Likewise with *psychoanalytic theory*, some of the stages (for example, Erikson's 'autonomy') reflect Anglo-Saxon ideals which are not universally shared in all cultures. In some ethnic groups, collective thought and action are valued over autonomy. In some Japanese American families, a sense of belonging and collectivism − not individual autonomy − are goals in child rearing. It could be argued that the individualistically oriented notion of autonomy in Western views of child development represents a powerful, but minority, view of how children do and should develop.

Cognitive developmental theory is less criticised by Trawick-Smith (1997), who considers it to be generally successful in explaining universal developmental processes across many different cultures. However, again he notes that autonomy is not valued in some cultures, and he also notes the specific cultural biases behind the theories.

Gender in child development

We have already referred to the power dimension with respect to imposing Western cultural norms on images of childhood and child development which are supposed to be universal. The same thing applies to gender. In Western societies, ideas about how children develop, how they should develop, and how they should be reared are very closely linked to gender power relations. We might ask, for example, how theories of child development have been influenced by the fact that child-developmental theorists are predominantly male. (In the lists previously provided, the only woman was Maria Montessori.) Burman (1994) answers that question by suggesting that the focus of developmental psychology has shifted from the child to the mother, and to the regulation of the adequacy of mothering. In other words, the history of child development can be seen as centuries of men telling women how they should bring up children.

Burman (1994), drawing on the work of Newson and Newson (1974) and Hardyment (1983), describes five historical stages in the kinds of advice given to mothers over the centuries. These are:

1. The stage of religious morality.
2. The stage of physical health and survival.
3. The stage of mental hygiene.
4. The stage of understanding and meeting children's needs.
5. The individualism and fun morality stage.

In the stage of religious morality, when infant mortality was so high, the emphasis was on saving the soul of the child: that is, on preparing for the next world as the child might not survive in this one. Children were viewed as being born sinful, and harsh methods were needed to ensure that the child moved from a state of sin to a state worthy of salvation. Consider for example the two following quotes:

> 'Break his will now and his soul will live.' (Susan Wesley to her son John (1703–91), founder of Methodism in the eighteenth century, cited by Newson and Newson, 1974, p. 56)

> '[Children are] beings who bring into the world a corrupt nature and evil dispositions, which it should be the great end of education to rectify.' (More, a popular nineteenth-century writer, cited in Hendrick, 1994, p. 39)

Rousseau was also aware of the high infant mortality rate, but viewed the implications of this differently. He 'points out that many children will die young, having spent their lives preparing for an adulthood which they never achieved; and he asserts the right of a child to be a child, and to be happy in it' (Cunningham, 1995, p. 66).

The second stage of advice to mothers, emphasising physical health and survival, is often said to have started after the First World War, but it could be argued to have begun at least 20 years before that, with the introduction of health visiting. As described by Sanders (1999), the origin of health visitors (called 'health missioners' or 'sanitary visitors') can be traced back to the series of cholera epidemics in the latter half of the nineteenth century and to the subsequent legislation (the Public Health Act 1872). The continuing high rates of infant mortality gave rise to the infant welfare movement, in which mother and baby clinics were set up so that mothers could learn how to care for their babies properly. By the middle of the twentieth century, infant mortality in developed countries had dropped to such an extent that losing a child was considered to be unlucky rather than an expected part of everyday reality.

With survival generally ensured, the third stage of advice to women came into play: advising mothers on the mental hygiene of their offspring. Again, Rousseau is of interest here. Rousseau married an illiterate serving girl (Thérèse) with whom he spent the rest of his life. She gave birth to five children, but Rousseau had them all placed in a state foundling home. He later considered this action wrong, but said he had insufficient money to bring them up. As noted by Crain (1992, p. 9), 'Many people have found Rousseau so deficient as a man that they have refused to take his ideas seriously, especially on education. How can a man who abandoned his own children to an orphanage have the audacity to prescribe the right upbringing for others?'

On the other hand, Rousseau was very pro-woman in his ideas about the rearing of children. Consistent with the rest of his thinking about the importance of allowing the child to develop naturally, he considered that children needed the nurturance provided by a mother rather than the training and discipline that a father might attempt to provide. He was at odds with the Renaissance notion that the father should take responsibility for how the children are reared because of concerns that their mother would 'spoil' them.

> You say mothers spoil their children and no doubt that is wrong, but it is worse to deprave them as you do. The mother wants her child to be happy now. She is right, and if her method is wrong, she must be taught a better. Ambition, avarice, tyranny, the mistaken foresight of fathers, their neglect, their harshness, are a hundredfold more harmful to the child than the blind affection of the mother.
>
> (Rousseau, 1993 (orig. 1762), p. 5)

However, whilst he was clear that the nurturing environment should come from the mother, he was equally clear that the necessary direction should come from the father, acting in the role of 'governor'.

Consider how Rousseau's rather indulgent tone differs from the work of Watson and Truby King in the early half of the twentieth century. We have already looked at the work of John Watson in relation to the induced phobia of 'little Albert'. On the basis of his very strong belief about environmental influences, Watson prescribed how children should be treated by their mothers. He too was concerned that mothers might 'spoil' their children.

> Loves are home made, built in. The child sees the mother's face when she pets it. Soon, the mere sight of the mother's face calls out the love response. ... So with her footsteps, the sight of the mother's clothes, of

her photograph. All too soon the child gets shot through with too many of these love reactions.   (Watson, 1928, p. 75)

He continues:

> ... remember when you are tempted to pet your child that mother love is a dangerous instrument. An instrument which may inflict a never healing wound, a wound which may make infancy unhappy, adolescence a nightmare, an instrument which may wreck your adult son or daughter's vocational future and their chances for marital happiness.
>
> (Watson, 1928, p. 87)

He believed that parents should behave towards their children like strict executives, and like a good employee, the child was to learn to obey rules and fulfil performance expectations. He believed in very rigid schedules concerning both feeding and toilet training, advocating methods (e.g., enemas for toilet training) that by today's standards might be considered to be abusive.

This kind of rigid thinking about the discipline that children 'need' to acquire, was continued in the work of Truby King, a New Zealand stockbreeder who 'applied principles he developed rearing cattle to the upbringing of children' (Burman, 1994, p. 52). Developing the concept of 'the Truby King Baby', he advocated 'the establishment of perfect regularity of habits, initiated by feeding and cleaning by the clock' (Newson and Newson, 1974, p. 61). He advocated the beginning of bowel training at three days of age.

The fourth stage of advice to parents is the stage of understanding and meeting children's needs, which Burman (1994) describes as being influenced by psychoanalytic theory, placing an emphasis on 'lay ... emotional as well as physical needs, and ... continuity of care' (p. 52). In keeping with our emphasis here on gender issues, however, it should be noted that psychoanalysis was very biased in its consideration of boys and girls. As noted by Trawick-Smith (1997), psychoanalytic theories tend to view the development of male children as normal or ideal and to portray unique features of female development as deficits. For example, the process of separating from parents and becoming an autonomous person is important for boys, while attachment and intimacy are the norm for girls. Yet psychoanalytic theorists view separation as healthy and interpret intimacy as over-dependence or failure to separate.

The fifth and final stage is described as the individualism and fun morality stage, identified as beginning after the Second World War. The rise of affluence and the availability of choice are seen as related to notions of parents enjoying their baby/child. However, even this can take on the form of a prescription, and a mother who does not feel the kind of enjoyment she is told she ought to feel may well believe that this is due to a deficiency in herself. Of interest in this context is the fact that most of our post-natal services are aimed at 'high-risk' mothers, whereas it is the 'low-risk' mothers who are apt to expect that having a baby will be 'fun' and who may run into trouble when the reality does not meet their expectations.

We have briefly described a number of theories of child development, tracing them back to their origins in the work of either Locke or Rousseau, and commenting on their cultural and gender implications. There are two further theories of child development that we will now consider: attachment theory and social ecological theory. These are both considered fundamental for people engaged in work with children. Neither is really influenced by Locke or Rousseau – attachment theory because it is more of a micro theory, dealing with a very specific and focused aspect of child development, and social ecological theory because it really is *sui generis*, i.e., in a class of its own.

Attachment theory

This section looks at the concept of attachment, its definition, background, and application. To begin with, let us consider what attachment is. Attachment can be defined as:

> any behaviour designed to get children into a close, protective relationship with their attachment figures whenever they experience anxiety. (Howe et al., 1999, p. 14)

This definition has several components which should be highlighted before we look at the origins of attachment theory more closely. First, the actual behaviour is one of proximity seeking. Whilst this may be closely related to other aspects of the child's development (emotional security, relationship quality, identity, etc.) the actual behaviour is one that can be observed. It contrasts, for example, with the following definition of attachment by Banyard and Grayson (1996, p. 217):

> Attachment refers to a strong emotional tie between two people. In developmental psychology, the term attachment is often taken to mean the emotional tie between the infant and the adult care-giver.

Secondly, Howe et al. (1999) are careful to avoid identification of the attachment figure as the mother, the father, or even the 'primary caregiver'. There is an element of tautology in defining attachment in terms of attachment figures, but it does avoid the difficulty of being overly prescriptive. Finally, the behaviour can be elicited by any experience which causes anxiety, not just separation. The presence of a stranger, or a novel but menacing experience, may trigger the attachment response.

John Bowlby (1907–90) is generally credited as being the founder of attachment theory, but its roots can be traced further back to the ethologists of the early twentieth century, and from there even to Darwin in the nineteenth century.

Darwin was one of the first to study infant behaviour by direct observation. He kept a baby journal in which he recorded the visible changes in his eldest child, Doddy, from the time he was born. Thus Darwin introduced a useful technique for gathering data as well as a scientific approach to studying children's behaviour. Within the context of his wider theorising about the development of species, Darwin created the opportunity for studying human behaviour by learning from animal behaviour – species develop, societies develop, man develops. As noted by Kessen (1993), it is from Darwin that we derive the notion that by careful observation of the infant and child, we can see the descent of man. The debt to Darwin is apparent in Bowlby's statement,

> the only relevant criterion by which to consider the natural adaptedness of any particular part of present-day man's behavioural equipment is the degree to which and the way in which it might contribute to population survival. (Bowlby, 1969, p. 87)

Bowlby was also influenced by ethologists such as Konrad Lorenz (1903–89) and Niko Tinbergen (1907–88) who described imprinting, an instinctive pattern of behaviour in animals which must occur at a certain period of life (if it does not occur then, it will not occur at all), which is irreversible, and which produces a proximity-seeking behaviour. As evidence of the process, Lorenz had baby ducks and goslings imprint on him, so that instead of forming a line behind the mother duck (or goose), they lined up behind him, and followed him around. Bowlby's debt to the ethologists is clear in the following:

> We may conclude, therefore, that, so far as is at present known, the way in which attachment behaviour develops in the human infant and becomes focused on a discriminated figure is sufficiently like the way in which it develops in other mammals and in birds, for it to be included, legitimately, under the heading of imprinting. (Bowlby, 1969, p. 273)

Work by Harry Harlow (1905–81) on rhesus monkeys in 1958, further contributed to Bowlby's thinking on attachment. In Harlow's experiments, baby rhesus monkeys were reared on dummy monkeys, and the lack of the social contact that a real monkey would have provided was found to have dramatic social consequences for the babies later in life. In a variation on the experiment, two dummies were provided, one soft and cuddly, and the other hard but able to provide food. The monkeys were found to spend most of their time clinging to the soft and cuddly dummy, only leaving for short periods to feed off the other. However, these monkeys too grew up to be socially inept, and later studies, which incorporated *some* amount of social contact, suggested that it is the social contact that is more important than either the 'soft and cuddly' feeling or (within reason) the food.

According to Bowlby (1969) human infants aged 6 months to 5 years 'attach' to caregivers and the caregivers bond to the babies. He described any failure in this attachment/bonding process as 'maternal deprivation', and concluded that maternal deprivation could lead to psychopathic and affectionless personality types. He suggests,

> many forms of psychiatric disturbance can be attributed either to deviations in the development of attachment behaviour or more rarely, to failure of its development.   (Bowlby, 1977, p. 202)

Bowlby collaborated with James and Joyce Robertson who produced a series of films of children in separation situations, highlighting the impact of factors such as gender, the age of the child at separation, familiarity with the setting in which the child was cared for, the type of care setting, contact with the attachment figures, and so forth. The situations in the films are listed below:

- A two-year-old goes to hospital
- John, aged seventeen months, in a residential nursery for nine days
- Kate, aged two years, five months, in foster care for twenty-seven days
- Thomas, aged two years, four months, in foster care for ten days
- Lucy, aged twenty-one months, in foster care for nineteen days
- Jane, aged seventeen months, in foster care for ten days

A comparison of two children (John and Jane) of the same age highlights just how different the impact can be. John spends nine days in a residential nursery where he arrives in the middle of the night without preparation, whilst his mother is in hospital. Jane, on the other hand, is fostered by Joyce Robertson. In anticipation of the planned stay, she has visited the Robertson home and become familiar with Mr and Mrs Robertson. She is in receipt of one-to-one care, with the same caregiver, all the time she is there. The outcomes are very different. For John the experience is traumatic, and in the commentaries to the films the Robertsons indicate that there are long-term negative consequences. For Jane, there are occasions of distress, but they are not overwhelming, and overall the experience seems to be positive, without long-term ill effects. The work of the Robertsons has been extremely influential. Two examples of this are the closing of residential nurseries during the 1960s and 1970s, and the extension of hospital visiting schemes to include open access for parents of young children. We will revisit the issue of separation when we discuss 'looked-after children' in Chapter 6.

The work of Bowlby has not been without its critics. Most significant has been the reassessment of the concept of maternal deprivation by Rutter (1972), who was particularly critical of focusing separation and attachment issues solely on the mother. He comments,

> Schaffer and Emerson (1964) found that the sole principal attachment was to the mother in only half of the eighteen-month-old children they studied and in nearly a third of cases the main attachment was to the father.   (Rutter, 1972, p. 17)

Rutter notes that the separation experiences of children are treated as if they were a separation from the mother only, whereas, 'in fact they consist of separation from mother *and* father *and* siblings *and* the home environment' (p. 48). He goes on to identify those factors that mediate the short-term effects of maternal deprivation, such as the age, sex and temperament of the child, the previous mother–child relationship, the child's previous experiences of separation, the duration of the separation or deprivation experience, the presence of other familiar people, and the nature of the circumstances during the separation/deprivation. If one were to take all of these factors and put them into a worst scenario/best scenario framework, it could be seen that the impact of separation from the mother for a child may be extremely damaging, or have minimal consequences, or be somewhere in between depending on the circumstances of the separation.

Rutter also looked at those factors that modify the long-term consequences of separation. In considering the impact of the separation from the parents he noted the various impacts of multiple mothering, transient separations, and prolonged or permanent separations. He considered the type of child care, the presence of good relationships between child and caregiver, and the opportunity to develop attachments to other adults. As with short-term separations, he also considered the impact of the age, sex and temperament of the child. He concluded that children who had mentally ill parents or histories of family discord, whose behaviour was difficult to change, who did not mind messiness and disorder and who were markedly irregular in their eating and sleeping patterns were significantly more likely than other children to develop deviant behaviours.

In summary, in view of Rutter's work, separation in childhood is not necessarily damaging, and will not necessarily lead to damaged adults. That is not, of course, to say that it should be treated lightly, and one should always be mindful of the potentially damaging impact.

Another influence on Bowlby's thinking was the psychoanalytic school of thought. Bowlby had considered a number of alternative foundations for the development of attachment behaviours, and concluded that they were not incompatible, and could operate together. For example, he considered that attachment as a means of protecting vulnerable youngsters from predators did not contradict the need for the infant 'to learn from the mother various activities necessary for survival' (p. 274).

Vera Fahlberg (1988) developed the attachment model further, using a needs arousal and fulfilment model, with two cycles, to understand the development of attachment and bonding between infant and caregiver. In the arousal and relaxation cycle, the child experiences a need leading to displeasure (arousal) which is followed by satisfaction of the need by the caregiver and quiescence on the part of the child (relaxation) until a further need arises. The need could be anything requiring action on the part of the caregiver (hunger – the child needs to be fed; too much sun – the child needs to be moved into the shade; messy nappy – the child needs to be changed; boredom – the child needs stimulation). This cycle is initiated by the child and its continuous operation leads to the development of trust, security and attachment on the part of the child. However, the actions of the caregiver bring about an obvious satisfaction of the need (for example, the child stops crying) and this success is satisfying to the caregiver. The caregiver may then initiate a 'Positive Interaction Cycle'. Here, the caregiver initiates positive interactions with the child, which produces positive responses on the part of the child. The child's positive responses in turn lead the caregiver to initiate more positive interactions with the child. The continuous operation of this cycle leads to the development of self-worth and self-esteem (presumably on the part of both caregiver and child). In other work, Fahlberg has clarified the distinction between the attachment and bonding processes. Attachment is seen as the child's responding pattern in the cycle; bonding is seen as the development of positive (and rewarding) responses on the part of the caregiver. Attachment is what the child does; bonding is what the caregiver does.

These cycles set the patterns for later life. Children base their views and expectations of the world on how they are responded to and how their needs are met. Parents, too, may base their future behaviour on how the child responds. If they feel that they are unable to satisfy the child (for example, the child continues to cry despite all their efforts), they may get frustrated and disheartened and make no further effort.

As part of her work, Fahlberg has produced very clear observation checklists for practitioners assessing attachment. These are differentiated according to age: birth to one year, one to five years, primary school children, and adolescents. For each age group, the checklists take into account both what the child does and what the parent(s) do. Another aspect of Fahlberg's work incorporates the needs of children at various ages into a life task model. She describes the various 'tasks' that children must accomplish in order to fulfil their needs as they go from stage to stage in their development. These are briefly outlined here.

1. *Basic tasks in the first year of life*
   1.1 The meeting of dependency needs;
   1.2 The building up of trust and feelings of security, i.e., attachment;
   1.3 The beginning of sorting out perceptions of the world.
2. *Basic tasks of the toddler years*
   2.1 The need to develop a sense of autonomy and identity;
   2.2 Continued sorting out of perceptions of the world and the need to relate to an increasing number of people, to learn their reactions and to respond;
   2.3 Period of rapid language acquisition needs lots of stimulation – particularly with spoken language.
3. *Basic tasks of pre-school children (3–6 years)*
   3.1 Continuing individuation and self-proficiency in the family setting, learning to care for self; bathing, dressing and toileting, but may still need help. Needs opportunities to play with children of own age as well as family members;
   3.2 Dramatic change in conceptual functioning.
4. *Basic tasks of primary school age children (6–12 years)*
   4.1 To master problems experienced outside the family;
   4.2 Increased academic learning;
   4.3 Acquisition of gross motor skills.
5. *Basic tasks of adolescents*
   5.1 Psychological separation from the family;
   5.2 Identity issues.

Another theorist concerned with attachment was Mary Ainsworth. With her colleagues (Ainsworth et al., 1978), she developed a procedure for empirically measuring a child's attachment. The procedure is called the 'Strange Situation', and consists of eight 3-minute episodes during which the child is brought into a strange room with his or her mother, is joined by a stranger, and is separated from the mother, who later returns. Raters measure the child's reactions to both separations and reunions. The actual procedure is described below.

- *Stage 1*   The infant and her mother are brought into a comfortably furnished laboratory playroom and the child has an opportunity to explore this new environment.

- *Stage 2*   Another female adult, whom the child does not know, enters the room and sits talking in a friendly way, first to the mother and then to the child.
- *Stage 3*   While the stranger is talking to the child, the mother leaves the room unobtrusively, at a prearranged signal.
- *Stage 4*   The stranger tries to interact with the child.
- *Stage 5*   Mother returns and the stranger leaves her together with the child.
- *Stage 6*   Mother then goes out of the room leaving the child there alone.
- *Stage 7*   Stranger returns and remains in the room with the child.
- *Stage 8*   Mother returns once more.

The video record is scored in terms of the child's behaviour towards the person in the room: seeking contact, maintaining contact, avoidance of contact and resistance to contact. On the basis of this measure, Ainsworth and colleagues described four basic types of attachment (exclusive of a very small category of children subsequently described as non-attached).

The main type is Type B, a secure attachment pattern. These children cry during separation, but are easily soothed upon reunion when the mother returns. They seek and maintain contact during the reunion.

Types A and C both describe types of insecure patterns of attachment: anxious/avoidant and anxious/ambivalent respectively. In Type A, the anxious/avoidant type of insecure attachment, the child shuns contact with the mother after she returns. Either the mother is ignored or the child's welcome is mixed with other responses, such as turning away or averting the gaze. The stranger and the mother are treated similarly. In Type C, the anxious/ambivalent type of insecure attachment, the child is very upset during the absence, but is not easily consoled upon the mother's return. The child resists contact, but there is some proximity-seeking during the reunion. The child is ambivalent about reunions after separations. He or she resists comforting from the stranger.

After these three categories had been described, another category, Type D (disorganised), was added because not all of the children observed fit easily into the previous three categories. Type D (disorganised) is characteristic of families where there has been parental pathology, child abuse, or other indicators of very high social risk. The child appears dazed or confused or is made apprehensive by the separation, and shows no coherent system for dealing with either the separations or the reunions. The child's behaviour may suggest fear and confusion about the relationship and what to expect from it.

That being said, it is interesting to note that Lamb et al. (1985), in their observation of 32 children who had been maltreated or abused either by the mother or by someone else, found that maltreatment by mothers was associated with a marked increase in the number of insecure (especially anxious/avoidant) patterns of attachment. However, where the maltreatment was by someone other than mother, the pattern of attachment to the mother seemed to be unaffected.

Finally, it is useful to consider attachment in a cross-cultural context. Woodhead (1998) conducted a study of early child-care and education programmes in India, Mexico, France, Venezuela and Kenya. He found that patterns of attachment in all of the countries followed a similar course, peaking between 10 and 15 months. He also found differences in a number of aspects related to attachment: for example, the numbers and patterns of attachments, the ways in which caregivers respond to infant distress, and the regulation of close relationships within families. He reminds us that the findings of Bowlby in relation to attachment were in the context of commissioned work reflecting postwar concerns about the impact or otherwise of separation on children who had been in day care whilst mothers contributed to the war effort. In that sense he observes,

> evaluations of day care that rely on the standard classifications of secure and insecure attachment prescribed by the 'Strange Situation' (Ainsworth et al., 1978) may misinterpret the emotional adjustment of children for whom separation and reunion has been a daily recurrence. (p. 9)

In this context, we should be aware that separation and reunion is a daily occurrence for many of the children social workers work with today. Many of them are cared for outside the home while their parents work.

Coming back to cross-cultural comparisons, Barnes (1995) summarises the work of Van IJzendoorn and Kroonenberg (1988), who prepared a meta-analysis of attachment studies across different cultures, looking at West Germany, the UK, Holland, Sweden, Israel, Japan, China and the USA. They used the Strange Situation categories. Whilst attachment patterns appeared in all of the countries, there were variations between the countries. Sanders (1999, p. 30) notes that the findings highlight.

> some very strong differences in the proportion of these three types of attachment patterns in children in different cultures, making a tendency to generalise about attachment across cultures something to be undertaken with extreme caution.

Like other issues previously discussed (e.g., autonomy *vs.* collective responsibility), the different patterns of attachments in different countries may be a reflection of different values associated with child rearing in those countries. These values will be internally consistent with other aspects of the roles of children and parents within the societies.

Social ecological theory (Bronfenbrenner)

It would be fair to describe the ecology of human development theory (Bronfenbrenner, 1977, 1979, 1986, 1989) as existing in a class of its own. It too is a way of understanding how children (and adults) grow and develop but it differs from all other theories of child development in one important respect: they are chronological and linear; the ecological model, though it incorporates a temporal component, is not. Instead, it places a primary emphasis on linking all the different systems influencing the individual (e.g., cultural, social, economic).

Bronfenbrenner (1979) expressed dissatisfaction with the traditional ways of understanding child development in that their exclusive focus was invariably the immediate setting of the individual, and they ignored wider societal impacts on how children develop. This is certainly true of all of the child-development theorists we have so far considered. Likewise, Bronfenbrenner was critical of those disciplines which are more social in their orientation because of their methodological limitations. In this sense there are close parallels with Durkin's (1996) notion of the need for social developmental psychology. For Durkin, the fundamental difficulty was that developmental psychology was not social and social psychology was not developmental.

Ecological thinking appears to be on the verge of gripping the imagination of those who are involved with children either as practitioners or as child-welfare educationalists. Some would argue it is not before time, considering that it has been around for nearly a quarter of a century. As suggested by Barrett (1998, p. 268):

> As stage models have become less useful, models which allow more precise classification and measurement of the environment have grown more necessary. Bronfenbrenner's (1979) *Ecology of Human Development* has emerged as by far the most cited and influential reference in developmental science.

Whilst the extent of its influence is perhaps more debatable than suggested by Barrett, there can be no doubt that interest in Bronfenbrenner's model is increasing. One of the real benefits for students and practitioners alike is that such a model enables them to see their clients in the widest possible social contexts. In the hurly-burly of everyday casework, it is easy to lose sight of the wider picture, and indeed, keeping in mind the wider picture is an ongoing struggle with which every practitioner should be engaged. But the wider picture is often devalued, first because of its seeming lack of relevance to everyday work, and secondly because of the inability of practitioners to actually do anything about the wider context within which their clients find themselves. For example, Blackburn (1991, 1993) looks at the issue of poverty and the strategies that practitioners can adopt to address it. She notes (1991, p. 8) that 'the fact that poverty is an everyday reality for a growing number of families means that work with families needs to be based on a clear understanding of the meaning, causes and dimensions of poverty in Britain today'. She also notes powerful barriers to addressing poverty: practitioners not believing they have a mandate to address it, and practitioners feeling overwhelmed by the enormity of the problem.

Perhaps one of the reasons why ecological theory is not applied as extensively as it might be is because the concepts are rather difficult to understand. Readers of Bronfenbrenner struggle with his material. They struggle for two main reasons. First, Bronfenbrenner is not easy to read. Like the work of many other child-development theorists (Freud, Piaget), there is an abstruse quality to the text that makes it difficult to get through. And like earlier theorists, he has created new words (neologisms) in order to express the ideas contained within the theory. As we continue in this chapter, we will encounter 'chronosystems', 'ecological transitions', 'microsystems', 'mesosystems', 'exosystems', and 'macrosystems'. To make matters worse, he has located these new words in a series of definitions (1–14), propositions (A–H) and hypotheses (1–50).

The main thrust of the ecological model is the adaptation between the individual and his or her environment. Bronfenbrenner defines the ecology of human development as follows:

> the scientific study of the progressive, mutual accommodation, throughout the lifespan, between a growing human organism and the changing immediate environments in which it lives, as this process is affected by relations obtaining within and between these immediate settings, as well as the larger social contexts, both formal and informal, in which the settings are embedded. (Bronfenbrenner, 1979, p. 21)

You see why a whole text written like this would be difficult to follow.

The mutual accommodation mentioned in the definition is the result of the individual and the environment interacting with each other. The individual plays an active role in influencing the environment, which in turn exerts an influence on the individual, which takes into account that previous influence, and so on. It is a synergistic (combined) cycle of influence between the changing individual and the changing environment.

The environment itself is seen as a complex set of systems within systems. In the opening paragraphs of his book, Bronfenbrenner (1979) uses the image of a set of Russian dolls, but it is perhaps easier to visualise the model as four systems represented by four concentric circles (see Figure 2.1). These four systems are given the labels: microsystem, mesosystem, exosystem and macrosystem (micro = small; meso = middle; exo = outside; macro = large or great).

The four systems are illustrated in Figure 2.1.

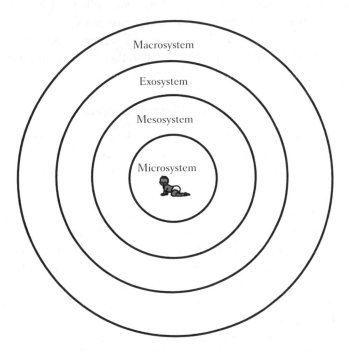

Figure 2.1 Bronfenbrenner's ecology of human development

The *microsystem* (small system) is defined as:

> a pattern of activities, roles, and interpersonal relations experienced by the developing person in a given setting with particular physical and material characteristics. (Bronfenbrenner, 1979, p. 22)

Examples of the microsystem would be the home, the school, and the workplace. It is this level to which most traditional theories of child development restrict themselves. Wherever there is a setting in which the child is physically present, there is a microsystem for his or her development. Considerations of the quality of care in the family environment come under this system. Family therapy is based largely in this system. Notions about the quality of out-of-home care (for example, in nurseries and playgroups, and other preschool care) are based in this level of system. For any one child, there is not one microsystem, but many. This is true at any one period of time, but becomes more true as the child grows older. In fact, one way of understanding child-development microsystems as the child grows is by considering their proliferation in number and complexity. To begin with, the child is largely rooted in the family system. As he or she grows, the child moves into the school system, and learns to move back and forth between these two microsystems. As the child gets older still (and becomes more independent), the child moves more and more between many different microsystems. By the time children become adolescents, they may have not one, but several different peer groups to which they relate in different ways.

The *mesosystem* (middle system) is defined as comprising:

> the interrelations among two or more settings in which the developing person actively participates (such as, for a child, the relations among home, school, and neighbourhood; for an adult, among family, work, and social life).   (Bronfenbrenner, 1979, p. 25)

Examples of the mesosystem would be interactions between family, school, peer group and church. Bronfenbrenner describes the mesosystem as a 'system of microsystems' (Bronfenbrenner, 1979, p. 25). It is a system comprising the network of the different microsystems of the child. In the last 25 years we have seen considerable thinking about the concept of 'partnership with parents', and it is here that the concept is most easily illustrated. Consider, for example, the influence of the relationship between parents and teachers in handling a nine-year-old boy's behavioural difficulty. In the first case, the parents and the teachers are able to discuss the problem so that a concerted and consistent approach can be adopted in both home and school (let's say, for example, a behavioural programme). The parents do not feel threatened by the teacher, who treats them with respect and values their contribution. They do not feel defensive, as if they are being accused of causing the difficulty that the school then has to deal with. In the second scenario, however, the parents do feel threatened, as if someone is pointing the finger of blame at them. They therefore work less effectively with the school in developing a home/school strategy. There may be a number of resulting difficulties. The problem may not be able to be resolved at all. The solution of the problem may be situation specific (it continues at home but not at school, or vice versa). The problem may take longer to resolve than necessary. The point for our purposes here is that the nature of the relationship between the school and home, *in itself,* is an influence on how the child will develop.

As another example, consider two of the microsystems of an adolescent, the family and the peer group. The nature of the relationship between the adolescent's parents and the adolescent's peer group is likely to exert an influence on the young person that is distinct from the two separate influences respectively. Perhaps the adolescent will identify more completely with the peer group, in defiance of his parents, or less completely, in compliance with his parents' wishes.

Of course it is important to remember that the influence is reciprocal. Not only does the nature of the relationship between parent(s) and school influence the child, but the child influences the nature of that relationship. The same is true in the case of the adolescent and his or her peer group.

The *exosystem* (outside system) is defined as:

> one or more settings that do not involve the developing person as an active participant, but in which events occur that affect, or are affected by, what happens in the setting containing the developing person.
>
> (Bronfenbrenner, 1979, p. 25)

Examples of the exosystem include the world of work, the neighbourhood or local community, the mass media, agencies of government (local, state and national), communication and transportation facilities, and informal social networks. The exosystem is the most challenging to understand, but its main features are that it does not contain the individual and that it is localised (although it may reflect locally the operation of national factors).

Understanding the impact of the exosystem on the individual is a two-stage process. The first stage is to demonstrate the impact of the exosystem on the individual's microsystem. The second stage is to demonstrate the resulting impact of the microsystem on the individual. If either is absent, then the system is not an exosystem for the individual. This also works in reverse; that is, the individual may exert an impact on his or her microsystem in a way which has wider repercussions beyond the microsystem. For example, a child might interact with his peer group in a way that causes disruption in a youth centre and affects the local community.

The *macrosystem* (large system) is defined as:

> consistencies, in the form and content of lower-order systems (micro-, meso-, and exo-) that exist, or could exist, at the level of the subculture or the culture as a whole, along with any belief systems or ideology underlying such consistencies. (p. 26)

Examples of the macrosystem can be both explicit (for example, laws, regulations and rules) and implicit (for example, belief systems as they are reflected in custom and practice). It is here that we see another influence on Bronfenbrenner's thinking about child development. Nearly ten years earlier he wrote a book (Bronfenbrenner, 1970) in which he raised a question about how the cultural differences between the USSR and the USA in bringing up children affected the children's lives. The main dimension he looked at was 'concern of one generation for the next', concluding that the greater investment of adults in the lives of their children in the USSR contrasted with the trend to age-segregated peer-group influences in the USA. He wrote that:

> children in the USA are more likely to be cruel, inconsiderate or dishonest, that fewer of them are polite, orderly, kind or helpful, that many are selfish and few have any real sense of responsibility. In contrast, Soviet children develop a concern for others and feeling of community at an early age.   (Bronfenbrenner, 1970, sleeve notes)

It is at the level of the macrosystem that we can consider the ways in which children internalise values in relation to gender, disability, race, sexual orientation, and so forth. An important part of the macrosystem is the way in which ideologies at the national level (based on power definitions of what is 'normal') operate at the local level, through books that the child reads, television, the behaviour of adults, and a host of other influences. We can understand macrosystem influences best when we are able to compare them with the macrosystem influences of other cultures: for example, Bronfenbrenner's contrast between the results of child-rearing practices in the USA and the USSR.

Now we come to the concept of ecological transition, which takes account of changes over time. Such a transition is defined as:

> whenever a person's position in the ecological environment is altered as the result of a change in role, setting, or both.
>
> (Bronfenbrenner, 1979, p. 26)

Examples of ecological transitions are the birth of a new baby, the arrival of a sibling, the child's first day at school, beginning work, or the loss of a significant person from the microsystem. Indeed any loss from the microsystem, any addition to it, or any change in the way the components of the microsystem relate to each other could entail an ecological transition.

One of the main advantages of an ecological orientation towards child development is its congruence with anti-discriminatory practice. It exhorts the practitioner to look widely at the influences on a particular child in a particular place, and in doing so challenges the practitioner to become aware of how structural inequalities within society are played out in the very immediate situations that the practitioner encounters. However, a continual difficulty for the practitioner is how to put theory into practice. The recent *Framework for the Assessment of Children in Need* (Department of Health et al., 2000) encourages practitioners to think widely in their assessments:

> The care and upbringing of children does not take place in a vacuum. All family members are influenced both positively and negatively by the wider family, the neighbourhood and social networks in which they live (p. 35)

These ideas, however, stop at the exosystem level of analysis. Whilst the guidance does not go so far as to prescribe that macrosystem factors should be part of the assessment, it is argued here that they are very significant, and are integrally related to an understanding of the child in his or her situation. A consideration of the macrosystem for an individual child is important because it calls upon the practitioner to locate his or her practice in the widest possible political and social contexts, and can serve as a secure basis for developing anti-discriminatory practice.

In this chapter, we have looked at the different sides of the nurture–nature debate as illustrated by the work of Locke and Rousseau and the developmental theorists who followed them. We have discussed cultural and gender issues in child development, and have touched on attachment theory and social ecological theory. In the next chapter, we will focus on the skills needed to work with children and families.

Some exercises

Exercise 2.1   Nature/nurture

Consider various aspects of how children develop, and share views on the extent to which they are determined by heredity or by environment. Some examples (but please use more) are:

- intelligence
- temperament
- physical attributes (consider different kinds, stature, body shape)
- personal likes and dislikes
- abilities/talents (e.g., music or art)

Exercise 2.2   Spare the rod

Consider from the perspective of learning theory the effectiveness of physical punishment on a child in relation to:

(a) the impact on the non-desired behaviour;
(b) the learning of the legitimacy of aggression by children.

Exercise 2.3   Spoiled goods?

Consider the meaning of the word 'spoil' in everyday usage. What does it mean? How is that concept applied to 'spoiling' a child? How does it reflect societal expectations about the role of children?

Exercise 2.4   Separation experiences

Consider any separation experience you may have had in your life (or that of someone very close to you). What factors made the separation worse? What factors made it better?

Exercise 2.5   Applying the ecological model

Take any well-known individual (it could be real or fictional) about whom there is a sufficient quantity of biographical information. Describe all the factors you can in relation to the four systems (microsystem, mesosystem, exosystem, macrosystem) that impinge on that individual.

CHAPTER 3

Skills in working with children and families

Objectives

In teaching and training it is customary to divide the requirements needed to undertake a particular kind of work into knowledge requirements, skills requirements and value (or attitude) requirements. This chapter deals with skills requirements. Knowledge is a matter of what a person needs to *know* in order to do the work; values or attitudes refer to how the person needs to *feel*; skills are what the person needs to *do*. It is very difficult to learn how to do something by reading a book – practice skills can only come with time and experience – but a book can tell you what types of skills are necessary to be able to undertake effective work. When you have read this chapter, you will not be a skilled practitioner, but you will have an idea of what skills need to be mastered and how you might begin to acquire these skills.

A good starting point is the principles contained in the new government guidance on assessment (Department of Health et al., 2000, p. 10). These principles describe assessment, but they can be seen as underlying the entire process of intervention. The principles require that assessments:

- are child centred;
- are rooted in child development;
- are ecological in their approach;
- ensure equality of opportunity;
- involve working with children and families;
- build on strengths as well as identifying difficulties;
- are inter-agency in their approach to assessment and the provision of services;
- are a continuing process, not a single event;
- are carried out in parallel with other action and provision of services; and
- are grounded in evidence-based knowledge.

The skill is to apply these principles to children in a variety of different situations. The children you work with may be in the 'looked after' system. They may be children in need living with their families in the community. They may be abused children. They may be children being placed for adoption. Despite the children's different situations, many of the skills you will need to work with them are the same. This chapter will deal first with skills needed to work with children, and then consider skills needed to work with families. Obviously these two sets of skills are not mutually exclusive and there will be some overlap.

Skills needed to work with children

Any work with a child must be based on a very thorough understanding of children's development and of the needs of the particular child being worked with. The child's needs will be identified through an assessment of the child's situation (and remember that an assessment is a continuing process not a single event, as indicated in the principles listed above). Then the needs must be addressed through specific activities related to specific goals, and the degree of success in meeting the needs must be evaluated both on an ongoing basis and at the end of the work.

The way you work with children changes depending upon the age of the child. If the child is four, you might get down on the floor and play with a puzzle or a doll; if the child is fourteen, puzzles and dolls are not the way to go. As children grow older, the more the work undertaken with them resembles work undertaken with adults. Adolescents are in the transition between childhood and adulthood, and are usually more interested in where they are going (adulthood) than where they have come from (childhood). Certainly, any indignity arising from a teenager's experience of being treated like a child will interfere with future work. Another general principle is that work with adults is more direct than work with children. You can usually talk directly to adults about relevant issues whereas you might need to communicate indirectly with children through some intermediary device like a doll or toy telephone.

Although communication with children is usually *indirect*, it may be *directive* or *non-directive*. For the most part, work undertaken in social services departments by social workers is directive work. This means that the work is highly focused. It is focused not only in the sense that it has a clear purpose but also in terms of how active the worker is in providing a structure for the child during the session. In directive work, the worker gently suggests moving from one issue to another, from one method of working to another. In non-directive work, by contrast, the worker provides an environment in which the child's natural propensity to play can be actualised, and looks at how the child uses the opportunities made available through play, to find self-expression. In fact, very little work is completely directive or non-directive, and most can be described as a mixture of both with a varying degree of emphasis on one or the other. Non-directive work is usually undertaken by more specialised therapeutic agencies (for example, child and family clinics), but even within the therapeutic services there are debates on the relative merits and efficacy of directive versus non-directive approaches.

Let us now turn to the more specific skills needed to work with children. Some of these are:

- ability to maintain clarity of focus;
- ability to recall the experience of being a child and to relate that to the work in hand;
- ability to get children to talk or express themselves;
- ability to feel comfortable in the presence of children and to have them feel comfortable with you;
- ability to facilitate children's play;
- ability to decentre from an adult perspective to engage the child;
- ability to continue working uninterrupted despite the emergence of painful and disturbing material;

- ability to respond to the different vocabulary, idioms, and expressions of children;
- ability to be the diplomat.

Ability to maintain clarity of focus

There are a number of reasons for undertaking work with children, and it is important to be absolutely clear about what the reason is. Is it to assess the child? Is it to enable the child to express a view? Is it therapeutic? Is it a mixture of these? Unfortunately, these reasons are not always separate and distinct. Assessment is an ongoing process, continually modified on the basis of work done with the child. It may well influence and be influenced by therapeutic intervention, each informing the other as the process unfolds. To take another example, advocacy work undertaken with a young person for the purpose of enabling him to express views about being looked after, may well act therapeutically by giving him a strong sense of personal validation, even if the process is not one that is explicitly intended to be therapeutic. But it would be an unwise advocate who confused her role and began trying to use advocacy work to achieve therapeutic objectives.

Advocacy for children is a field of work that has only seriously begun to develop since the implementation of the Children Act 1989 with its very heavy emphasis on the voice of the child. An advocate's primary objective is to express the words of the child; and, indeed, one might view the role of an advocate as having parallels with the role of a translator. The role of the translator is to aim for the most accurate possible translation across the two languages, without any embellishment or modification, no matter what the translator himself thinks. If the client says something that might be mis-construed, or which, when translated, may go against the client's interests, that is not a matter for the translator.

In advocating for a child, the role of the advocate is to provide informa-tion to the child and to convey the child's views to those who are charged with the responsibility for making decisions concerning the child. It is the child's rights and views that are promoted through advocacy, not his or her welfare. Rights and views may be in conflict with welfare. The most obvi-ous example is where a child wishes to return to live with a father who has sexually abused her. She may feel that the disclosure and the open knowl-edge will be enough to protect her. Professionals may feel concerned that she will continue to be at risk. Here we have a situation of potential con-flict between the professionals and the advocate: the professionals may feel that the advocate does not appreciate the harm to the child if she returns home, and is not acting in a way that will promote the child's welfare. It is then the advocate's task to clarify for the professionals the distinction between their role and his: it is they who are responsible for the child's welfare; it is his role merely to inform the child about the options available and convey the child's views. The advocate may have to make this distinction clear to the child as well. If she erroneously believes that he has the same decision-making powers as the professionals do, she may not trust him enough to express her views truthfully.

Ability to recall the experience of being a child and to relate that to the work in hand

Most of us cannot recall what it was like to be a child. Certainly we may recall memories of things that have happened to us. We may create a synthesis between what we recall, what we think we recall, and what others have told us, and call it 'memory', but the real sense of being a child is for many a clouded image. Some may recall happiness, others a melting pot of psychological pain, anger, helplessness, sadness, recognised and unrecognised loss, fears of rejection, and a feeling of being misunderstood. These are powerful emotions for a child to have to deal with, and therefore by the time 'normal' people reach adulthood, many of these experiences have been adjusted to in a way that perhaps drives them from memory. Consider the following, for example:

> The truth about childhood, as many of us have had to endure it, is inconceivable, scandalous, painful. Not uncommonly, it is monstrous. Invariably, it is repressed. To be confronted with this truth all at once and to try to integrate it into our consciousness, however ardently we may wish it, is clearly impossible. The capacity of the human organism to bear pain is, for our own protection, limited. (Miller, 1992, p. 1)

Miller is not talking about the distorted, disturbed and disrupted childhood of the abused child, but the powerful emotions behind the ordinary upbringing of the ordinary child in not unusual circumstances. While working with a child who has experienced abuse, the worker may well be confronting ghosts from her own past. It is vital that this is understood, so that the worker does not try to resolve her own problems through the work undertaken with the child. It is not uncommon for workers to be attracted to areas in which they have had some personal experience. A worker who was sexually abused in childhood, for example, may feel that she has much to offer other victims through her personal understanding of their trauma. Convinced that she has worked through her own experience, she will not consciously use her client to benefit herself but, nevertheless, the child's story may trigger a feeling in her which she had not resolved as thoroughly as she had thought. Supervision and self-awareness on the worker's part are both vital to ensure that this potential difficulty is kept in check.

A second, perhaps less emotionally laden barrier to recalling the experience of being a child is simply the vast distance between the developmental stage of the young child and the developmental sophistication of the adult. The language and thought of the adult are different from the language and thought of the very young child. For infants (for example, those in the Piagetian sensorimotor stage of development), the world is an experience of fleeting images and impressions which may exist briefly in time and space. Trying to recall such experiences is similar to trying to translate the stream of consciousness of James Joyce's *Ulysses* into a more prosaic, structured and grammatical form of text. Even the older child who has not yet developed the mental apparatus to handle concepts of object constancy (in both space and time), may find abstract reasoning, logical thought and reciprocity in relationships very difficult. Helping the child to achieve an understanding of adult decisions, actions and concepts may be enormously challenging. One of the very important examples here is the child's conception of time. Depending upon age, the 'here and now' can be a state that will exist forever, and notions of 'tomorrow' or 'later' may be the equivalent of 'never'.

In this sense, it is useful to be reminded of the totality of experience in very young children. Loss is loss forever, of the other and of a large part of the self. It is not a matter of 'I'll see you later', because for the very young child there is no 'later' and the sense of 'I' and 'you' can still be largely undifferentiated. Anger, on the other hand, is a rage that destroys. The experiences of hunger, frustration and pain are all extreme; they are not experienced as a temporary state that will get better, but rather as 'This is what it will be like forever.'

ACTIVITY
- Consider your first memory. To what extent is it your own recall? To what extent is it the recall of what others have told you?
- Look around the room you are in. Consider the sights and sounds you experience. Then try to imagine how they would appear without the continuity that locates them in time and space. Consider, for example, how it might feel to close and open your eyes with wonderment at seeing the same things? Consider how the sounds might be if you had no previous understanding (through experience) of the causes of those sounds.

Ability to get children to talk or express themselves and ability to feel comfortable in the presence of children and to have them feel comfortable with you

Not everyone feels comfortable around children. Children have a tendency to say whatever comes into their heads ('Mummy, how come that man only has one leg?'). Children do not have adult qualities of self-restraint, the ability to delay gratification, and an appreciation for the needs of others. Children are noisy and frequently destructive. They say the wrong things, cry at the wrong times, and demand almost unceasing attention.

To work effectively with children the worker must be comfortable around children. If this does not sound like you, then you may need to evaluate quite soon whether this is the place for you. Comfort around children can be learned (most parents learn it) but it may take time, and involve a considerable amount of self-reflection. The worker needs to be secure enough in himself that he is not excessively perturbed when the child asks why he is bald, why he has that spot on his nose, or mentions some other embarrassing attribute. To help the child to talk, he needs to relate to the child in a way that is different from how other adults relate to children, and initially at least the novelty of that approach may make the child curious, but in a cautious way. Talking to the child in a way that encourages the child to express a view, that says in effect that the child is worth talking to, and is an important person in his or her own right, may be something the child is not used to.

Getting down to the same physical level as the child, to address the child more as an equal, does serve to reduce the barriers to communication, but it is also something that may strike the child as odd, at least initially. After a time, it may make the child more comfortable, and the child's level of comfort with the worker is a primary factor in engagement.

Because children tend to be more open in their expression of feelings, it is easier for the worker to gauge a child's comfort level than it would be with an adult. However, when the child is uncommunicative, there are other indicators of comfort. Children who are distrustful of the worker, or at least cautious, will keep a safe physical distance. They will only approach the worker or allow the worker to approach if they are relatively comfortable. Another indicator is the extent to which the child engages in, or allows the worker to engage in, dialogue or other types of interactions (e.g., joint play). The worker should be aware of eye contact and other body language here, always keeping in mind that the messages conveyed by body language vary from culture to culture. A third indicator is the degree to which the child is able to stay 'on task' in terms of activity when the worker is present. The child who is excessively anxious is unlikely to be able to continue to play or concentrate on the task in hand.

Children, and in particular younger children, can be quite anxious about people whose appearance is simply different. If they are not used to men with beards, then the mere fact of the worker having a beard may make them wary. Similarly, they may be anxious about an unfamiliar skin colour or any physical peculiarity. Certainly, in time, they will come to adjust (or to use a Piagetian concept, the child will come to accommodate eccentric appearance as part of the way that adults appear), but not before they have mentally struggled unsuccessfully to assimilate it into their existing picture of the world. Some children adjust quickly, others take longer, and the issue for the worker may well be how long he needs to wait for the child to adjust. Patience will usually prevail but in the worst possible case it might be necessary to assign another worker. The bearded and rejected worker must then be sufficiently self-confident to accept that it was his beard that was rejected and not himself.

Ability to facilitate children's play

Play is an absolute prerequisite for work with young children. If a child cannot play, she cannot be helped, and therefore, the first stage with a child who cannot play is to help her to learn how to play. From there the work can begin. There are three fundamental principles underlying using play to work with children. First, play is the child's medium. The child feels comfortable with play. Playing with the child sends the message that the adult values what the child does, and this message empowers the child. Secondly, play, like other techniques, is a method of making the 'inner world' of the child external. It is a projective tool in that it takes what is inside the child, puts it outside the child, and there allows it to be the focus of attention by the child and the worker. It acts as a screen upon which the child is projecting herself. There is nothing the child can create in the context of play that is not a reflection of the child's inner self and that inner self's relation to the world. The child who makes the bear eat up the little boy, demonstrates at the very least an awareness that there are creatures called 'bears', that they can eat people (sometimes a little poetic licence needs to be allowed), and that children are vulnerable to dangers from other living creatures. The worker may be able to take the scenario further, by asking, 'How does that boy feel about being eaten by the bear?'

A third principle of play as a medium of working with children (and this is particularly true in non-directive play approaches) is that it relies on an inner drive of the child to health and reparation. Given a supporting environment that does not direct that certain things need to be done at certain times, the child will use the equipment available to address issues of significance to herself – possibly as a way of learning to understand something she does not yet understand. The worker is thus more of a facilitator and observer of the healing process than a prime mover. It is not the worker that heals the child; the child heals herself, but the worker provides the context in which the healing can occur. Of course, healing may not occur, but at least the opportunity has been provided.

One of the difficulties of working with children is that this is often seen to be the province of experts: child psychologists, child psychiatrists and play therapists all lay claim to the special skills and knowledge that are needed to understand children, and a social worker with none of these specialist qualifications may feel that she ought to leave well alone. It is useful here to make a distinction between play therapy, and direct work with children using play as a medium. Child-welfare workers do not provide therapy in the sense that their primary goal is to reduce the child's trauma. Instead their role is to assess or monitor the child's situation in order to provide the appropriate services. One such service may be to refer the child to a 'child expert' so that therapy can be provided, but meanwhile the worker must communicate with the child in order to find out what is needed. As with all clients, the worker will communicate in the way that is most likely to elicit a valid response, and for a child that way is through play. After all, no worker would hesitate to try to communicate with an adult on the grounds that a psychiatrist is more qualified to do it. Engaging in play as a medium of communication is therefore a perfectly legitimate occupation but engaging in 'play therapy' is not.

As a practical example of the difference between play as communication and play as therapy, we might point to the interpretation of the significance of communications from the child. If a child draws a picture of a person without arms, a worker who is trying to communicate might well say, 'It's hard to do things without arms. How does the person feel about that?' But the same worker should steer clear of interpreting the drawing as a reflection of the child's internal sense of helplessness. That kind of interpretation is the province of the experts.

We see here, again, the importance of clarity of focus. It is the coordination of the efforts from different professionals that is the hallmark of effective practice, but such coordination only works if each professional is clear about her own role and purpose as distinct from the roles of other professionals on the team.

Ability to decentre from an adult perspective to engage the child

Direct work with children operates at the interface between the world of children and the world of adults. We cannot expect children to be eager to talk to us about issues of concern to adults, even if they are also issues of concern to the children themselves. For children, sitting down face to face with an adult and talking about things that they have perhaps not talked about before is not an easy matter. The interview situation may be familiar to the worker, but to the child it is artificial. It may require social skills (taking turns to talk, waiting until the speaker is finished, using eye contact appropriately) that the child has not yet acquired. It may require cognitive skills (for example, sustained concentration) that the child is still developing. It may require a level of self-denial (or endurance) that the child is not yet ready for. Therefore, above all else, work with children must be undertaken in a way that engages the child. It has to be appealing, it has to be comprehensible, it must be age appropriate, and it must be fun (or at least not excessively tedious). This is not to say that direct work techniques cannot be used to address painful material, but it should be the content that is painful, not the process.

A very good example is provided by Bray (1991) who describes her work as a social worker with Shaun, a child in a children's home. The work gets off to a very unpromising start. Shaun is not around when she visits, despite his knowing she was coming. When he arrives they sit opposite each other in green plastic chairs, and she proceeds to go through the agenda she has mentally prepared, telling Shaun about the threat of exclusion from school, changes in his mother's circumstances, and the forthcoming meeting with his foster carers. Shaun says, 'Can I go now?' and the social worker is left feeling angry and bemused at the lack of connection. For Bray it was the beginning of thinking about how to approach work with children in a different way, how to avoid adult-centred agendas in the actual work with the child, and how to find a different medium for communication in which the child will be engaged. This is not easy and means abandoning many preconceived notions about the importance of getting answers from children about the questions adults want to ask. It means that the worker must meet the child on his own terms, in his own place, using his own language. And for younger children especially, this language is the language of play.

The attitudes of colleagues can make this even more difficult than it is already. It is obviously faster, even if less effective, to have the child talk to the social worker in her place, on her terms, in her language. It is faster still not to talk to the child at all, obtaining the needed information instead from adults who think they are familiar with the child's situation. In a busy social-services child and family team, where there may be great pressure to allocate cases, taking a long time to work with a child, at the child's pace, using methods which may seem slow and unfocused, is not likely to be viewed with favour. Even though more experienced practitioners recognise that direct work with the child is a necessity not a luxury, the worker may still feel that she has to justify the time spent with the child. From the point of view of colleagues, she could be using that time to initiate other interventions that might be seen as more useful, at least in the short term.

A final point to note about decentring from an adult perspective is the extent to which the child is expected to share everything with the worker. No child, or anyone else for that matter, can be compelled to share information and we should allow the child the dignity of choosing what he wants to share. A more difficult decision for the worker is to what degree she should let the child know the consequences of sharing before the information is shared. For example, if a child says that abuse has reoccurred the worker must take steps to deal with that and a possible consequence may be that the child is constrained. If the worker points out the possibilities, the child may conceal the information and his welfare may be jeopardised. If the worker does not point out the possibilities, she has deceived the child but can address his welfare because she has the relevant information. On the other hand, the child might not trust her ever again. With older children, the worker might decide to be open about the consequences, and trust the child to make an informed and correct decision about what to share. But it is always a difficult situation, and with younger children it is even more complex.

Ability to continue working uninterrupted despite the emergence of painful and disturbing material

The material that children disclose to workers can be very painful and distressing. If the worker is to provide a useful service to the child, she must not be thrown off course by the content of what is said. It is not unheard of, particularly in the early days of interventions with children who had been sexually abused, for workers to require temporary breaks during the sessions, for the purpose of regaining their composure.

We know from foster carers (Macaskill, 1991) that children frequently do not disclose all of the abuse that they have experienced at once. There is a pattern of disclosing physical abuse before disclosing abuse of a sexual nature, and often there is a progressive unfolding of the extent of the sexual abuse. Foster carers describe the process as one in which the child seems to test you out to see how much you can cope with. If you seem able to cope with what you have been told without being shocked or thrown off course, then later the child may tell a little more. The implications of this for the social worker are self-evident. She needs to be able to maintain equanimity in the face of shocking material. Training helps, and so does the capacity for self-care. It may seem a truism to say that if you can't care for yourself, you can't care for anyone else, but many social workers lose sight of themselves in other people's traumas, and losing sight of yourself is a sure recipe for disaster. There is a large literature on burn-out, vicarious traumatisation and post-traumatic stress disorder, which describes the consequences of repeated exposure to traumatic experiences, both one's own and other people's. There is not space here to go further into that, but the importance of self-care cannot be over-stressed.

Ability to respond to the different vocabulary, idioms, and expressions of children

As already noted, the language of children is different from the language of adults. One of the areas where this is particularly important is work with abused children. For example, one of the exercises used in basic training to enable people to understand sexual abuse and work with sexually abused children is to brainstorm on the range of terms used to describe male genitalia, female genitalia, and various sexual acts. In part, this exercise is used to desensitise people to the shock-value of the terms used (important in connection with the previous section). However, in part this exercise is designed to familiarise trainees with the wide range of terminology so that they will be familiar with euphemisms and idiosyncratic terms when children use them.

In the same way, it is helpful to be familiar with slang expressions, which can change almost overnight. A word of warning here though. It is one thing to understand slang and quite another to attempt to use it. Children feel patronised by adults who try to 'come down' to their level by using their slang, and they have a very natural tendency to laugh when the adult gets it wrong. It is more respectful to the child and more comfortable for the worker to use ordinary age-appropriate language, with words and sentence structures that the child will easily understand.

Ability to be the diplomat

Children will frequently ask questions which the worker will find very difficult to answer. Why didn't my parents want me? Why was I the one to be adopted when others in the family weren't? Why was it me my father abused? These and other questions can present a dilemma for the worker – not whether to tell the truth (lies are always counterproductive), but how much of the truth to tell at the moment, and, most importantly, how to tell it. The first step is to understand the question. The child who asks why his parents didn't want him is not asking for reasons why he couldn't live at home. The real question behind all three of the questions above is, 'What is wrong with me that ... ?' Of course what the child who couldn't live at home needs is personal validation. He needs to feel that despite appearances to the contrary, he is an individual with intrinsic worth and reasons to feel good about himself.

The child who was adopted has the same need. One of the issues for an adopted child is why her parent(s) didn't love her enough to keep her. Strategies for dealing with this frequently tend to emphasise the material circumstances surrounding the parents (they couldn't afford to keep you), or letting the child know that, although she was given up by one set of parents, she was especially selected by others. Both of these strategies have difficulties. The child may know other families living in poverty who do not give up their children. And it is all very well to be specially selected but if you hadn't been given up by your own parents in the first place – the people who are supposed to love you – you wouldn't have been available for selection.

It is usually considered important, when faced with difficult questions by children, to present the information as factually as possible, being careful to avoid any condemnation of the parents. However, one also has to be careful not to go too far in the other direction, or the child may develop fantasies about absent parent figures, or add to already existing fantasies.

Sometimes the worker needs to convey 'bad news' to the child. For example, the parent no longer wishes to have contact with the child; a decision has been taken *not* to return a child to his or her parents; the foster carers can no longer look after the child. Again, in these cases, the worker must not only deal honestly with conveying the information but must be sufficiently skilful to convey the reason for the news in a way that makes sense to the child without being too hurtful. There is no formula that any text can provide to help you here: it is a matter of your own skill, your own judgement, your own human empathy with the child's situation.

Skills needed to work with families

We have deliberately considered the skills of working with children first, for two reasons. One reason is to remind you that the prime reason for intervention in the lives of children and families is to promote the welfare of the child. As stated by the Department of Health et al. (2000, p. 13):

> Working with family members is not an end in itself; the objective must always be to safeguard and promote the welfare of the child.

The other reason is to remind you that, as adults, workers often find it easier to communicate with other adults (the parents), and therefore it is a greater challenge to find and develop the skills necessary to communicate with children and enable them to communicate with you.

Now we will consider some of the skills needed for working with the parents and with the families as a whole. We will look at:

- ability to work in partnership with parents;
- ability to be honest and open even when the information you have to share is unpleasant or painful;
- ability to communicate with adults;
- ability to negotiate;
- ability to provide counselling, warmth, empathy, understanding;
- ability to tolerate people's pain and anger;
- ability to work effectively with groups.

Ability to work in partnership with parents

As we noted in Chapter 1, one of the key elements of the Children Act 1989 is that it promotes partnership between parents and local authorities. In the 1990s, 'partnership' and its companion, 'empowerment' have become buzz-words within social-welfare practice. However, partnership is an ideal, and as such, is unlikely to be totally attainable within practice.

For many, the idea of partnership is flawed because of the very real differences in power between social workers and clients. When compared with parents, who frequently come from the most disadvantaged sectors of the community, social workers have extensive knowledge of the legislative context in which they operate. They have a large-scale organisation behind them providing professional, legal and administrative support. They have several years of training to prepare them for their role, and they are likely to have at least some experience of the matters with which they are dealing. Critics of the concept of partnership claim that even to maintain the existence of partnership is disempowering because it represents obfuscation, an attempt to obscure the very real power differentials in the relationship. Others however (for example, Tunnard and Ryan, 1991), maintain that partnership, as intended under the Children Act 1989, must be redefined in order to change practice. They note, for example, 'For us, partnership is not about equal power, but about people working together towards a common goal' (p. 67). This can be illustrated in the process of assessment. Even where there is conflict, the extent to which social workers and parents work in partnership is based on the degree to which they can reach an understanding about the common objectives of the social-work intervention process, and the role that each should play in achieving those objectives.

The concept of partnership is integrated into many provisions of the Act, and into some of the changes that have been made from previous legislation. The main partnership provisions of the Act relate to the requirements to ascertain the wishes and views of parents when working with children in need or with children who are being looked after. Colton et al. (1995a), in their study of family support under the Children Act 1989, did just this.

As part of their study, Colton et al. (1995a and 1995b) talked to 122 children in need within the terms of the Act, and with their parents. Many of the parents interviewed felt that social workers were too concerned with the welfare of a single child and not sufficiently concerned with the welfare of the family as a whole; in other words, they were concerned with protection at the expense of family support. Likewise, some parents with disabled children, while grateful for the help they were receiving, believed that this help should be extended to their other children, whose 'normal' lives were being disrupted by their sibling's disability.

Truancy was a further major concern for a large number of the parents, who were intensely frustrated by the seeming inability of any authority to enforce the law regarding school attendance. These parents were also reluctant to talk to teachers and tended to believe that social workers should act as intermediaries between the family and the school, the police and the school, and the special and local schools. Parents felt in addition that temporary placement in a special school following difficulties in the local school could do more harm than good if gains were not maintained when the child returned to the local school. These gains tended not to be maintained because there was little communication between the special and local schools.

A good deal of concern was focused around the accommodation of children. Some parents confided that children were being returned home from local authority accommodation before parents were ready to cope with the responsibility. The lesson here might be that reunification, though a worthy goal, only works when the groundwork has been thoroughly prepared and the timing is right. It is easy to assume that parents mourn the loss of their children and want them back as quickly as possible; and, for many, this is indeed the case. Others, though, while not wanting to admit it in case they are seen as 'bad' parents, are thoroughly relieved that the rude, destructive, trouble-causing child has gone. They need time to come to terms with their feelings about their child and they need help to cope with the kinds of behaviours they will have to face when the child comes home. No doubt, they need help also to change their own behaviours with respect to the child; and all of this is an inherent part of the reunification process.

Another concern was the relatively high amount of assistance provided to foster parents to care for a child. This was resented by birth parents, particularly when the child spent a lot of time at the birth parents' home. A further cause of resentment was the benefits afforded to accommodated children when compared with non-accommodated siblings. Moreover, children returning home after being accommodated tended to resent the loss of the benefits they had formerly enjoyed. Social workers here seem damned if they do and damned if they don't. Providing for one seems to lead inevitably to jealousy on the part of the other, yet provision is required under the terms of the Act, and resources do not allow for indiscriminate provision. It is perhaps a case of viewing the needs of the child in the context of the needs of the family and ensuring that siblings and birth parents are not ignored.

Finally, Colton et al. (1995a and 1995b) examined partnership between families and social-work agencies. Most parents did feel that they had participated in decision-making, and two-thirds felt that social services had helped them in bringing up their children, and they particularly appreciated the provision of emotional support. The partnership element most lacking between agencies and families was the sharing of information. Only 29 per cent of the children interviewed felt that their social workers had told them things they needed to know, and only 13 per cent of parents felt that they knew enough about the kinds of services available to help them (from other agencies as well as social services). Social workers tended to provide children only with the kind of information that seemed relevant and beneficial under the circumstances, and withheld information which could potentially be damaging – such as not telling a 16-year-old girl that she was entitled to leave her foster home to move in with her boyfriend. There are echoes here of the 'diplomatic' skills needed to work with children discussed earlier, where the issue was how much of the truth to tell and how to tell it. However one feels about the social worker's action in this particular circumstance, Colton et al.'s study did show that relying on social workers to provide verbal information did not work well overall. The authors' recommendations for more effective dissemination of information included the following:

- Prepare information leaflets for parents, covering such common concerns as: hyperactivity; working without losing benefits; child support; parent support groups; behaviour management; harassment by an ex-partner; personal development programmes for men; entitlements when leaving care; and so on.
- Have social workers distribute the relevant leaflets (including leaflets from or about voluntary agencies and community groups), providing additional verbal explanations where necessary. Such provision of written material often helps to dispel parents' suspicions that information about entitlements is being deliberately withheld.
- Utilize other ways of disseminating information: for example, holding film shows and public meetings, or erecting information booths in public places such as shopping centres.
- Develop a multi-agency strategy on how information is to be produced, publicized and delivered.

Even in child-protection work, the trend has been towards increasing partnership, and one impact of this, as a result of the Children Act 1989, is the greater involvement of parents in child-protection conferences which look at issues of risk to their children. Whilst there have been real problems with the implementation of this practice, it is now generally accepted that parents should participate in child-protection conferences. For some parents, however, participation means little more than physical presence. It is easy for them to be intimidated by the authority figures at the table with them, difficult for them to argue, easy to feel at the end that they were no more than a rubber stamp, called there to reinforce decisions already made. If there is to be any real partnership, the impetus must come from workers who genuinely desire the parents' input and have the ability to make the parents feel comfortable and empowered in an alien setting.

Ability to be honest and open even when the information you have to share is unpleasant or painful

Parents are not always honest with social workers, particularly when there are issues of abuse (Department of Health, 1991a; Reder et al., 1993), but it is important for social workers to be scrupulously honest in all their dealings with parents. Sometimes this is difficult, particularly when sharing unpalatable decisions with the parents, such as the decision to hold a child-protection conference, the decision to place a child's name on the child-protection register, the decision to withdraw, or not provide, financial support for a child to attend nursery (or indeed any family-support service), and of course, the decision to apply for a care order for the child to be removed from the care of the parents. Sometimes other unpleasant information needs to be shared with parents: you haven't been able to secure the service for the parent that you were attempting to get; you haven't been able to do something very important for the parent that you had agreed to do.

Like any unpleasant task, telling the parent this tends to be put off because there is always something more important that you have to do right now. Also, like any unpleasant task, it gets more difficult the longer it is delayed. Honesty with parents includes sharing information in a timely manner, using all the skills you possess to convey what you have to say in the least hurtful and most productive way.

Ability to communicate with adults

We have already discussed the skills needed for working with children, and some of the skills needed for working with adults are similar. However, whereas with children the major obstacles to communication are developmental differences, with parents the obstacles are more likely to stem from social class and cultural differences. One of the lessons one learns very soon in practice is that there are ways and ways of saying the same thing, and finding the right way is vitally important. A temptation when one has to say something unpleasant is to lapse into jargon. Official-sounding phrases that are usually incomprehensible to the parent can distance the worker from the whole proceedings, allowing her to believe that she has said whatever it was without putting it into so many words. Sometimes, the use of jargon is not intentional: it is just a matter of the worker unconsciously trying to increase her own comfort level by using language that is familiar to herself. But jargon is only communication if it is used as a convenient shorthand with other professionals who know what it means. With parents, it is more often a process of exclusion: the worker is essentially saying, 'I belong to a professional club and you don't.' It is very important, therefore, to use only words that the parent will understand, taking into account the parent's cultural background and social class.

Social class is a delicate area. It is easy to pretend that social class does not exist, that we are all equal as people and class distinction is something that is better ignored. However, class distinction does exist. It is one of the realities that affect all other aspects of client's lives, and to ignore it does no-one a service. A worker might well be seen as hypocritical if she tries to pretend to a client – whose awareness of the social hierarchy is probably acute – that they are both on the same social level. Most often they are not, and this is something that must be dealt with honestly, and without patronising the client. Again, there are no formulae to help you here. It is your own skills, your own personal qualities of warmth and empathy that will count.

Another point to be aware of is that much of our communication with each other is not verbal at all but comes through body language. If you are assuring your client that her situation is immensely important to you whilst backing towards the door, you are sending mixed messages, and the message which will come across with most force is your desire to escape. Be aware of your body language, and do your best to ensure that your tongue, your eyes, your hands and your feet are all saying the same things.

This is particularly important when you need to confront or challenge people. Issues about non-compliance or disguised compliance (Reder et al., 1993) must be addressed, not swept under the carpet, and they must be addressed clearly so that there is no possibility of mistake. A good example here is work with sexual abusers. The worker often needs to confront abusers who deny what they have done or the extent of the abuse. If the client has lied, the lie needs to be pointed out, but the focus of the worker's remarks should be this particular lie, with no implication that the client is, in general, a liar. This may seem a subtle distinction – a liar, after all, is a person who lies – but it is very important to distinguish the person from the act. A child who has done a bad thing must not be labelled as a bad child. Similarly, a client who has lied must not be branded as a liar but is simply a person who, in this particular instance, has told a lie.

Being willing to confront does pose certain risks for the worker, even if done with the utmost care and discretion. Even the most skilful worker may at times trigger an extremely aggressive response, and it is a matter of judgement to be able to predict when a client might pose a personal danger. If there is a possible danger, it is not brave to confront it alone: it is just foolhardy. Take another worker with you or ask for the protection of the police. If you are alone when the situation arises, leave as rapidly as possible. At all times, consider your personal safety first when dealing with potentially aggressive clients, remembering that you can't look after anyone else if you can't look after yourself.

Ability to negotiate

One of the very curious aspects of working with children and families is the success of the family therapist. Almost any family therapist will tell you that when families arrive, it is very rarely family therapy that they are looking for. They expect that their problem will be fixed, and the problem, in their eyes, is usually the family member who is causing all the trouble: the 8-year-old who will not go to school; the 13-year-old who stays out all night; the 14-year-old who is involved with drugs. The other family members expect that their role in the 'fixing' process will be to provide the therapist with the necessary information and possibly provide moral support to the one who is being fixed.

The first job of the family therapist, therefore, is to persuade the family that it is the family system that needs to be addressed, not the behaviour of the offending member. Perhaps this idea will be introduced gradually, but if the therapist cannot negotiate with the family about what needs to be done, nothing will be accomplished. The fact that something often is accomplished says much for the negotiating skills of family therapists. Other social workers too experience similar problems. We know from research (see, for example, Mayer and Timms' classic work *The Client Speaks*, 1970) that a mismatch between client and worker expectations leads to poor outcomes. Perhaps the client expects material assistance while the worker hopes to increase the client's ability to cope with the situation as it is. Unless the worker is able to negotiate with the client what result can be expected from their work together, the worker will be frustrated, the client disappointed, and nothing will be done.

Negotiation is a vital skill for social workers. They do not need to be Henry Kissinger, but they do need to understand the importance of trying to find ways out of an impasse that allow the other party dignity, and a feeling of having achieved their goals. A very interesting story is told about two sisters who both wanted the same orange. They could not agree over who should have the orange and so, in a spirit of compromise, they cut the orange in half and divided it equally. One sister then went home, squeezed the juice from the orange and threw away the peel; the other went home, used the peel in a cake she was baking, and threw away the rest. Although the division was fair, had the sisters been able to negotiate the outcome with reference to their needs, they would have both had twice as much.

The important phrase here is 'with reference to their needs'. When there is conflict, it is vital in negotiation to identify clearly your own needs, interests and expectations and to help the other parties to identify theirs. Sometimes, the conflict will turn out to be about means rather than ends, and then the process can be addressed rather than the objectives. Even when the conflict concerns the objectives, there may be some overlap, where common action can be mutually beneficial.

Objectives (or interests, needs and expectations) should always be expressed specifically, avoiding generalisations. For example, the worker should not say to a parent that she wants what is best for the child. This does not specify what the worker thinks is best (which is probably the nub of the conflict) and, worse yet, it implies that the parent does not want what is best for the child. Similarly, a worker who proclaims that 'the child's welfare is paramount' will probably produce defensive parents who believe that the worker thinks she has more of an interest in their child's well-being than they do.

Having noted the pitfalls, let us now turn to the principles. The following are some principles of negotiation from Fisher and Ury (1991) that lend themselves to working with parents.

1. Participants are problem-solvers.
2. The goal is a wise outcome reached efficiently and amicably.
3. Separate the people from the problem.
4. Be soft on the people, hard on the problem.
5. Proceed independent of trust.
6. Focus on interests, not positions.
7. Explore interests.
8. Avoid having a bottom line.
9. Invent options for mutual gain.
10. Develop multiple options to choose from; decide later.
11. Insist on using objective criteria.

12. Try to reach a result based on standards independent of will.
13. Reason and be open to reason; yield to principle, not pressure.

Of particular interest here is the emphasis on negotiation as a creative process. Fisher and Ury describe negotiation as a problem-solving process; they suggest *inventing* options for mutual gain and *developing* multiple options. Creativity is not an attribute that tends to be emphasised in social-work training, but there is no doubt that the ability to find creative solutions to problems is a major asset for a social worker.

Another point of interest is the recommendation to proceed independent of trust (principle 5). Social workers tend to believe that trust is paramount and nothing can be accomplished without it. Doubtless it is paramount and it should always be aimed for. On the other hand, it is not always present (in international negotiations it is almost never present) and it is quite possible to negotiate in good faith without waiting for a trusting relationship to be established. Principle 12 suggests that agreements may be reached about specifics if there is agreement about the broader principles (for example standards) underlying the issue. This then makes the discussion one of trying to reach agreement about how to operate on the basis of standards about which there is agreement. This may also de-personalise the issue from an 'I want, you want' position, moving towards a 'we both want'.

Ability to provide counselling, warmth, empathy, and understanding

There are other situations in which a counselling approach is required. The provision of rapid support, advice and guidance when parents have just received the news that their child has a disability ('early counselling') may be a very useful way of helping them to cope. When parents have experienced the loss of a child, a counselling approach is likely to be beneficial, perhaps provided by a specialist counselling service. Marital counselling may be provided by organisations such as Relate. You will be able to think of many other situations where counselling is appropriate.

The third element of a growth-promoting relationship is empathic understanding. This relies on the ability of the worker to imagine what the client may be experiencing, relating it to her own nearest experience to that of the client. Empathy also draws on the ability of the worker to be an active listener. This means fully hearing what the client has to say, relaying what one has heard back to the client for clarification and confirmation, and not jumping in prematurely with answers and solutions. Empathy can be a suspect concept from the point of view of the client, on the grounds that 'you can't know what it's like until you've been there'. For example, workers are frequently asked by parents, 'Do you have children?' The implication here is that, if you don't, you have no right to be telling me how to bring up mine. Workers should not become defensive – it is not a sin to have no children – and the question, anyway, might provide a good lead in to having the client tell you how *she* brings up children.

Ability to tolerate people's pain and anger

Responding to another's pain and sadness is not easy. There is sometimes a tendency to do anything to get away from the experience: bring the interview to an end; suggest a cup of tea; change the subject; heartily tell the client not to dwell on it. Another temptation is to try to 'fix it': suggest things the client might do; promise to do something yourself. The most difficult thing to do is to sit in silence while the client cries. Allowing a client to feel what she is feeling without trying to move her on to something else is a very important skill. You must be able to contain your own pain in order to allow your client to experience hers.

Loss of a child is a particular example. People who have experienced such a tragedy may well find that others around them are ready to move on long before they themselves are ready. Even those friends who were most supportive during the weeks following the loss may reach a stage after several months when they are no longer comfortable hearing the person talk about the lost child. 'It's time to move on with your life,' they say bracingly, and it is most important that the worker does not convey, implicitly or explicitly, the same thing. The clients themselves are the only judges of when it is time to move on.

Coping with a client's anger is also a difficult task. Despite their best intentions, social workers do things that make people angry. It is no use thinking that because a difficult decision was justified and the justification was explained to the client, the client will not be angry. A decision to remove a child, for example, even when made and explained with the utmost care, sensitivity and fairness, is likely to make the parent extremely angry. As with pain and sadness, the best approach is to allow the parent to experience her anger. However, there is a world of difference between anger and aggression. Physical and verbal threats and menacing behaviour should not be tolerated and, as previously discussed, the worker must be aware of any risk to her personal safety.

Ability to work effectively with and in groups

It is important to feel confident about working in groups and with other professionals. Most child-care social work is delivered by social workers operating in teams. These teams may be more or less specialised, but they will generally adopt a coordinated approach to assessment and intervention work. During the last quarter of a century, there has been a much greater emphasis on working together with other professionals in a range of children's services. Teamwork is no longer the exclusive prerogative of child protection (if indeed it ever was) and many of the decisions to be made will be undertaken by a group of professionals coming together to develop a coordinated plan. These professionals may come from different agencies and represent several different disciplines.

A good example of this kind of inter-agency and multi-disciplinary working is the case conference. Case conferences to consider the situation of all children who are at risk of abuse were recommended by the report into the death of Maria Colwell (Department of Health and Social Security, 1974). In the case of Maria Colwell, it seems that there were a number of professionals who each held a different piece of information about the situation, but no-one understood the situation in its entirety because there was no mechanism for putting the pieces together. The case conference constitutes the required mechanism, and its purpose is to make mutual decisions about what should be done next, to ensure the welfare of the child. This is not as easy as it sounds. Consider two of the barriers.

First, meetings involving a number of professionals are expensive. The time spent needs to be justified, and therefore the purpose of the meeting must be clear. It is generally accepted that case conferences – and committees in general – should *coordinate* work, not undertake work. Much of the work (for example, risk assessment, locating a foster home) needs to be done outside the committee, and the role of the committee is primarily to decide which tasks need to be undertaken, to allocate those tasks, to monitor progress on the tasks, and to ensure that new plans are made when the tasks are either not being achieved, or are unachievable.

Secondly, professionals have different backgrounds and approach issues in different ways. The most conspicuous example of this is the difference between the social and medical models of disability or illness. A physician treating a child with diabetes, for example, is treating the diabetes and does so by prescribing diet and medication. A social worker, working with the same child, is treating the whole child in the context of her family and may be more concerned with the effect of the diabetes on the child's and the family's life. Both of these perspectives are quite legitimate and, if the social worker and physician can respect each other's views, their cooperation will be fruitful. Perhaps the social worker can persuade the child to follow the diet when her friends are eating sweets; perhaps, on the social worker's advice, the physician can modify the insulin injection regime to fit more conveniently with the child's routine. If, on the other hand, the social worker believes that all physicians are only interested in diseases, not in people, and the physician believes that social work is a waste of time, it is the child and family who will suffer from the conflict.

Another area of conflict can arise from the different perspectives of social workers and the police. In a situation of alleged sexual abuse, for example, the police focus is to gather evidence that may be used in laying criminal charges. The social worker's focus is to protect the child. It is very difficult to achieve both ends at the same time (in a joint investigative interview, for example, involving both the social worker and the police) and the result may well be mutual recriminations, with both parties feeling that the other has intruded on their turf and prevented them from carrying out their function.

Turf and territory tend to be important considerations for professionals. Psychologists might argue that only they have the skills and training to administer and interpret pencil-and-paper measuring instruments (to measure such things as marital satisfaction, for example). Nurses and social workers might both argue that it is only they who ought to be doing discharge planning for patients coming out of hospital.

Terminology is another bone of contention. Social workers might say that the word 'patient' is disrespectful, implying that the person is an object with no control over his or her own life or treatment (and that medical staff use that word because they do, in fact, see people that way). Physicians might counter that the word 'client' is hypocritical. 'Clients' in the world of commerce are people who pay for services, and social workers' 'clients', who often do not pay, are not clients at all but rather consumers of services. A social worker's real 'client', is the funding body or the taxpayer, and (our hypothetical physician might say) social workers would do well to remember that.

What is to be done about all this? How do we remove the barriers of jealousy, resentment and misunderstanding so that professionals from different disciplines can work together in ways that are beneficial to children and families?

Education is one way. First, students who are being taught within their discipline should be taught the functions and perspectives of other disciplines in a manner that allows them to respect and understand what other people do. Next comes joint training. Professional development training in sexual-abuse investigations, for example, might include both social workers and police officers. So might training in how to handle situations of domestic violence. Training in the medical examination of a woman who has just been sexually assaulted might include physicians, social workers and the police. Through joint training, professionals can learn each other's perspectives, goals and problems. If they work together after the training, and if they are given time to debrief and discuss, they might even grow to like and respect one another.

However, effective interdisciplinary work is not just a matter of cooperation between individuals, necessary though that is. It is something that needs to be structured, paid for and valued by the various organisations and agencies for which the individuals work. Attitudes need to change, in short, from the top down as well as from the bottom up.

As well as working *in* groups, workers need to be able to work *with* groups. The last thirty years have seen the expansion of group work from an extremely specialist method of working, undertaken only by a small number of specially trained professionals, to a method that is considered to be in the repertory of every qualified worker. Groups are very powerful tools, now used in a wide variety of situations, with a wide range of client groups. Consider the following examples:

- group work with abusers, to mobilise peer pressure to acknowledge denial and minimisation;
- groups for parents of children with a learning disability;
- groups for mothers of sexually abused children;
- groups for children who have been sexually abused;
- groups in family centres, for a wide range of practical activities;
- groups for victims of domestic violence to share their experiences;
- groups for parents of teenagers;
- parenting groups.

One of the main purposes of the more therapeutically oriented groups is to break down the isolation that people often feel. For the sexually abused teenager who, in the context of the secrecy surrounding sexual abuse, has felt that she is alone in this terrible experience, it is often astounding to find that others have been coping with similar experiences, and remarkably, have been experiencing similar consequences. Another positive impact of groups is that people who have felt extremely damaged by what has happened to them (for example, being abused, losing a child), begin to realise that they have something to offer others who are in a similar situation. They begin to find a capacity for growth, and their self-esteem is enhanced when others respond positively to their experience and perhaps their advice.

Of course, any group situation can also have negative aspects: faction formation, scapegoating, groupthink, domination by some group members, and dismissal of the opinions of others. The group facilitator must watch for these and use the most appropriate means to ensure that the group process is one of empowerment, not one of compounding the disempowerment its members may already have experienced.

We will leave the discussion at this point and move on to talk about the distinction between prevention and protection. In this chapter, we have looked at the skills needed to work with children and families. In the next chapter, we will consider prevention and family support.

Case examples

Case example 3.1 Helping troubled children

There follows a number of scenarios in which children may experience adjustment or personal difficulties. For each of them, consider the following:

1. What emotional difficulties might the child be experiencing?
2. How might the child, directly or indirectly, be helped?
3. Are there any particular means of communicating with the child, or methods of working that might suggest themselves in this particular situation?

(1) Paul is 6, and is the youngest of three children. His mother and father have just separated, several months previously. It is an acrimonious parting, and Paul has not seen his father since the separation.

(2) Kylie is 12, and is the oldest of three children. Her father comes home regularly in a drunken condition, and frequently (at least once a month or so) assaults her mother. Her mother has considered moving, but feels afraid to do so.

(3) Richard, who is West Indian, is 8. He has been fostered, on his own, with a white family for two years, in an area where there are very few other black children. It has always been planned that he should move, and now it is suggested that he should go to live with a black family in a more culturally diverse neighbourhood.

(4) June (7) finds it difficult to make friends at school. Her father left home when she was 3 years old, and she has regular contact with him. Since last September, she has complained most mornings of stomach ache so severe that she does not feel she can go to school. On the few occasions when her mother has kept her home the stomach pains have apparently subsided in a few hours.

(5) Michael (11) has just transferred from a very small rural primary school to an urban secondary school because his family relocated. Over the course of his first term in secondary school, a gang of boys have been intimidating Michael, and taking his lunch money off him. He has been afraid to tell anyone about it.

(6) Andrew is 5 years old. His concentration is very poor and at school his temper tantrums are so severe that the school is considering exclusion. His older sister no longer enjoys playing with him, and his parents are finding it difficult to deal with his behaviour.

Case example 3.2   Overcoming barriers to working with families

There follows a number of scenarios in which parents may experience difficulties in working with social workers. Consider what those barriers might be, and how they might be addressed in work with the family.

(1) Mary is 17 and has a child, Paul, aged 18 months. She is a single parent, and is still under a care order, which will lapse when she is 18 years old. She has been provided with housing through a supported housing scheme, and she has found the support provided very helpful. Recently there has been concern about her care of the child, and her social worker is calling around to see her.

(2) Mr and Mrs Anthony are a West Indian couple living in a London borough. Mr Anthony recently used a belt on his 13-year-old son for 'cheeking' him. The school reported the welts, and a social worker, who is white, is calling around to meet with Mr and Mrs Anthony to discuss the incident. Mr Anthony does not understand what the fuss is about; he experienced the same type of discipline when he was growing up in the West Indies.

(3) Anne (23) is a single mother, living next door to her own mother in an English village. She has been in an escalating cycle of drug usage, and is now regularly injecting. She is involved in prostitution to support her drug habit. Whenever she takes the drugs, she ensures that her son Dean (3 years, 6 months) is with her mother next door. Her mother doesn't approve, but is glad that she has enough control of the situation to leave her son there; but she is uncertain whether the drug usage will remain under control. The health visitor has referred Dean to social services.

(4) Megan (38) and her husband have a child (Sian, aged 2) with Down's Syndrome. The health visitor has referred them to the social services for respite care, as Megan is occasionally very tearful, and generally is very tired and run down. Both Megan and her husband are Welsh speaking; the social worker calling to see them doesn't speak Welsh. He is going to be discussing the provision of respite care, and other possible services that might help Megan and her husband.

(5) Mrs Ali has left her husband with her three children aged 3, 5 and 7 to go into a refuge, following his continued violence towards her over the

last five years. Her command of English is very limited, and most of her dealings with people are undertaken through her oldest child. The workers at the refuge are concerned about the impact of the domestic violence on the children and wish to discuss this with Mrs Ali.

Case example 3.3 *Working across professional and disciplinary boundaries*

Mrs Jones is 25 and has a six-week-old baby boy. He is her first child. She lives with her husband. They live in Grangetown, Cardiff, in a modest, privately-owned, small terraced house. The health visitor has been to see her and using the Edinburgh Post-Natal Scale considers that she is at high risk of post-natal depression; the Health Visitor has shared her concern with the GP to whose practice she is attached. The GP feels that the Health Visitor should strongly advocate medication, which he would then prescribe. The Health Visitor believes that there is time to explore the benefit of post-natal support networks and weekly support visits from herself before embarking on chemical treatment.

1. How might the different professional backgrounds influence their perceptions as to the causes and remedies of post-natal depression?
2. How might their different roles influence their perception of the difficulties associated with becoming a parent?

CHAPTER 4

Prevention and family support

In Chapter 3, we looked at the skills needed to work with children and families. In this chapter, we will discuss prevention and family support.

Objectives

After reading this chapter, you should know the theoretical positions of prevention and protection on a continuum of services to families and children. You should understand the difference in practice between preventive and protective services, and between reactive and proactive approaches to prevention. You should also have an understanding of the distinction between primary, secondary and tertiary prevention; and this may inform your view about the state's right to interfere with the way that parents bring up children. You will know the legislative context of services for children in need and their families, including the duties of local authorities. You will have a fuller understanding of some of the issues within the provision of family-support services, for example, 'partnership with parents', the distinction between 'family support' and 'intensive family preservation services', and the difference between 'child-focused' and 'family-centred' services. You will also be introduced to the concept of quality in family-support services.

Let us begin by considering the continuum of services to families and children.

A continuum of services

Services to children and families may be placed on a continuum from preventive to protective services (see Figure 4.1). At the far left 'preventive' end of the continuum, universal services such as health care, education, and access to income are provided for everyone. Such services are non-stigmatising because they are universal and they provide the basic foundation of security, education and health that may prevent families and children from becoming 'at risk'. Obviously, the success of their preventive function depends on the degree to which they are sufficient, readily accessible, and disbursed in a manner which does not carry a stigma.

If the provision of universal services does not prevent families from becoming at risk of child abuse or neglect, one or more of a range of family-support services can be provided to ensure the child's safety while preventing the need to remove the child from home. For example, a social worker may go into the home on a regular basis to help parents learn non-violent methods of discipline and interact more positively with their child.

If these efforts fail and the child must be removed, protective services come into play. Such services may comprise some form of out-of-home care such as foster or residential care, and they are often seen as indicators of failure: failure on the part of the parent to parent adequately, and failure on the part of the social worker to prevent the child's removal. From a more

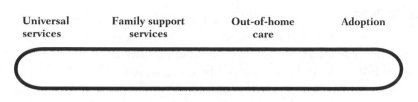

| Universal services | Family support services | Out-of-home care | Adoption |

Figure 4.1 Prevention/protection continuum

positive viewpoint, however, a temporary separation can allow time for the parents and the child to do the work necessary to enable them to live together again successfully. Thus, a protective service such as foster care can also be a preventive service if it prevents permanent family breakdown.

In cases where the child has been removed and where attempts to reunite the family are unsuccessful, adoption may be considered. Adoption appears at the far right 'protective' end of the continuum and, indeed, it is a service that protects the child by providing a safe and stable environment. Nevertheless, it is also preventive in that children who are nurtured by adoptive parents are less likely to become 'at risk' of child abuse or neglect when they themselves become parents. Thus, the ends of the continuum may be joined to form a loop.

Preventive and protective services

We have said that child-welfare services run on a continuum from preventive to protective services. There is sometimes a very fine line between prevention and protection. Indeed, depending on what it is we want to prevent, we could theoretically classify all services as preventive. When we provide universal services, such as health care and education, we are trying to prevent some children being at a disadvantage compared with other children. If some children are at a disadvantage despite our efforts, we provide services to prevent them being neglected or abused. If they are neglected or abused anyway, we provide services to prevent them being removed from their homes and families. If they must be removed, our services are aimed at preventing permanent separation: and, if permanent separation becomes inevitable, we try to care for them in such a way that they will grow into competent adults whose own children will not be at a disadvantage compared with other children. Thus, our preventive efforts come full circle.

However, differently phrased, these same efforts could be theoretically classified as protective. Universal services are designed to protect children from such threats as disease, illiteracy, the general effects of poverty, and the poor parenting that often results from life stress. When universal services are insufficient, family-support services aim to protect children who are neglected or abused or are at risk of being neglected or abused. If protection can be assured while the child remains at home, so much the better. If not, the child is protected by being separated from the family and is reunited only when safety concerns have been addressed.

In practice, the term 'prevention' is usually used to designate those services that are provided to prevent the child being separated from the family. If the child must be separated, then the investigation of alleged abuse or neglect, the child's removal when necessary, and all subsequent services are viewed as 'protective' services. This division between 'prevention' and 'protection' at the point of the child's removal is purely arbitrary since all services, both before and after, lie on the same continuum. However, we sometimes forget that the division is arbitrary. Many social workers view prevention and protection as separate, even opposite, services and this is an attitude which has very real consequences. The most damaging of these consequences is the perception that removing the child implies the failure of prevention: a failure that is laid at the door of both the social worker and the parents. Since removal is associated with failure, accommodating the child outside the parental home becomes a demonstration of failure, with all the accompanying stigma. The parents, having 'failed' in their parental role, may be viewed as 'bad' parents, by social workers, by foster carers and, worst of all, by their children and themselves. Children, too, are stigmatised. They cannot live at home, as other children do, and they may feel that this is because they are 'bad' children, seen as such by their parents, teachers, peers, caregivers and social workers.

Section 17 of the Children Act 1989 stipulates that the provision of accommodation for a child should not be viewed as failure by either the family or the social worker. However, it is usually not possible to change ingrained attitudes merely through legislation. Since actions follow from attitudes, it is often not possible to legislate actions either. The Act may include specific duties to be discharged by local authorities but, inevitably, some interpretation will be necessary to translate a written duty into a particular action taken with a family. The duty will be interpreted differently depending on the perceived needs of the family, the resources available, and the value base of the person doing the interpreting. Thus, the same duty may result in different actions by different local authorities and even by different social workers within the same authority.

Naturally, written guidance has been provided in conjunction with the Act to help with the interpretation, but it is almost impossible to write anything with sufficient clarity and lack of ambiguity to ensure that it is always interpreted by everyone in the same way. Thus, though obviously helpful, the guidance itself is open to interpretation, and specific services made available to families will still differ between authorities and social workers.

In this chapter, we will look at what the Act says about prevention, and the difficulties that have arisen with respect to interpretation.

The meaning of prevention

We have already said that, whereas all services might be viewed as preventive in theory, in practice, preventive services are only those services that prevent the child being removed from home. Holman (1988) considers that the key to the meaning of prevention lies in its aim or purpose: deciding what it is that we want to prevent. If we want to prevent children being disadvantaged – that is, if we want to prevent them becoming at risk through disadvantage – we must take some positive steps to accomplish this. This is the *positive* approach to prevention. In Holman's (1988) view, a positive view of prevention entails the promotion of policies and practices aimed at preventing children from failing to enjoy, in their own homes, the kind of parenting, the freedom from suffering, the standards of living and the quality of community life which are considered reasonable for children in our society.

If, on the other hand, separation is what we want to prevent, then we will not worry about providing services to prevent children being disadvantaged: we will merely react to prevent separation when their disadvantage puts them at risk. We are then taking a *reactive* approach to prevention. A reactive approach is defensive in nature. It concerns policies and practices which prevent the unnecessary separation of children from their parents and their placement away from home in public (or voluntary) care or custody. It also prevents children who are separated from having to remain in care unnecessarily, and it prevents them being stopped from maintaining physical and/or emotional links with their natural families. The approach that we tend to take in practice is the reactive approach.

Holman (1988) has defined prevention more fully, including both reactive and positive approaches, by identifying seven dimensions of prevention:

(i) preventing children being received into public or voluntary care away from their families;
(ii) preventing children entering custodial care;
(iii) preventing the neglect or abuse of children;
(iv) preventing the effects of poor parenting on children;
(v) saving children from those disadvantages in their homes and communities associated with lack of income, amenities and social experiences;
(vi) preventing children from having to remain in care (rehabilitation); and
(vii) preventing the isolation of children in care.

An earlier definition of prevention, still in use, employs terminology derived from the world of medicine and distinguishes three levels of prevention:

(i) *Primary prevention* comprises those services which give general support to families and reduce levels of poverty, stress, insecurity, ill-health, or bad housing. The aim of primary prevention is to ensure that all families have the basic necessities which make good parenting possible.

(ii) *Secondary prevention* is help offered after problems have arisen within families. Such services are likely to be restricted to those felt to be at 'special risk' (for example, children at risk of neglect or abuse) or who require special priority (for example, children with disabilities). Secondary prevention includes support and encouragement for parents in times of stress, welfare-rights approaches aimed at alleviating hardship, and initiatives designed as alternatives to care and custody.

(iii) *Tertiary prevention* seeks to prevent adverse consequences to children spending time in substitute care. It includes attempts to ensure high-quality substitute care and reunification of children with their families.

Bringing together the old and new terminologies, we might equate primary prevention with a positive approach to prevention and secondary prevention with a reactive approach. Tertiary prevention, though certainly included within Holman's seven dimensions of prevention, may be regarded as falling within the purview of protection.

Legal duties of local authorities and social workers

We come now to look at the duties regarding prevention which are laid down in the Children Act 1989, and the context within which those duties were formulated.

A major debate in child welfare concerns the degree to which the state has the right to interfere with the way that parents bring up their children. At that period in history when children were regarded as property, the state had no right, and some people at the extreme Conservative (or right-wing) end of the political spectrum would still argue that the state has no business, let alone duty, to intervene in the private lives of families. According to this view, parents' rights are paramount. At the other end of the spectrum, people would argue that bringing up children concerns us all and the state has an absolute right, indeed a duty, to override the parents' wishes when parents are not caring for their children adequately for any reason. In other words, the child's rights are paramount. Most social workers take a middle ground, believing that the best interests of the child must come first but, given this, parents' rights, wishes and parental authority must be upheld by the state to the greatest degree possible.

The Children Act 1989 supports the latter view, seeking a balance between protecting the child and supporting the family. Under Section 17 of the Act, local authorities have a general duty to safeguard and promote the upbringing of children in need. To this end, they must facilitate the upbringing of children by their own families through providing services to both the child and the family. The term 'family' includes anyone with parental responsibility and anyone the child is living with.

This duty is restricted to 'children in need'. Hence, it is not proactive in the sense that services are universally provided to all; but it is proactive in the sense that local authorities are expected to seek out children who may be in need in their area and provide services to prevent family problems developing. A reactive approach, as we have learned, would involve waiting until the problems had already developed before intervening.

A prime question here is: Who are 'children in need?' The concept of 'need' is obviously relative. Probably no child living in the United Kingdom is 'in need' if compared with children living in the developing world. On the other hand, almost every child in a poor community is 'in need' if compared with children in a richer community. There is some merit to the idea that whole communities may be 'in need' and it is the community rather than the individual child or family which ought to be helped.

The Children Act itself gives only a very broad definition of what is to be understood by 'in need'. 'Children are in need if they require local authority services to achieve or maintain a reasonable standard of health or development, or they need local authority services to prevent significant or further impairment of their health and development, or they are disabled' (Section 17, Children Act 1989). The Act gives no clear indication of what is to be understood by 'a reasonable standard of health or development' or by 'significant or further impairment'. Again, the terms 'reasonable standard' and 'significant impairment' are relative, depending on what community is chosen for purposes of comparison and what standards of health and development are common in that community. The Act does say that these matters must be judged with reference to *'all other children in the local area, not only those who live in a similar, and possibly quite disadvantaged, community to that of the child in question'* (our italics; Children Act 1989). This would seem to indicate that local authorities are expected to set higher standards than those found in the poorest communities; neither are they permitted, under the Act, to limit services to those children at risk of abuse. On the other hand, the Act does instruct local authorities to give priority to those children who are 'most vulnerable'. Hill and Aldgate (1996, p. 7) note that these ambiguities have 'allowed some authorities to close their doors to all except those seriously at risk. Such an approach is in danger of undermining the family support emphasis of the Act.'

The definition of need in the 1989 Act covers three categories of children: children who are not likely to maintain 'a reasonable standard of health and development' without services; children whose health and development are likely to be 'significantly impaired' without services; and children with a disability. This definition is broad enough to include any child who could potentially be helped by the provision of services: more children than social services departments could practically serve. Thus, it is often left to the social worker to decide how 'need' should be defined.

Colton et al. (1995a,b) carried out a comprehensive evaluative study of services for children in need in Wales under the 1989 Act (funded by the Welsh Office). This study included an examination of how social workers define need in practice. Colton and colleagues interviewed 103 front-line social workers, 21 leaders of social-work teams, 6 principal social workers and 16 Assistant Directors of Social Services with responsibility for child care. The interviews revealed that social workers interpreted the concept of need in a wide variety of different ways, with little agreement as to how a child 'in need' should be defined. There was also little agreement on how much guidance had been provided regarding the concept of need, and what that guidance said. Despite the wide variety of individual definitions of need, two lines of thought were prevalent among social workers. First, social workers believed that 'reasonable standard' and 'significant impairment' are opposite sides of the same coin; that is, a child who does not meet reasonable standards of development is significantly impaired. Secondly, a child who is 'significantly impaired' is one who is in need of protective services. Thus, by extension, all children who might be said to be 'in need' at all are in need of protective rather than preventive services.

Given the lack of adequate guidance on the concept of need, social workers were using material primarily formulated for use in child-protection work. This obviously reinforces, if it did not cause, the common belief that children 'in need' are in need of protection. Social workers were relying on their own experience as professionals and parents; the criteria used most often to decide whether a child was 'in need' were whether the child was reaching developmental milestones and receiving adequate basic care.

In addition, Colton et al.'s study asked managers to rank-order categories of children who would have priority for service under ideal circumstances, and also categories of children who did actually have priority. Proactive prevention came much higher on the 'ideal' than the 'actual' list, showing that managers wanted to give more emphasis to preventive work but in practice concentrated resources on children at risk of abuse and neglect. The level of services available to support families was judged by both managers and social workers to be generally inadequate.

In the same vein, several other research studies have examined the implementation of services for children in need under Section 17 of the Act. For example, Aldgate and Tunstill (1995) found that local authorities were far more likely to see children for whom they already had a degree of responsibility as being 'in need' compared with other children in the community. Some 78 per cent of the authorities studied gave high priority to children at risk of harm and 74 per cent to children at risk of neglect or in care, but only 12 per cent gave high priority to children living in homes where the gas, electricity or water was disconnected, and 11 per cent to children excluded from school.

Colton et al. (1995a,b) argue that, if it is departmental policy to move away from an emphasis on protection towards proactive prevention, then procedures for accomplishing this must be specified. Such procedures might include:

- discouraging social workers from using protection material to guide them in preventive work by issuing alternative guidance designed to emphasise prevention;
- developing guidance materials in cooperation with other statutory and voluntary agencies;
- establishing indicators for prevention work along the same lines as the *Working Together* material (Home Office et al., 1991);
- issuing the guidance in joint training sessions together with other statutory and voluntary agencies.

As we have discussed, it seems that both local authorities and the social workers they employ have wide discretion in deciding which children are 'in need' of service, and often disagree. Nevertheless, there is some agreement on a number of categories (not mutually exclusive) of children who should be regarded as 'in need' within the terms of the Act. These include:

- children with disabilities;
- children at risk of abuse and neglect;
- children who are delinquent, or at risk of becoming so;
- children separated from their parents because of divorce, separation, hospitalization, parent in prison, immigration restrictions, and so on;
- children being looked after by local authorities;
- children with caring responsibilities (e.g., teenage parents, children of parents with disabilities);
- children whose home conditions are unsatisfactory (e.g., those who are homeless, in temporary or substandard accommodation, or in accommodation for homeless families);

- children who may be broadly defined as living in poverty and at high risk of family breakdown. (Colton et al., 1995a,b)

As might be expected, there is a relationship between the types of children 'in need' who are to receive services and the specific purposes for which these services are to be provided. It follows, for example, that if a service is directed at children who are at risk of ill-treatment or neglect, then the purpose of the service (and the concomitant duty of the local authority) is to prevent ill-treatment and neglect. Thus, the duties imposed by the Act on local authorities indicate the purposes for which family-support services should be provided. These duties are:

- preventing ill-treatment and neglect;
- reducing the need to bring care or related proceedings;
- reducing delinquency and criminal proceedings against children;
  minimising the effects of disability on children with disabilities;
- promoting family reunification and contact.

Now we have considered to whom services ought to be provided and why, the next question has to do with the nature of the services themselves. What sorts of services should local authorities provide? The Act refers to a variety of services that may be necessary to support families, including: advice, guidance and counselling; occupational, social, cultural or recreational activities; home helps and laundry; travel to services; holidays; family centres; accommodation for children and families; accommodation/cash assistance for rehousing abusers; assistance in kind; cash assistance; and day-care and out-of-school activities. The Act also stipulates that services should be provided in a non-stigmatising way, and should enhance the authority of parents. Children should participate in decision-making, and service provision should be sensitive to the needs of ethnic minority communities. Participation in decision-making is discussed later in the chapter, and service to ethnic minorities is discussed in Chapter 7.

As we have seen, local authorities are expected to seek out children in need in their area and provide services to them to prevent problems developing. The process of seeking out children in need includes publishing information about available services, and developing strategies which encourage children and families to come forward. It also includes facilitating the provision of services by others. The Act recognises that social services departments cannot provide the full range of necessary services themselves. Therefore, it enables them to call on other departments within local government – for example, leisure and recreation, health and education – to assist. This approach is particularly important in relation to children with disabilities whose state of health often requires special educational provisions to be made available (Hill and Aldgate, 1996). However, assistance is not limited to other government departments. The Act also allows social services to request – and fund – assistance from voluntary and private agencies. Hill and Aldgate (1996, p. 7) rightly note that, while the voluntary agencies have a vital role to play in service provision, particularly of an innovative or specialist nature, consistency and continuity of provision of services is not always compatible with a market economy.

Contexts of family support

Let us now look at the contexts of family support: that is, the conditions which must prevail in order for family-support services to be provided – as the Act stipulates – in a way that is non-stigmatising, enhances the authority of parents while taking children's wishes into account, and is sensitive to the needs of ethnic minority communities. The first of these contexts is poverty.

Poverty

Although the Act encourages a proactive approach and does not permit local authorities to limit services to children at risk of abuse, we have seen that, in practice, authorities are constrained by limited funds to focus their attention on children who are already abused or neglected or are at imminent risk of becoming so. Holman (1988) sees a reason for this. He believes that proactive family-support services can only be effectively provided in a society which is working towards diminishing the gap between the rich and the poor. However, for much of the past quarter of a century, Britain has moved in the opposite direction. Social polarisation has occurred and levels of child poverty have increased (Colton et al., 1995a,b).

Holman (1988, p. 211) correctly states that social deprivation remains closely associated with 'children having to leave their parents and ... suffering severe disadvantages within their homes'. He therefore argues for a coherent strategy on the part of central government in relation to primary prevention. In his view:

> there can be little doubt that government policies directed at reducing poverty, improving the health of lower-income groups, and the provision of adequate housing for all would do much to prevent children having to endure either of these two outcomes.

Significantly, when asked what services they would like but were not receiving, the parents in Colton et al.'s (1995a) study of children in need in

Wales gave first priority to material goods and better housing. The study also found that, although children living in poverty are 'children in need' under the 1989 Act:

(a) social services departments in Wales could not provide data on the number of children living in poverty; (b) because of limited resources, children living in poverty were accorded lowest priority in terms of service provision, despite the desire of managers to engage in more preventive work; (c) services designed to alleviate poverty were provided inconsistently to users depending on the particular social worker involved; and (d) given the resource constraints, child care managers could see little hope of altering the situation.   (Colton et al., 1995a, p. 102)

Some groups of children are particularly vulnerable to poverty. According to the LIF (Low Income Family) Statistics, over three-quarters of children growing up in lone-parent families were living in poverty compared with 18 per cent in two-parent families (Child Poverty Action Group, 1996). Likewise, Colton et al. (1995a, p. 30) reported that in the UK, people from ethnic minority groups experience disadvantage in many areas of their lives.

Reviewing the comparatively large body of research on the practice of child and family social workers funded by the Department of Health, Thoburn (1997, p. 291) reports that:

All these studies show that children most in need of additional child welfare services tend to come disproportionately from certain groups in society. Amongst those who are over-represented are children from single parent or reconstituted families; those who are badly housed and living in deprived areas, and those whose families subsist on incomes below the recognized poverty line. The parents and children tend to have more physical and mental health problems than the general population, and children of mixed racial parentage tend also to be over-represented.

Colton et al. (1995a,b) argue that perhaps more than any other factor, poverty threatens the practical achievement of effective family-support services. The successful implementation of Part III of the Children Act, and indeed, community care policy more widely, necessitates that poverty be placed again at the centre of the policy, practice and research agenda. Quite simply, there is no substitute for action at the national level to tackle primary poverty. However, at the local level, social-welfare agencies and local authorities might develop anti-poverty strategies to help improve the financial circumstances of their service users. Such strategies would comprise three elements.

First, policy-makers and senior officers within social-welfare agencies must acknowledge their own status as major resource holders. They have the capacity to invest in the human, physical and social fabric of impoverished communities by establishing local offices in these communities, employing local people, and purchasing goods and materials from local vendors. Secondly, within social-welfare organisations, traditional welfare-rights activities are presently located at the margin of organisational activity. Such activities need to be reaffirmed as part of mainstream work. An approach is required which recognises and seeks to redress the unfairness and discriminations within the system. Thirdly, with regard to the wider anti-poverty strategies of local authorities, the development of Credit Unions, cooperative buying schemes and Bond banks can do a good deal to improve the financial circumstances of groups in poverty. Moreover, they do this in ways which build upon the networks of mutual support that exist even within the most disadvantaged communities.

Ruxton (1996) suggests a number of measures to help families out of poverty. With regard to lone parents, he calls for an appropriate mix of employment training, child care, social security and maintenance arrangements. He also advocates specific action to improve the employment prospects of all young people, including those with inadequate qualifications and/or those who leave the education system prematurely. Further, he argues for an appropriate range of welfare benefits for low-income families and young people. These should be set at an adequate level and uprated on an annual basis. Finally, he recommends a comprehensive range of support services at a local level to counter the effects of poverty and social exclusion. These may include family and community centres, debt counselling services, credit unions, child health clinics and care and education services.

Having touched on the issue of poverty, we will now look briefly at another contextual factor related to family support: the way that services are organised.

Organisation of services

A second contextual factor in providing family-support services is the way that these services are organised. Research indicates that the organisation of service delivery as a whole is often incompatible with the concept of family support contained in Part III of the Children Act 1989 (Colton et al., 1995a,b). For example, rather than providing employment for local inhabitants, social service departments tend to draft in workers from outside the area, and operations are often directed from remote headquarters rather than locally. Indeed, it is difficult to escape the impression that social services departments are designed to operate in ways that are bound to be self-defeating, and that frustrate any effort to develop effective family-support services, or to fashion an authentic partnership with parents, children and local communities.

An important family-support service, as we shall see later in the chapter, is the family centre. Here too, Colton et al.'s (1995a,b) study showed that the statutory sector has been slow in establishing these centres and does not always allow them to be run in ways that empower local inhabitants while boosting the local economy.

Types of family-support services

Having discussed two of the contexts of family support, let us look now at the types of family-support services which are provided. It might be noted that some family-support services are provided at a national or departmental level while others are community-based and are sometimes referred to as community prevention programmes. Let us begin with a brief, general discussion of community-based prevention programmes.

Community-based prevention programmes

In North America, a good deal of attention has been paid to community-based prevention programmes, a generic term which encompasses various types of family support and family preservation programmes and services.

Family-support services may be defined as:

> Community-based activities designed to promote the well-being of vulnerable children and their families. The goals of family support services are to increase the strength and stability of families, increase parents' confidence in their parenting abilities, afford children a stable and supportive family environment, and otherwise enhance child development. Examples include: respite care for parents and caregivers, early developmental screening of children; mentoring, tutoring, and health education for youth, and a range of home visiting programs and center-based activities, such as drop in centers and parent support groups.
>
> (General Accounting Office, USA, quoted in Whittaker, 1996, p. 117)

By contrast, '"intensive family preservation services" are brief, highly intensive services generally delivered in the client's home with the overarching goal of preventing unnecessary out-of-home placement' (Whittaker, 1996, p. 118).

Expanding on this, family preservation services are:

designed to help families alleviate crises that, if left unaddressed might lead to the out-of-home placement of children. Although more commonly used to prevent the need to remove children from their homes, family preservation services may also be a means to reunite children in foster care with their families. The goals of such services are to maintain the safety of children in their own homes, when appropriate, and to assist families in obtaining services and other support necessary to address the family's needs.

(General Accounting Office, USA, quoted in Whittaker, 1996, p. 118)

Whittaker (1996) notes that 'family support' and 'intensive family preservation' are the two dominant expressions of a shift away from child-centred to family-focused service. He distinguishes the following essential foundations on which family-oriented prevention rests:

- *Partnership* – the meeting of clients and professionals on common ground and as a unified team.
- *Mutuality* – creating an atmosphere where clients and professionals communicate openly about the most sensitive of concerns in a relationship built on openness, mutual respect and trust.
- *Reciprocity* – where we truly operate on ... the 'helper principle', where giving help and receiving help goes both ways and between all the key players: professional to client, client to professional, professional to professional, and client to client.
- *Social assets* – where assessment begins not by looking at what is going wrong in clients (deficits), but at what is going right (strengths).
- *Resilience* – where we are always alert to those protective factors and mechanisms that blunt and divert the effects of known risk factors and permit individuals, families and groups to overcome extraordinary and difficult life situations.
- *Optimization* – where our goal is always on creating the conditions within which each individual, each client family, group and neighbourhood fully exploits its developmental potential.
- *Natural healing* – where our search is for those approaches to change which draw fully on the clients' ability to heal themselves through ritual, celebration and reflection.
- *Social integration* – where our work with the 'private troubles' of individual clients is seen in the context of raising public social concern about the critical function of individuals, families, small groups and neighbourhoods in maintaining social order and promoting public safety.

- *Coherence* – here used ... to describe processes through which individuals, families and groups discern a sense of meaning beyond the struggles of day-to-day existence.
- *Hope* – Finally, person-in-environment practice is about fostering a sense of hope: hope that things can change for the better, that the power for change resides within, that someone is listening ... and cares.

(Whittaker, 1996, pp. 123–4)

Now that we have noted some basic principles underlying community-based prevention programmes, we will turn to a few specific examples of such programmes. First, though, we should look briefly at who provides the programmes – community child-care teams – and the process through which the programmes are provided.

ACTIVITY

The reader may find it helpful to identify prevention programmes that exist in his or her local community. Consider who provides these programmes. Are they examples of primary, secondary or tertiary prevention?

Community child-care teams

Family support services are often provided through community child-care teams. As we have seen, in England and Wales, Section 17 of the Children Act 1989 requires local authority social services departments to provide a range of services for children in need. This responsibility is devolved to community child-care teams. Parents or children may seek help directly from these teams, or they may be referred by another agency (Thoburn, 1997).

When contacted, the child-and-family social worker must assess whether any child in the family is 'in need' under the terms of the 1989 Act and decide how the identified need can best be met (Thoburn, 1997). Some children may be in need of protective services. In such cases, the social worker is first required to seek to prevent the child suffering maltreatment or further maltreatment through the use of family-support provisions. There is also a formal child-protection administrative system designed to ensure a coordinated interdisciplinary response to children who may be suffering significant harm as a consequence of maltreatment. If parents do not cooperate fully and compulsory measures are required to protect the child, the social worker may apply to the Family Proceedings Court for either a supervision order or care order (Thoburn, 1997). These court orders will be discussed in Chapter 5.

The children served by community child-care teams have been characterised as 'victims, volunteered or villains', or a combination of the three.

'Victims' are children who have received less than adequate parenting, and may have been neglected or abused. The 'volunteered' are children whose parents request help. Such help may include placement away from home because the parents are unable to care for their children due to factors such as personal or interpersonal stresses, deprivation or disability. 'Villains' are older children whose difficult, delinquent or anti-social behaviour gives rise to concern on the part of either their parents or the authorities (Thoburn, 1997). It should be noted that 'villains' have usually been 'victims', and there is much merit in the argument that early preventive work – which still has low actual priority – would go far towards alleviating the rage and frustration which older children often demonstrate in the form of delinquent acts.

The daily work of the child-and-family social worker is a combination of assessment, social-care planning, and the provision of a social-casework or therapeutic service to children, parents and other relatives, on either an individual or group basis. The precise mix will vary with each case. Social-care planning requires skills in negotiation, mediation and advocacy. Complex cases, especially those involving the likelihood of significant harm to the child, necessitate that the social worker is effective in working with multi-disciplinary groups: a task which requires diplomacy, flexibility, and an ability to recognise and work within various, and occasionally conflicting, political frameworks. It is also essential that the social worker is skilled in direct work with children of different ages and with parents whose problems range from poverty to mental illness or learning disability. In addition, skills in recruiting, training and supporting volunteers, who may provide support or advocacy, are of increasing importance (Thoburn, 1997).

The exercise of professional discretion is a key part of the work of child-and-family social workers. In Thoburn's view,

> they are the 'general practitioners' of the child welfare system in the United Kingdom and retain responsibility for the assessment and reassessment of the needs of the child and family, and for the provision of a varied and flexible casework service. The results of their decisions will be life enhancing or life threatening.   (1997, pp. 294–5)

Thoburn (1997) further notes that as a consequence of the emphasis on family support enshrined in the Children Act 1989, child-care social workers and managers have been encouraged by government to change their role from 'expert' to 'partner'. She argues that this has not been without opposition from child-and-family social workers who have worked in an era when high status was attached to skills in therapeutic methods, such as family therapy, or specialist aspects of work, such as child-abuse investigation and assessment, or permanent family placement.

The partnership-based practice required by the 1989 Act undoubtedly still demands the skilled delivery of therapeutic and protective services, but it also necessitates negotiation skills, and curtails some of the power of the professional social worker to decide on the methods to be adopted. In short, the skilled technician must also be a skilled negotiator. Thoburn (1997, p. 295) affirms:

> Child and family social work went a long way along the path of technical competence and practice dominated by official procedures. Consumer and outcome studies have … shown clearly that neither will succeed in either engaging families or in achieving positive outcomes for children without the accurate empathy, warmth and genuineness which have long been known to be associated with effective practice.

It remains to be seen whether social workers are able to abandon the status associated with the 'expert' role and accept that the real 'experts' with respect to a family's functioning are the family members themselves.

Thoburn identifies five pointers to positive practice by child-and-family social workers, derived from the principles for practice required by the Children Act 1989 and its guidance (for example, Department of Health, 1991b,c). These pointers also derive from two important social-work values: respect for individuals, families and communities; and a commitment to maximising the rights and freedoms of children and parents and giving them as much choice as possible in the provision of services. The five pointers – factors which Thoburn believes to be particularly important – are as follows:

- Prevention (of family disintegration);
- Protection (of the child and other vulnerable family members);
- Permanence (the importance of the child's sense of);
- Partnership (with family members and with other professionals);
- Preparation (of the social worker and of family members before important meetings, courts, etc.).

Community-based teams may provide the services discussed in the following sections. It should be noted that the examples of services selected for this text are by no means exhaustive.

Social networking

One type of family-support service is social networking. Networking is a valuable method in the social-work repertoire that can be deployed in a wide range of preventive work with children and families.

Network analysis has largely developed from systems theory. A systems approach to social-work practice may be used to analyse the complexity of forces – biological, psychological, social and cultural – operating in the relationships between social work and the informal social-support networks of a child or family (Reigate, 1996). Network analysis allows the social worker to understand clients' informal support networks (extended family, friends, church etc.) from their perspective. It also tells the worker what supports are *not* available so that she can assess how clients' social networks serve to help or inhibit their capacity to cope in the community.

A good deal of work on the potential of social networks to complement and support formal caring provision has been undertaken in the United States (Reigate, 1996). In the United Kingdom, the Barclay Report highlighted the vital role performed by informal caregivers, mutual aid groups and volunteers in the provision of social welfare to local communities (National Institute of Social Work, 1982). The report advocated that, in addition to undertaking their traditional tasks of counselling and casework with individuals and families, social workers should engage in ameliorative and preventive work with communities. In short, social workers are urged to create, stimulate and support networks in the community. The report proposed a new model of worker, the community social worker, a hybrid between community worker and social worker.

More recently, the Griffiths Report proposed that local authorities should arrange the delivery of packages of care, turning first to informal caregivers and neighbourhood support (Griffiths Report, 1988). These proposals were given legislative expression in the NHS and Community Care Act 1990. At first glance, it seems perfectly reasonable to seek informal help before formal processes are put into place, but an alternative interpretation is that agencies are seeking to avoid their own responsibilities by placing the responsibility on the community. Reigate (1996, p. 216) warns that 'social workers should respond with caution to pressures to use alternatives to formal provisions, particularly in times of economic restraint when agencies may be seeking to cut the costs of providing care and support to vulnerable people'. Thus, it is important to emphasise that, in mobilising community-based support systems, social-network analysis is a method that attempts to complement rather than replace statutory provision.

Working with social networks requires knowledge of the different types of networks and the part they play in the lives of clients. Knowledge of the communities in which clients live is also essential, particularly in relation to assessing current needs and the possibilities for developing new kinds of community support. Reigate (1996) distinguishes the following five strategies that may be useful in building upon social networks:

1. *Building on the personal links of clients* – e.g., relatives and neighbours – to help solve clients' problems or to enlarge clients' circle of support.

2. *Linking clients with volunteers* who have the experience and/or skills to tackle the clients' problems.
3. *Bringing together those with similar experiences or problems*, thus facilitating the formation of informal mutual aid networks aimed at: (a) developing further sources of support; (b) sharing knowledge; (c) building on existing community networks.
4. *Identifying and building on existing local networks* – e.g., neighbours or communities – with the aim of promoting social functioning and organisation.
5. *Forming groups to address local needs* through engagement with formal and informal groups (e.g., voluntary organisations, trade unions, churches, and formal agencies).

Reigate (1996) argues that networking enables the social worker to synthesise informal and formal welfare provision. In order to do this, workers need to be aware of: (a) the perceptions of clients; (b) how social networks serve to promote or inhibit coping; (c) the impact which formal intervention has on informal networks; and (d) the ways in which the social environment operates to strengthen or undermine the individual's social functioning (Reigate, 1996).

When undertaking network analysis, the relationship between individuals and their environments may be analysed at three levels:

(a) the *micro* level, which consists of the individuals' personal peer relationships or social support networks;
(b) the *mezzo* (or *meso*) level, where networks are examined in terms of issues of access to resources and social functioning;
(c) the *macro* level, which involves analysis of the relationship between people and more formal community organisations – for example, voluntary and political groupings, clubs, societies, etc.   (Reigate, 1996)

You will remember these levels from our discussion of social ecological theory in Chapter 2.

Let us turn now from theory to practice. What strategies might a social worker use to understand a client's social networks?

Social networking strategies

It has been suggested that clients should be asked to record their lives using structured diaries. A standardised format should be used which incorporates a structure that reflects what is already known about the general pattern of a specific client's day. Diaries for adults and children should be kept for a fortnight and a week, respectively.

The social worker then undertakes a follow-up procedure with the client, again using a standardised format or schedule. Having read the diaries, the social worker asks the client, first, about the three most important activities engaged in and/or places visited during the diary period and why they are so important; and secondly, about the three most important people in the client's life. The follow-up schedule is usually completed by the social worker in consultation with the client, sometimes with a support person present. Where appropriate, the follow-up schedule may be completed solely by the client. In addition, other schedules may be used to compile further information on self-management skills, daily living skills and social skills. The aim is to identify problems or issues in each area of functioning, what support may be required, and the implications for resource planning and provision.

Next, a summary is produced regarding progress in areas such as home management, social functioning, communication and general confidence. The client is also asked an open-ended question about what she feels she has learnt over the specified period. A further open-ended question is put to the client regarding any lack of progress. The social worker then produces a diagram of the client's networks based on information from the diary and schedules.

Such a diagram is sometimes called an eco-map. An eco-map is a drawing of the client/family in its social environment and is usually drawn jointly by the social worker and the client. Figure 4.2 is an example of an eco-map which portrays information relating to a couple, John and Sue Hickson, who are caring for Sue's elderly father and trying to bring up two children of their own. This is a second marriage for both John and Sue. John is partly supporting his two children by his first wife, and this first marriage is a source of both financial and emotional stress within his present family. Sue's elderly father, Paul, was diagnosed with Alzheimer's disease five years ago and now needs round-the-clock care since he has trouble sleeping at night, wanders around the house, and starts shouting when he becomes confused. He is cared for during the day by Sue's sister Jean, who also provides care for John and Sue's two children when they come home from school. Jean, who has two teenagers of her own, has recently said she can no longer cope with caring for Sue's family as well. John and Sue, who both work full time to make ends meet, are suffering marital discord, and there has been an allegation by his teacher that their eldest son, Mark, is being physically abused.

The social worker tries to depict the family in its social environment by drawing an eco-map (Figure 4.2), using the common symbols shown in Figure 4.3, and placing the client family in the centre circle. To draw an eco-map, the social worker must also know how to draw a genogram – that

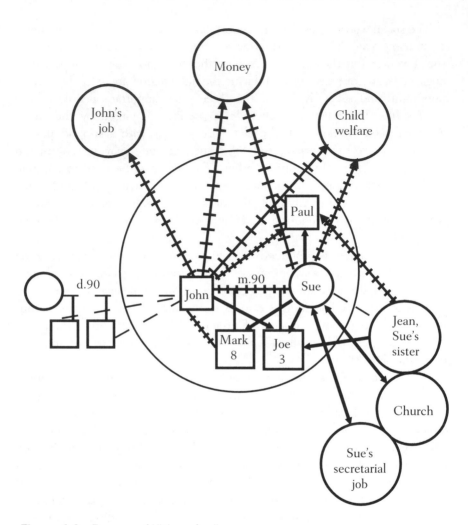

Figure 4.2 Eco-map of Hickson family

is, a family tree, or a diagram of the family's relationships over two or three generations. The common symbols used in drawing a genogram are shown in Figure 4.4.

As Figure 4.2 shows, John has a conflictual relationship with his father-in-law, Paul, his wife, and their eldest son, Mark. He has a positive relationship with his younger son, and a tenuous relationship with his divorced wife and his two children by her. Sue has generally positive relationships with her father and children but, as the arrows show, these relationships are giving on Sue's part and she feels that she gets very little back. It is apparent that an eco-map like this must be constructed with Sue's help if her feelings about the strength and direction of her various relationships are to be accurately portrayed. Similarly, other family members must tell

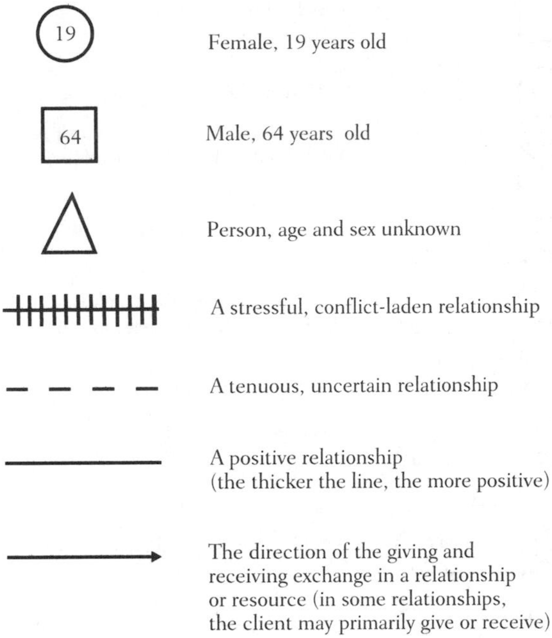

⬤ 19   Female, 19 years old

▢ 64   Male, 64 years old

△   Person, age and sex unknown

╫╫╫╫╫╫╫   A stressful, conflict-laden relationship

— — — —   A tenuous, uncertain relationship

————————   A positive relationship
(the thicker the line, the more positive)

————————➤   The direction of the giving and
receiving exchange in a relationship
or resource (in some relationships,
the client may primarily give or receive)

Figure 4.3 Eco-map symbols

the social worker how they feel about their own relationships. It can be quite revealing if, for example, a father says that his relationship with his son is strong and giving, while the son says that the same relationship is weak and conflictual. These discrepancies can give the social worker a place to begin when working with the family.

The outer circles on the diagram show other systems which are important in the family's life. For example, Sue has been a secretary for nine years and derives some energy from a feeling that she does well at her job. John's job, on the other hand, seems to be an additional source of stress for him. Sue has support from her church: John does not go to church and seems to have no support systems at all. Money is a worry for both partners: and the recent contact with child welfare is also very stressful. It should be noted, if it is not already apparent, that these maps are drawn *from the point of view of the family or individual whose relationships are being depicted*. For example, John and Sue might both feel that the relationship with child welfare is conflictual and energy draining, while the worker concerned might believe that it is strongly positive and gives support to the couple.

If the eco-map of the entire family system becomes complex and confusing, the social worker may need to draw separate maps for each family

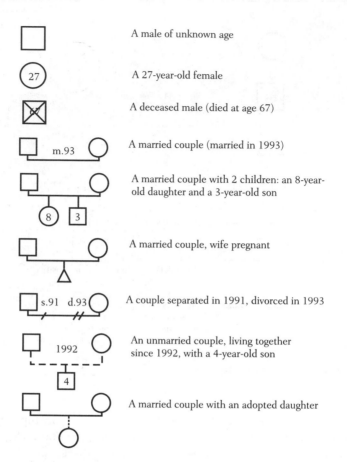

A male of unknown age

A 27-year-old female

A deceased male (died at age 67)

A married couple (married in 1993)

A married couple with 2 children: an 8-year-old daughter and a 3-year-old son

A married couple, wife pregnant

A couple separated in 1991, divorced in 1993

An unmarried couple, living together since 1992, with a 4-year-old son

A married couple with an adopted daughter

Figure 4.4 Genogram symbols

member, as shown in Figures 4.5, 4.6 and 4.7. Such separate maps will also be necessary if, as mentioned above, family members give conflicting information about their relationships with each other. In the Hickson case, for example, the social worker might well wish to draw separate maps for each of the children though these are not shown in the text.

The information collected through the eco-map and other forms of network analysis will help the social worker and the family to better understand the complexities of their social environment. This information may be used as a clinical tool to aid and direct work with the family, both immediately and for purposes of referral. It may also be summarised for use in case recording or to help in the monitoring of resources and their use over a given period. In addition, the network analysis will have significance in fieldwork assessments and reviews (Reigate, 1996).

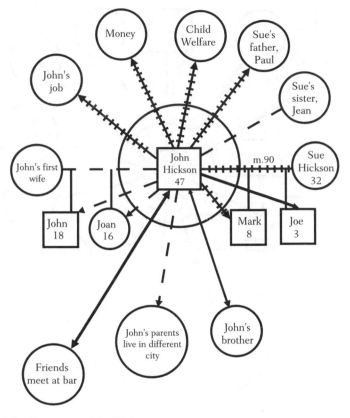

Figure 4.5 Eco-map – John Hickson

Neighbourhood services and family centres

A second initiative related to family support is neighbourhood services, particularly family centres. Under the 1989 Act, family centres constitute one of a range of family-support services which local authorities are required to provide 'as appropriate' in their area. Although these centres are formally recognised as a major element in preventive service provision, the phrase 'as appropriate' gives local authorities wide discretion over how many and what type of centres should be provided.

The term 'family centre' covers a range of community-based provision for parents and their children. Whilst there are many differences between facilities described as family centres, there are also common features. For example, they are located in neighbourhoods where there is a marked incidence of factors linked with family stress and the placement of children away from home. They emphasise family strengths rather than labelling families as problems and they do not stigmatise users. Their services are

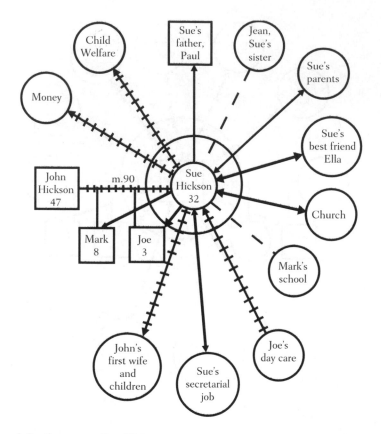

Figure 4.6 Eco-map – Sue Hickson

more accessible to local communities and more responsive to people's felt needs. They work with the parents as well as the children. They emphasise user participation, including control by users over such matters as the activities taking place in the building and the development of new services. They are committed to increasing the self-confidence and self-esteem of users, and they pursue preventive objectives (Holman, 1988).

Smith (1996) examined the operation and effectiveness of six family centres through the eyes of users. The centres were directly administered or supported by the Children's Society. Two of the centres worked mainly with referred clients and offered direct counselling, access visits, play sessions and advice on parenting skills, budgeting and diet. Two were 'neighbourhood centres' running various activities, some of them open to anyone and some available only to referred clients. These centres also provided counselling and space to other community groups in the form of office facilities and meeting rooms. The last two centres were run by local organisations and had adopted, or were planning to adopt, a 'community

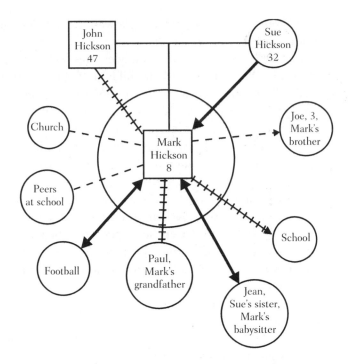

Figure 4.7 Eco-map – Mark Hickson

development' perspective. They provided space to other groups, and amenities and facilities for use by the local community; they encouraged local
people to identify issues and needs, and worked closely with local groups
and other professionals. Despite the differences in approach between the
centres, they were all situated in highly disadvantaged communities with
high levels of unemployment, low incomes, lone parents, and large families.
One community also had a high proportion of black and ethnic minority
households.

The parents interviewed in Smith's (1996) study identified common
issues of concern in relation to bringing up children. These included the
importance of safe neighbourhoods, the difficulty of 'making ends meet',
and depression and health problems. Parents described difficulties of
bringing up children as a lone parent, the need for day care so that parents
could go out to work, the importance of free time, the value of social contact, and the importance of support networks – friends, family, baby sitting.
They also indicated a desire to learn about child development.

A major finding was that levels of need were very high both among users
referred by social workers and among those attending by choice, particularly where the latter were lone parents. It was also found that large numbers of children who were not living in families referred to the centres by

social workers and were not considered 'at risk' were nonetheless growing up in highly disadvantaged circumstances.

Encouragingly, most users felt that the family centres had had a positive impact on their own lives and those of their children: 97 per cent said they would recommend the centre to someone else; 86 per cent said that the centre had made a difference to them; and 84 per cent said the centre had made a difference to their children. Moreover, the family centres were seen as: accessible – a safe place to go, with welcoming staff; available – there was always someone to talk to; a community resource – to use the phone, get a lift, hire a room for a celebration; and a collective resource.

Smith concludes that all three types of family centre helped parents and their children. However, in view of the high levels of disadvantage found in many areas, she also considers that, over the longer term, the type of centre which gives open access to community members and supports existing community resources is likely to benefit more families than centres which are accessible only through social-work referrals.

Holman (1988) notes that family centres were first established by the major voluntary child-care agencies in the 1970s, including National Children's Homes (NCH) and the Children's Society. Local authority social services followed suit in the 1980s. However, by contrast with the voluntary societies, the establishment of family centres represented only a minor part of the statutory sector's response to social need. While progress has since been made, research suggests that family centres have still not been given the pivotal role in the activities of local authorities that effective family-support services necessitate (Colton et al., 1995a,b). Family-support services should play a central role in the delivery of services and need to be decentralised on a local neighbourhood basis.

Video Home Training

Video Home Training (VHT) is an innovative and increasingly popular technique for helping children, young people and their families. Janssens and Kemper (1996) note that, at the time of writing, VHT had already been used in the Netherlands for more than ten years. VHT is characterised by short-term, home-based, filmed video-feedback of family interaction.

The basic assumption underpinning VHT is that a child's behavioural problems are related to dysfunctional interaction between parents and child. Thus, the goal of VHT is to improve parent–child relationships by resolving communication problems between parents and their offspring. VHT seeks to improve the quality of parental communication by stimulating the kind of interactions which are seen as forming the basis of good communication. Such positive interactions include parents and children displaying attentiveness to one another, looking at each other when speaking, using a friendly tone of voice, and so forth.

VHT is informed by social learning theory (remember Skinner and Bandura – see the section on 'Cultural issues in child development' in Chapter 2). First, VHT reinforces positive communication: desired behaviour increases because the video home trainer emphasises that the parents are able to react appropriately to their child's behaviour, and rewards and encourages positive interaction. Secondly, the home trainer applies the principle of negative reinforcement. During VHT, parents can observe that, owing to their own changed behaviour, the behaviour problems of the child decrease: this encourages them to respond appropriately to the child in future. In addition to reinforcement, VHT utilises the modelling principle, which holds that many behaviours are learned through imitation. While talking to the parents, the home trainer consistently applies the communication principles of VHT, thus serving as a model. The parents also serve as models for themselves in that the video recordings allow them to carefully observe their own positive behaviours.

Following an initial meeting on referral, the video home trainer visits the parents at their home, and explains the nature and purpose of VHT. If the parents agree to participate in the training, appointments are made for the forthcoming weeks. In the first week, the video home trainer records a typical sequence of everyday interaction involving the whole family, such as a meal-time or game, for 10 to 20 minutes. In the second week, the home trainer reviews a selection of positive segments of interaction with the parents. This is done to show the parents that they are able to communicate with their children in a positive way. Reflections are made on significant non-verbal communication – which family members usually have not noticed before – and all positive interactions are encouraged. This 'immediate video-feedback approach' seeks to reinforce positive communication in day-to-day family life. Recordings made during one week are reviewed the following week with parents. This process is repeated until the video home trainer and the parents concur that the parents can interact positively or communicate effectively with their children without further support. The average duration of VHT is 8 months (Janssens and Kemper, 1996).

Janssens and Kemper's (1996) research demonstrates that VHT is effective in improving the quality of parent–child communication and reducing children's behaviour problems. However, their research examined the short-term effects of VHT and they note that further research is required to establish whether VHT has lasting effects on communications processes and children's behaviour problems.

Further work is also necessary to ascertain whether VHT has a positive impact on other aspects of family functioning. In the meantime, Janssens and Kemper take issue with those who appear to regard VHT as a panacea for solving all the problems of families in need. In their view, this is too ambitious, and the use of VHT should be limited to attempts to resolve communication problems within families. Other social-work methods must be adopted to tackle other difficulties.

Group-work approaches

Some parents and children have needs that lend themselves to group work; and we said, in Chapter 2, that social workers must be comfortable working with groups. Some self-help groups are organised and led by the participants themselves, but most child-welfare clients will benefit, at least in the beginning, from the services of a trained group facilitator. The purpose of group work is usually either therapy (directed primarily towards effecting change in the participant's personality or interpersonal relationships) or education (focusing on imparting knowledge that can be expected to have a positive effect on family life), or some combination of the two. Change is made possible by providing a supportive, safe environment where participants feel comfortable disclosing problems and can benefit from the help of other group members who share the same difficulties. Often, groups are run by male and female co-facilitators who select participants, organise and oversee group activities, model such skills as male–female interactions and conflict resolution, and monitor group dynamics so that no one individual becomes too dominant or is victimised by the others. Participants are selected for the group on the basis of characteristics important to group cohesion: for example, problem areas and gender in groups for male sexual-abuse perpetrators; age in groups for teenage parents; and problem areas in groups for parents of mentally disadvantaged children. The only criterion for exclusion is usually a perceived inability to function as a group member, due to mental disadvantage or behavioural or attitudinal problems.

Most groups consist of 10 to 14 two- to three-hour sessions, run once or twice a week; 10 to 14 sessions is often considered to be the longest time for which participants can be expected to keep their commitment to attend. However, if group cohesion occurs and a process of meaningful interaction emerges within the group, participants may miss the sense of security the group affords and wish to continue for longer than the allotted period. This is rarely possible since other groups must be run for other participants; and, indeed, many group facilitators complain that the process of change has just begun when the group is over. Often, group work is offered in conjunction with other services such as individual casework or community work, where the process of change might continue. However, where group work is the only service offered and the group cannot be extended because of resource constraints, facilitators do sometimes encourage the group to continue on a self-help basis. They explain that they are not 'the experts': group participants have learned and will continue to learn from each other.

Crisis support services

An important aspect of agency policy concerns the provision of an out-of-hours service when the social worker known to the family is unavailable. The emergency service provided by most agencies out of office hours is rarely a *social work* service. Client files are often not accessible to the duty worker: the worker does not know the family, is unable to contact the family's social worker, and so may be unable to take appropriate steps to resolve the crisis situation.

Local authority social workers are usually discouraged from giving their home telephone numbers to clients, for obvious reasons. Neither is it reasonable to expect that social workers, who are under considerable stress during working hours, should be expected to be available out-of-hours as well. Nevertheless, most specialist units (dealing, for example, with special needs or highly disturbed children) do provide an emergency service which is based on being able to access the family social worker. Paradoxically, such access is often reserved for foster parents, who have high skill levels and are more likely than the average caregiver or client to be able to deal with the crisis by themselves. However, as Thoburn points out (Thoburn et al., 1986), merely knowing that the social worker *could* be accessed if necessary builds confidence and may in fact lead to a less frequent use of the emergency service since the caregiver, with a back-up in place, now feels more able to try to resolve the crisis before calling in the social worker.

Thoburn et al. (1995) argue that it is the duty of all managers involved in child-care work to establish an adequate emergency system which is accessible and welcoming to all clients, where there is the possibility of access to client records, and where the family social worker can leave messages about clients together with suggested ways of handling foreseeable difficulties.

In cases where the agency does not provide an adequate emergency service, or for families who are not presently involved with an agency, help in crisis can usually be accessed through such community services as suicide crisis lines, sexual-assault centres, drug/distress centres, AIDS/HIV crisis lines, women's shelters, child-abuse hot lines, and so forth. Many communities sponsor drop-in centres; for example, crisis nurseries where parents who are feeling temporarily overwhelmed can leave their children and obtain advice and referral information, in addition to immediate assistance.

Homemaker services

Homemaker service is provided to enable children to receive care in their own homes when the parent, for any reason, cannot fulfil parental and homemaking responsibilities. In such instances, child welfare will provide a person (usually a woman) trained in child care and home management who comes into the home for a few hours or more a day, and sometimes for 24 hours a day. In addition to the help provided by the homemaker, child welfare will try to facilitate the provision of other social or health services needed by family members.

Homemaker service was originally conceived as a short-term emergency service to hold families together in a crisis. While it still serves this purpose, the present conception permits its application to a broader range of situations. For example, it may be part of an intensive effort at family preservation, where the homemaker acts as a role model and educator to the parent in addition to providing hands-on help. Matters addressed by the homemaker may include such things as how to discipline a child, and child-rearing techniques in general; problem-solving strategies; nutrition; budgeting and house-keeping; and safety.

Homemaker services can be helpful in a variety of situations. If a parent is temporarily ill or absent, the presence of a homemaker will prevent haphazard babysitting arrangements, children scattered among relatives, or no care at all. In cases of abandonment, a homemaker can spare the children the added trauma of leaving familiar surroundings while authorities try to locate their parents or make other arrangements for their long-term care. A child with a marked handicap may consume parental energy to the detriment of the other children or there may be a period of psychological turmoil while the family adjusts to the handicap. Here, the homemaker can provide support to help the parents cope constructively. She may also provide reliable observations pertaining to the child's development which will enable the parents and the agency to develop a sound plan for the child's care and treatment. If a child has a serious illness, perhaps a terminal one, the homemaker may enable the parents to balance the care of the ill child with the needs of the other children in the family. If children are at risk of being apprehended due to neglect or abuse, the homemaker may combine education in child-rearing with the kind of warm support which will enable the parent to accept instruction and advice.

The preventive, protective and therapeutic usefulness of the homemaker service has been demonstrated in a variety of socio-economic groups and problem situations. It is an economical service compared with the cost of most out-of-home care for children; it is less stressful than foster care, especially when a number of children are involved; and it accords with the

value of family preservation. Nevertheless, it tends to be insufficiently sup-
plied and continues to be primarily an urban service although it has been
shown to be feasible in rural areas. Lisbeth Schorr (1991) has identified
points of possible conflict between effective services in general and bureaucratic methods which may help to explain this. For example, most government programmes are funded according to categories, and people have to
fall into the category to be eligible for the service. A service which encompasses many categories (or sometimes no category at all) may not be provided because the proposed recipient cannot be fitted into an appropriate
categorical slot. Further, a service which requires flexibility and front-line
worker discretion may be at odds with the traditional training of professionals and managers and with conventional approaches to ensuring accountability. Intensiveness and individualisation are at odds with pressures to
ensure equity despite insufficient funds. A long-term preventive orientation
is at odds with pressures for immediate payoffs. Finally, Schorr (1991)
notes that a programme's ability to evolve over time is at odds with the per-
vasiveness of short-term and often unpredictable funding.

Shorr (1991) recommends creative funding approaches such as the
decategorisation of certain categorical funds. These approaches could be
directed to geographic areas that are at risk, so that eligibility for service
would be linked to residency in the area, not to individual failure or need.
Shorr argues that channelling money from various government agencies to a
small geographic area would create a 'critical mass' of services that would
be sufficient to make a difference at a relatively low cost. Such an approach
would address the argument – mentioned earlier – that it is whole areas
and not individual children in those areas which are 'in need'.

Day care

Day care defies simple description because day-care provisions are so
varied. In general, day care can be divided into three major categories. The
largest category, unregulated day care, consists of caregivers who operate
independently of any regulatory agency, even though they may be subject
to licensing or regulation by the local authority in whose area they live. The
second category consists of caregivers who also operate independently
but comply with government regulatory requirements, are periodically
inspected and may lose their licences if any complaint is substantiated. The
smallest category of caregivers, though it is growing in importance, consists
of regulated homes functioning as part of a child-care system or network
under the auspices of an umbrella sponsoring organisation.

Family day care offers several advantages to parents and children. Parents
can often find daycare close to home, which makes transportation easier.

A good relationship with the care provider might ease difficult situations such as special needs on the part of the child or an unusual work schedule on the part of the parent. Some providers will even offer emotional support to the parent, information on access to other services, and advice regarding such things as child developmental stages, how to discipline, how to persuade children to eat or take a nap, and so forth. From the child's perspective, day care offers the stimulation of playing with other children and relating to other adults within the comfort and safety of a familiar setting.

The major disadvantage of day care is the lack of accountability. A parent who drops off a child in the morning has little idea of what occurs in the home during the day. The vast majority of care providers are not licensed or regulated and are not part of a network of providers. They work independently and without supervision. Often, they do not have the training to provide planned experiences for the children aimed at promoting cognitive development, and some may have taken the job simply to earn money while they stay at home with their own children. Levels of care vary from loving and competent care by experienced providers to abusive care by depressed and isolated women: and parents, whose choice of day care often revolves around location and cost, may not know which type of care their child is receiving. In addition, homes operated by individuals are often short-lived because the provider may decide to move, or have another baby of her own, or go out to work, or simply stop caring for other people's children.

Educational requirements for caregivers in child centres vary, and many caregivers, especially in rural areas, find it difficult to access training opportunities because of lack of time and money, and too few places in post-secondary early-childhood-education programmes. To alleviate the situation, at least in part, it is recommended that post-secondary institutions should provide coordinated training and education opportunities for the early-childhood workforce, expand their focus from centre-based preschool care to a full range of early-childhood services and family-support programmes, and provide additional courses to enable caregivers to increase their skills in the following areas: guiding children with behaviour challenges; providing culturally sensitive care and inclusive care for children with special needs; and working with young children in changing environments which include different work patterns and part-time and flexible child-care arrangements. To make the training more accessible, they should develop better credit and transfer procedures between institutions and reduce the barriers which limit access to training for some populations.

To further complicate the training issue, there has been little work done in the area of home-based care on which to base decisions about what constitutes good education for caregivers and how it should be delivered and supported.

Most providers derive a great deal of satisfaction from their work, but their benefits and working conditions leave a lot to be desired. The majority of caregivers do not receive paid benefits such as sick leave, retirement and pension plans, and medical benefits. They work long hours and face higher than average risks of physical injuries, infectious illness and stress. These factors contribute to caregiver turnover, which has a negative impact on quality care.

Petrie et al. (1995) carried out a survey of out-of-school play and care services for school-age children, a broad term which includes playschemes, after-school clubs, adventure playgrounds, out-of-school centres and day camps. The Children Act introduced a requirement that such services should be regulated if they took children under eight. The Act also requires that local authorities should provide out-of-school services for children in need.

The Petrie survey revealed numerous shortcomings in both day and open-door provision. Examples of good practice were found, but overall standards were unsatisfactory. The survey found that, out of the school services studied: 10 per cent did not keep an accident book; 15 per cent did not take up staff references, and 50 per cent did not do so for volunteers; 21 per cent had no kitchen area; 57 per cent had no policy on equal opportunities; 64 per cent had no hygiene procedures; and the majority of staff had no formal qualifications.

Candappa et al. (1996) examined day-care services for children under eight in England. More than 95 per cent of such care is provided by organisations (voluntary or private) in the independent sector. In England, there are currently over a quarter of a million childminders, day nurseries, playgroups, out-of-school clubs and holiday playschemes. Under the Children Act, all these provisions have to be registered and inspected annually. Roughly half of the playgroups and day nurseries and almost a quarter of childminders surveyed had accepted children placed by a social worker or health visitor. Although independent-sector providers were often ready to offer services to children in need, the potential of the independent sector was not fully utilised by local authorities.

Candappa et al. (1996) also found that the new statutory requirement that independent day-care services should 'have regard to' children's different ethnic and cultural backgrounds had limited impact on attitudes and practice. For example, almost a quarter of day-care providers in the study reported that the issue of equal opportunities and ethnic diversity was not discussed with them by the local authority when they were registered or inspected. Conversely, a large minority of day-care providers felt that too much emphasis was placed on equal opportunities by local authorities.

Similar findings were reported by a parallel study of day-care services for children in Wales carried out by Statham (1997). Whilst Welsh-language issues were being addressed by day-care providers, little attention was given to equal-opportunities issues and the need to help children develop positive attitudes in relation to cultural and racial diversity. Indeed, many day carers in Statham's study saw such issues as irrelevant to their role. As previously mentioned, Colton et al. (1995a,b) also found that insufficient priority was given to issues concerning ethnic, cultural and linguistic differences among service users in Wales.

Short-term accommodation/'respite care'

Under the Children Act 1989, the term 'accommodation' denotes out-of-home placements for children where the arrangements are made on a voluntary basis between social workers, parents and children. The 1989 Act repealed previous legislation concerning such voluntary arrangements, which 'placed sanctions on parents removing children from local authority care after six months' (Aldgate et al., 1996, p. 147).

The 1989 Act also introduced planned periods of respite care, of up to 90 days, as a single placement episode. Under Section 20 of the Children Act, local authorities are empowered to provide children with short-term breaks away from home as a means by which to support families and prevent family breakdown. As with the provisions for longer term voluntary care, the aim is to create a middle ground between keeping children at home and placing them in care. If accommodation is used as a form of family support, then children may not be living at home but they are still not formally in care (Aldgate et al., 1996).

Short-term placements, which used to be described as respite care, have traditionally been offered to families of disabled children. Aldgate et al. (1996) investigated their use in relation to other children in need. The study was funded by the Department of Health and was carried out in two parts over a four-year period. The first part reviewed 13 examples of short-term accommodation services for children other than those designated 'disabled'. This showed that effective short-term accommodation was being provided to a wide range of families, and children of all ages, by both statutory social services and voluntary agencies.

The second part of the study followed the progress of 60 families through a period of short-term accommodation, 'mainly in two city local authorities, looking at expectations, progress and outcomes from the perspective of children, parents and social workers' (Aldgate et al., 1996, p. 150). The accommodation typically involved two- or three-day visits to the caregiver's house at weekends. No child stayed away for more than four days at a time. The authors found that the provision of short-term accommodation met parents' expectations to a large degree, particularly in relation to the immediate benefits of time for themselves (which lived up to the expectations of 93 per cent of parents) and recuperation (which met the expectations of 86 per cent of parents). The longer-term benefits for parents included feeling less lonely and being able to cope with everyday life (which met the expectations of 96 per cent and 76 per cent of parents, respectively). However, parents' expectations that their children's behaviour would improve were met in only a quarter of the cases.

The authors conclude that short-term care can help to redress the imbalance between child-abuse investigation and the provision of family-support services. They state (Aldgate et al., 1996, p. 159) that their study showed:

> an early response to family stress can provide simultaneously a protective and supportive service. Nor was there any evidence to support the myth that if families are offered accommodation, they will take advantage and abandon their children to long-term placements. Indeed, the contrary was evident. Out of 60 placements, only two turned into long-term arrangements. Parents showed themselves capable of responsible and responsive behaviour. For them a service which offered family support was indeed the best option. Their only complaint was that there was not enough of it.

With respect to short-term care for children with disabilities, Robinson's studies are of interest. Robinson et al. (1995) evaluated the quality of services for disabled children, and produced self-assessment materials which services could use to develop their provision in line with the principles in the 1989 Act. The study looked at two types of children's services: short-term care for over tens and day care for under fives. The researchers developed a number of tools to enable disabled children to articulate their views about the service they received. For children under five, observation schedules were devised to monitor the quality of provision. Two packs of evaluation methods were formulated – one for short-term care and the other for day care.

Robinson and her colleagues found that some authorities had elected to hold review meetings less frequently than required by the Act because they felt that regular reviews were unnecessary for children placed away from home for relatively short periods. Moreover, full child-care plans had seldom been produced for these children. Few had social workers and short-term care staff did not see care plans as their duty. Where reviews were held, they tended to focus on short-term arrangements at the expense of key issues such as whether the placement was appropriate for the child concerned. Colton et al. (1995a,b) also highlight problems with regard to services for children with disabilities under the 1989 Act.

Aldgate et al. (1996) note that short-term care can be offered either as a discrete service or as part of a package of care, and for the parent provides relief from the common stresses of parenthood, help with child management, and a link with the community for socially isolated families. For parents in difficult circumstances, it can provide relief from the stress of living in long-term poverty and relief for sick parents. It can also be a means of building parents' self-esteem and can act as an early diversion from potential physical abuse. For the children it can provide a different and relaxing experience, an alternative to long-term and/or full-time out-of-home placement and a relief from stressful family living.

The social worker has two important roles: as a direct service provider, and as an enabler. 'Social workers offer the resource of respite care – they also bring parents the opportunity of reflecting on their needs and of using counselling and support to look at how they might use their strengths most effectively to promote their children's welfare' (Aldgate et al., 1996, p. 150).

The provision of short-term accommodation requires careful consideration of the details of practice and the organisation of services. Aldgate et al.'s (1996) work indicates that the following issues may be important when arranging short-term accommodation. Family worries should be acknowledged and discussed in decision-making. There should be no hidden agendas; parents and children must have a clear picture of what short-term accommodation is and what it is not. The partnership should be rooted in reality; families must know what is realistically available and what choices are open to them. Written agreements are essential; they exemplify partnership by setting out what is expected of all parties. User families should be given some choice in the selection of the caregiver family; this reinforces a sense of partnership and commitment to the success of the arrangements. Meetings to help with selection are best held in the caregivers' homes; this provides parents and children with a good sense of how it feels to be there. Placement with a family of similar ethnic origin and religion is most likely to meet a child's needs and safeguard his or her welfare most effectively. However, caregiver families with different cultural, ethnic or religious backgrounds are often able to understand and value these aspects of the child's family life sensitively; and there should be an emphasis on this in training. Understanding and communication between user and caregiver families is essential; among other things, it is important to attend to the details of expectations about family life in both families. Children must know that their experiences are being considered and that they are being cared for by adults who are concerned about them and have taken the trouble to find out about their needs and wishes.

Issues in monitoring quality

Now that we have looked at some of the types of family-support services which may be provided, it is time to turn to issues of quality. How effective are the various services in giving support to families? How do we know when they have been effective? In other words, what criteria do we use to indicate success?

Whittaker (1996) identifies the following critical issues concerned with monitoring the quality of preventive initiatives: outcome measurement; specifying intervention components; training and technology transfer; and the problem of 'ecological validity'.

Outcome measurement

Whittaker (1996) reports that virtually all major providers of child-welfare services in the United States are reconsidering the definition of 'success'. This increased interest in 'outcomes' is primarily driven by financial considerations. Funding for services is increasingly tightly tied to clearly defined outcomes, specified time-limited interventions and constant monitoring. This has made agencies and practitioners 'acutely aware of the need to specify precisely the intended outcomes of their interventions and then to live with the results' (Whittaker, 1996, p. 119).

For example, *avoidance of unnecessary out-of-home placement* was chosen as the primary criterion of success in relation to intensive family-preservation initiatives. However, Whittaker notes that this caused major problems for researchers, policy-makers and practitioners. For one thing, 'placement' has been found to be a relatively low-frequency event which is difficult to predict. Secondly, it is now well known that 'placement' as an outcome is subject to a wide range of factors independent of services, including: formal and informal administrative policies; the presence or absence of resources; and the discretion of juvenile court judges. Thirdly, it appears that for some families there may be a need for a brief period of residential treatment for an emotionally disturbed child. Thus placement cannot necessarily be equated with failure; and indeed, in the UK, as we have seen, Section 17 of the 1989 Act stipulates that provision of accommodation for a child should not be viewed as failure by the family or the social worker.

In the United States, a number of tragic and well-publicised child deaths and some inconclusive research findings have fuelled a serious attack on the use of 'placement prevention' as the primary-outcome measure in intensive family preservation. In light of this, some have called for greater emphasis on child safety as the primary outcome of interest, and it is generally felt that there should be less focus on the physical location of the child and more on his or her development and the state of the family's functioning (Whittaker, 1996). We will look more closely at measures of children's development when we consider the Looking After Children (LAC) materials in Chapter 6.

Specifying intervention components

A related issue is the task of carefully specifying the intervention components of preventive programmes. Whittaker (1996, p. 121) astutely observes that

> model legislation is silent on the specifics of intervention while eloquent on its values. The result is all too often the veneer of reform without the substance. As is the case with all social welfare intervention, the central question is simple yet elusive:
>
> > What combination of treatment/education/social support/concrete resources for what duration of time and intensity will produce the outcomes of interest to differing types of children and families?

Although a good deal has been written about effective preventive programmes, their components have seldom been subject to rigorous empirical evaluation. In relation to family preservation, further research is required to establish the importance and contribution of caseload size, the teaching of cognitive problem-solving skills (such as anger management), and the mobilisation of social support, including the provision of concrete resources. Likewise, with regard to placement services, both residential and therapeutic fostering represent a series of 'black boxes' rather than a clearly specified and empirically validated set of interventions. Similarly, with respect to family intervention, fundamental questions about the length, intensity and nature of the intervention remain unanswered. Some of these questions have major implications for budgets as well as for treatment planning. For instance, 'family intervention' could mean any or all of the following:

- Periodic contact with a local and lightly trained family worker linked, perhaps, to mutual aid and self-help;
- Training in parenting skills from a highly skilled parent educator on a groupwork basis;
- Family therapy with a therapist trained to post-graduate level;
- Occasional consultation with a parent volunteer via telephone.

(Whittaker, 1996)

We cannot therefore talk about the 'success' of 'family intervention' without first defining both 'success' and 'family intervention'. We might talk instead about the success of a group designed to increase parenting skills where 'success' is an increase in skills as measured by the increased frequency of certain desired behaviours in parents' interaction with their children. However, we will probably not make the measurements necessary to enable us to hold any such conversation. Very rarely do social workers measure the results of their interventions with children and families, even when they know, specifically, what the intervention was designed to achieve. They may have a gut feeling that they were successful, but the feeling is rarely translated into objective evidence of success that others can use and evaluate. If we do not evaluate the results of our work with individuals, how can we evaluate the success of our agency's programmes? And if we do not know the effects of one agency's programmes, how can we gauge the effects of *all* agencies' programmes, nationwide, to bring us to an understanding of the effectiveness, or otherwise, of policies enshrined in legislation such as the Children Act? The next time you work with a child or family, think about one thing, specifically, that you want to achieve. Then think about an intervention you might use to achieve that. Then think about how you will know to what extent you have achieved what you wanted to. How will you objectively *know*? How could you demonstrate to others what you did and how well it worked? This is not an exercise: it is an integral part of your life as a social worker.

Training

When outcomes have been selected, and key interventions chosen, the third issue arising in preventive work with families concerns staff training and the utilisation of knowledge. Whittaker (1996, p. 122) describes the general approach to family-oriented prevention in the United States as a 'train and hope' strategy. He argues that:

> If intervention is the 'black box', training is the 'black hole' in most social services departments. To the extent that it exists, it is often didactic and diffuse as opposed to experimental and skill-oriented. ... its content is driven by the desires and interests of practitioners rather than either the demands of client families or relevant intervention research on 'what works'. Moreover, much of our training is patchwork, episodic with little attention given to follow-up, worker supports and either training needs assessment or evaluation.

In Whittaker's view, more attention needs to be devoted to the careful and systematic development of training in family-oriented prevention to ensure effective dissemination of innovative interventions. In other words, when you have done something new and clever with a child or family and you have demonstrated how well it worked (as discussed above), you need an opportunity to tell others about it so that they can do it too – and such opportunities need to be structured and regularly provided by the agency in which you work. And not only do you need to tell others in your agency about it – you need to tell people in other agencies and other disciplines. There need to be structured opportunities, in other words, for sharing information across professional and agency boundaries.

The problem of 'ecological validity'

In the field of prevention/intervention, ecological validity may be defined as follows:

> Does the environment experienced by clients in a service program have the properties it is supposed or assumed to have by the practitioner?
> (Whittaker, 1996, p. 123)

In other words, does the client's perception of her environment (family, friends, finances, physical living arrangements, etc.) fit with the social worker's perception? If it does not, it is apt to be the social worker's perception that takes precedence, probably to the client's detriment. Whittaker (1996, p. 123) considers that 'while environmental intervention lies at the centre of the mission of social work, it exists at the margins of its practice'. That is, we generally do not take the time to find out what environmental factors are important to the client and what those factors mean in the context of the client's unique view of the world. What does it mean to a deaf child, for example, that all of his peer group and his parents have normal hearing?

Whittaker (1996, p. 123) rightly argues that increased emphasis should be placed on ecological validity in all its forms:

> greater emphasis on culture, gender, and sexual orientation in crafting interventions; greater involvement of indigenous communities in the development of the intervention and its evaluation through participatory action research; greater focus on environmentally directed intervention and on 'situated practice' (i.e. practice that occurs in the real life environments of our client families, as opposed to the sterile context of the clinic or social agency).

In this chapter, we have talked about proactive and reactive preventive services and the categories of 'children in need' who are eligible to receive those services. We have also discussed the types of family-support services which might be provided and the difficulties of evaluating the effectiveness of our efforts. We will leave this chapter now and go on to discuss protecting children, in Chapter 5. We will look at the definitions, causes and consequences of child abuse, as well as child-protection procedures and legal considerations.

Case example

Case example 4.1   Salimah and Tasneem W

Salimah W (6 years, 3 months)
Tasneem W (4 years, 7 months)

Salimah and Tasneem are the daughters of Iris (23) and Mohammed (36). Iris and Mohammed have recently moved from the Welsh valleys to London in hopes of finding work. Mohammed emigrated to the UK seven years ago from Iran. He says that he was a doctor in his own country but his qualifications are not recognised here and he refuses any other sort of work, saying that it is beneath him. Iris, who is Welsh, has found a job as a cleaner. She does this job in the evenings when Mohammed is at home to look after the children. She earns very little but gives all her income immediately to Mohammed who manages the family's money.

Iris has no contact with her family. She says her mother threw her out when she became pregnant at 16 and she hasn't talked to any member of her family since. Mohammed has extended family in another part of London. Iris says that six or seven of them visit every month or so but they talk in Mohammed's language and ignore her because she produced only daughters and she is white. Mohammed says his family is supportive and he couldn't manage without them.

Salimah, who was in school in Wales, has recently started school in London, and it was Salimah's teacher who referred the family to social services. The teacher says that Salimah talks hardly at all, either to her or to the other children. She is always spotlessly clean when she comes to school and never gets herself dirty. She does what she is told but the school work seems to be beyond her. She is mercilessly teased by the other children and seems to be an intensely unhappy child. The teacher has never seen bruises but wonders about physical and sexual abuse.

Salimah's home is as spotless as herself and her mother as silent. There are no toys in evidence and no sign that children live in the house. On the social worker's first visit, Salimah and Tasneem sat quietly on the sofa beside their father and refused to speak to her. She did manage to get Iris alone in the kitchen for a few minutes but when they went back into the living room Mohammed did all the talking. Mohammed told her not to come again because he could look after his family and they were doing fine.

- What proactive preventive approaches could have helped this family?
- What micro, mezzo and macro factors come into play?
- What would you do now if you were the social worker?

Protecting children

In the previous chapter we discussed the meaning of prevention in the context of the Children Act 1989, and we looked at a few of the family-support services designed to prevent abuse from occurring. In this chapter, we shall focus on protection: that is, what happens when abuse or neglect are alleged or have actually occurred.

Objectives

When you have read this chapter, you should understand why agreed definitions of child abuse are so important and why figures on child protection registers fail to reflect the true extent of child abuse. You will encounter a number of perspectives on the causes of abuse, and the consequences of both physical abuse and sexual abuse. The concepts of risk and resilience are both discussed. In addition, the chapter looks at the attempt of the government to integrate family-support services and child-protection services: this is discussed in the context of the new government guidance on child-protection procedures and assessment, including the process of dealing with referrals, investigation/assessment, and child-protection conferences. The legal context of child protection is also discussed.

Abused children

Concern about child abuse can be traced back to the latter part of the nineteenth century in most EU countries. Since then, and in line with changing societal attitudes, awareness of child abuse has increased progressively, particularly over recent decades. In the 1960s, child battering was identified as a major cause of child injury and death. The 1970s and 1980s were distinguished by the 'discovery' of widespread sexual abuse of children both inside and outside the family. During the 1990s, increasing attention was paid to the abuse of children within institutions. In the UK, we have seen a number of scandals involving physical and sexual abuse of children and young people by care staff and teachers in residential-care and educational settings (Ruxton, 1996).

Four broad categories of abuse are recognised internationally: physical abuse, emotional abuse, sexual abuse and neglect. It is widely understood that official statistics represent only the tip of a rather large iceberg with respect to the true prevalence of child abuse (Giddens, 1989; Colton and Vanstone, 1996). Even so, the numbers of children placed on child protection registers do provide some idea of levels of violence to children in the UK. On 31 March 1998, there were 31,600 children on child protection registers in England. This represents 2.8 per 1,000 of all children under 18. The most common reason was neglect, followed by physical abuse, sexual abuse and emotional abuse respectively. This represents a reversal of the previous trend where physical abuse was much more likely to be the reason for registration than neglect. Girls were more likely than boys to be on a register because of sexual abuse – around a third of the girls as compared with a fifth of the boys (Ruxton, 1996).

There is increasing concern about child pornography and the sexual exploitation of children. The possession and dissemination of child pornography is an offence in the UK. A recent study estimated that there had been a 35 per cent rise in the annual number of police cautions administered to young people for soliciting (Lee and O'Brien, 1995). So-called 'sex tourism' is also a significant problem. Substantial numbers of men from the UK, and other technologically advanced countries, visit certain developing countries (e.g., the Philippines, Sri Lanka and Thailand) to buy sex from young child prostitutes. As noted by Sanders (1999), the UK, along with a number of other European countries (Sweden, France and Germany), have passed legislation to make it a criminal offence to travel abroad for the purpose of sexually abusing children. The Sex Offenders Act 1997 (Section 7(1)) prohibits this activity by specifying that:

> any act done by a person in a country or territory outside the United Kingdom which (a) constituted an offence under the law in force in that country or territory; and (b) would constitute a sexual offence to which this section applied if it had been done in England and Wales, or in Northern Ireland, shall constitute that sexual offence under the law of that part of the United Kingdom.

Over recent years, there has been growing professional awareness of other forms of abuse, not least domestic violence. Children are often the hidden victims of this problem. There is a relative lack of research on the impact of domestic violence on children. The first study in Britain showing the devastating effects of domestic violence was published as recently as 1994 (NCH, 1994). Based on information collected from over 100 women, who looked after 246 children, the study found that nearly three-quarters of mothers said that their children had witnessed violent incidents, and 67 per cent had seen their mothers being beaten. Ten per cent of the women had been sexually abused in front of their children. Most of the mothers believed their children were adversely affected in both the short and long term. The problems manifested by the children included: bed-wetting, becoming withdrawn, low self-esteem, violence and aggression towards others, problems at school, and problems in trusting people and forming relationships.

The definition and extent of child maltreatment

The term 'child maltreatment' is more widely used in North America than in the UK but it is useful in that it covers both child abuse and child neglect. In the United States, the Child Abuse Prevention and Treatment Act of 1974 has defined maltreatment as:

> the physical or mental injury, sexual abuse, negligent treatment or maltreatment of a child under the age of 18, by a parent who is responsible for the child's welfare, under circumstances which indicate that the child's health or welfare is harmed or threatened.

However, many people would argue that abuse is an act of *commission* while neglect is an act of *omission*: the two are different in kind and ought not to be grouped together. This argument raises the question of whether abuse is in fact different from neglect and how the two ought to be defined. We might say, for example, that while both abuse and neglect result in harm to the child's welfare, the former is deliberate while the latter is not, and so the definitions should revolve around the parent's motivation or intent. Now – at least from the practice standpoint – we are in the position of having to decide whether a parent who, for example, scalded a child's foot in too-hot bath water, intended the scald or just neglected to check the temperature of the water. It is often very difficult to determine motivation, particularly since 'accidents' can contain unconscious intended elements.

A second practical problem in separating abuse from neglect is distinguishing less than optimal care from care that is actually harmful. Can a 12-year-old, for example, be safely left alone for half an hour? Three hours? Overnight? Is it acceptable to discipline a child by slapping with the hand? With a belt? With a cricket bat? Examples of inadequate care fall on a continuum from the slightly neglectful to the grossly abusive. There is also a continuum regarding the actual harm experienced by the child: from subtle forms of emotional damage to physical injury to death. How serious must the harm be before we say it is abusive rather than the result of neglect?

We must also decide whether to include potential as well as actual harm in any definition of neglect. Some people might say that the 12-year-old could be left alone for half an hour but not overnight, on the basis that harm is more likely to occur the longer the child is left. Some might say that a toddler may be allowed to play on the stairs but should not be allowed to play with a knife. The degree of potential harm inherent in these examples is largely a matter of opinion, and it is almost impossible to write a definition of neglect which is neither too broad nor too narrow. A too-broad definition would include the average parent's every lapse of attention, while a too-narrow definition would exclude everyone but the most severely neglectful. Besharov (1985) has suggested that the deciding criterion ought to be the frequency or length of time (duration) over which the neglectful behaviour continues. A parent whose child comes home to an empty house on one occasion is not neglectful but a parent whose child always returns to an empty house is neglectful. Frequency and duration, again, each lie on a continuum, and there are no agreed-upon answers to the questions 'How often is too often?' and 'How long is too long?' Nevertheless, the idea of persistence (which might include both duration and frequency) has been incorporated into the 'official' definition of child neglect, which also includes the idea of severity (the seriousness of the harm incurred). This definition is derived from the Department of Health et al. (1999, paragraph 2.7, p. 6) guidance on inter-agency working with respect to child abuse, *Working Together*. It runs as follows:

> Neglect is the persistent failure to meet a child's basic physical and/or psychological needs, likely to result in the serious impairment of the child's health or development. It may involve a parent or carer failing to provide adequate food, shelter and clothing, failing to protect a child from physical harm or danger, or the failure to ensure access to appropriate medical care or treatment. It may also include neglect of, or unresponsiveness to, a child's basic emotional needs.

The official definitions of abuse, derived from the same source (paragraph 2.4, p. 5), divide abuse into three categories, physical, sexual, and emotional. The definitions are:

> Physical abuse may involve hitting, shaking, throwing, poisoning, burning or scalding, drowning, suffocating, or otherwise causing physical harm to a child. Physical harm may also be caused when a parent or carer feigns the symptoms of, or deliberately causes ill health to a child whom they are looking after. This situation is commonly described using terms such as factitious illness by proxy or Munchausen syndrome by proxy.

These definitions include potential (likely) as well as actual harm. Key terms such as 'development' and 'ill-treatment', which are somewhat nebulous, are drawn from the Children Act 1989 and are themselves defined in Section 31 of the Act:

- 'harm' means ill-treatment or the impairment of health or development;
- 'development' means physical, intellectual, emotional, social or behavioural development;
- 'health' means physical or mental health; and
- 'ill-treatment' includes sexual abuse and forms of ill-treatment which are not physical.

It may appear that this chapter has paid far too much attention to definitions of abuse and neglect which are ambiguous at best and will anyway have to be interpreted by the social worker with respect to individual cases. However:

> agreed definitions of child abuse are important for two reasons. The first is to establish a general framework within which policies designed to prevent child abuse can be developed and assessed. The second is to provide a set of technical definitions for identifying actions or circumstances which are taken to be abusive. These technical definitions are needed for statutory, legal, statistical, procedural and research purposes. (National Commission of Inquiry into the Prevention of Child Abuse, 1996, p. 1)

In other words, if we are to develop policies to prevent child abuse, we need to know what it is that we are trying to prevent; and if we are to count occurrences of child abuse we need to know what it is that we are counting. For example, one of the decisions for which technical definitions of abuse are needed is the decision about whether a particular child's name should be placed on the child protection register. The process by which a child's name comes to be placed on the register will be discussed later in the chapter. Here, it is sufficient to note that each child protection register lists all the children in the local area who are considered to be at continuing risk of significant harm, and for whom there is a child protection plan (Department of Health et al., 1999, p. 61).

At the end of March 1995, the names of 40,746 children were on child protection registers in the UK. In England, the number registered totaled 34,954 children; around 1 in every 300. Of these, 37 per cent were registered for physical injury, 32 per cent for neglect, 26 per cent for sexual abuse, and 13 per cent for emotional abuse, with 9 per cent registered for more than one category of abuse (National Commission of Inquiry into the Prevention of Child Abuse, 1996).

Unfortunately, the figures on child protection registers do not provide estimates of the true extent of abuse for a number of reasons. For example, not all children on registers have been abused; some are registered because they are thought to be 'at risk'. Registers mainly record abuse within families (intra-familial abuse) and generally exclude extra-familial abuse when the family can protect the child. Many children who are abused may not have their names on the child protection register; registers exclude large numbers of children who do not come to the notice of social workers but who have identical experiences to those registered. Those registered constitute only a minority of those referred to social workers; and, as well as the children referred to social workers, many more are involved in situations where abuse is likely. Children's chances of being registered partly depend on where they live; there is considerable geographical variation in definitions, interpretations and thresholds, reflecting local circumstance, practice and resources. Finally, the widespread practice of recording only one type of abuse reduces the apparent extent of emotional abuse in comparison with other types of abuse (National Commission of Inquiry into the Prevention of Child Abuse, 1996).

It is worth highlighting here that there is good reason to suppose that most cases of child sexual abuse do not come to the notice of child-protection agencies. As Colton and Vanstone (1996, p. 123) state: 'because the tabooed nature of sexual abuse impedes discovery and deters reporting, known cases are very likely to represent only a small proportion of the total number of cases among the general population'. Official figures for England indicate about 4,000 convictions and cautions for sexual offences against children annually. In addition, the names of some 17,000 children are on child protection registers for sexual abuse. However, the report of the National Commission of Inquiry into the Prevention of Child Abuse (1996, p. 14) estimates that as many as 100,000 children each year have a harmful sexual experience and that over a million adults may still be suffering the consequences of sexual abuse.

The report of the National Commission of Inquiry into the Prevention of Child Abuse (1996, p. 4) called for less tolerance of child abuse in general, based on a broader understanding and definition of what constitutes such abuse. The Report observed that 'child protection agencies tend to work to narrow legal and technical definitions of abuse, partly because of fears of widening the net for formal intervention or actions and partly because of the need to allocate scarce resources'.

The Commission argued that 'definitions of abuse should not be governed by the availability of resources. Moreover, if society is to become less tolerant of the abuse of children, there is a need for a wider definition of abuse than is generally accepted'. Thus, the Commission adopted the following broad definition of child abuse:

> Child Abuse consists of anything which individuals, institutions or processes do or fail to do which directly or indirectly harms children or damages their prospects of safe and healthy development into adulthood.
> (National Commission of Inquiry into the Prevention of
> Child Abuse, 1996, p. 2)

This definition covered a 'wide spectrum of damage' from 'actions resulting in criminal convictions' to 'the broader effects of poverty and deprivation'. It is also intended to reflect the principles contained in the United Nations Convention on the Rights of the Child – ratified by the UK government in 1991.

In seeking more realistic estimates of child abuse, the Commission's analysis went far beyond official categories and included a consideration of: poverty and homelessness, children living away from home, children in secure accommodation, school bullying and exclusions, young caregivers, and children and employment.

The Commission also considered racial harassment, from serious violence to name calling. The Commission's report noted:

> For some children there is no escape at school, on the journey to and from school or in the family's immediate neighbourhood. This can seriously constrain social and leisure activities and creates additional pressures on family relationships. (National Commission of Inquiry into the Prevention of Child Abuse, 1996, p. 21)

Currently in the UK, there is no system for recording racial harassment and there is a lack of national research. This is despite the fact that racial harassment is recognised as being widespread, and ethnic record keeping is known to be essential in dealing with institutional racism (Ahmed, 1986, 1994).

The Commission's report further noted that some organisations and their staff were unsuccessful in tackling racial harassment and in tackling the effects of policies which 'unwittingly exclude or disadvantage children from ethnic minorities. This creates distrust of those organisations and individuals and reduces willingness to seek help or support from them' (National Commission of Inquiry into the Prevention of Child Abuse, 1996, p. 21).

On the basis of its broad definition of child abuse, the Commission estimated that at least one million children are harmed each year. At least 150,000 children annually suffer severe physical punishment. Up to 100,000 children each year have a potentially harmful sexual experience. Between 350,000 and 400,000 children live in an environment that is consistently low in warmth and high in criticism. Around 450,000 children are bullied at school at least once a week. Over 4 million children – one in three of all children – in the UK live in poverty (National Commission of Inquiry into the Prevention of Child Abuse, 1996, p. 2).

The Commission's report contended that official statistics not only underestimate abuse but also divert attention from important issues.

> Their focus on an alleged incident or risk, with a single cause, masks the complex social, economic and personal problems which may have contributed to the abuse occurring, and which may not be addressed in child protection procedures. (National Commission of Inquiry into the Prevention of Child Abuse, 1996, p. 12)

In the same vein, the Department of Health emphasises the environment in which incidents of abuse occur:

> any potentially abusive *incident* has to be seen in *context* before the extent of its harm can be assessed and appropriate interventions agreed. An important part of that context is evidence about the ... *outcome* of abuse .... Long term difficulties for children seldom follow from a single abusive event; rather they are more likely to be a consequence of living in an unfavourable environment, particularly one which is low in warmth and high in criticism.   (Department of Health, 1995, p. 53)

According to *Child Protection: Messages from Research* (Department of Health, 1995), most cases which come to the notice of child-protection agencies involve children who are in need of support and protection but do not involve serious injury to the child. Whether a child is viewed as being in need of support and protection very much depends on the person doing the viewing. High tolerance on the part of the public and professionals for behaviours that are marginally neglectful or abusive will decrease the numbers of cases reported. The converse will be true if tolerance is low.

For example, while many people believe that any physical punishment of children is wrong (Newell, 1989) and contributes to their emotional maladjustment, others still believe in the right of parents to use physical force to discipline their children. The difficulty for those concerned with reporting child abuse is to differentiate between child abuse and reasonable discipline. Besharov (1990, p. 68) offers the following guidelines for deciding whether a particular physical punishment is 'reasonable':

- Was the purpose of the punishment to preserve discipline or to train or educate the child? Or was the punishment primarily for the parent's gratification or the result of the parent's uncontrolled rage?
- Did the child have the capacity to understand or appreciate the corrective purpose of the discipline? (Very young children and mentally disabled children cannot.)
- Was the punishment appropriate to the child's misbehaviour?
- Was a less severe but equally effective punishment available?
- Was the punishment unnecessarily degrading, brutal or beastly in character or protracted beyond the child's power to endure?
- If physical force was used, was it recklessly applied? (Force directed towards a safe part of the body, such as the buttocks, ordinarily is much more reasonable than is force directed towards vulnerable parts, such as the head or genitals.)

> **ACTIVITY**
>
> Think of a time when either you as a child, or a child known to you, were physically disciplined. Apply the Besharov criteria to it. Was it abusive?

Despite all our efforts to arrive at a generally accepted definition of what is meant by physical abuse, sexual abuse, emotional abuse and neglect, these concepts remain very much open to interpretation by the individual. Yet clear and accepted definitions are essential if professionals and the public are to know what behaviours to report, and child-protection agencies are to know when it is appropriate to intervene with families. A look at the history and a few of the suggested explanations of child abuse may not help us to resolve the dilemma, but it may at least increase our understanding of why a behaviour that is viewed as abusive by one person may be seen as natural and necessary by another. Sanders (1999) has reviewed the historical context of child abuse and child protection in both the UK and the USA and has drawn parallels between the developments in each country.

Understanding the causes of child abuse

There have been numerous attempts to explain child abuse, using different and often conflicting methodological approaches, levels of analysis, and theoretical perspectives. However, none of the theories advanced so far satisfactorily explains the full range of child abuse. At best, they offer only partial accounts. Thus, whilst they contradict one another in important ways, the different perspectives are perhaps most fruitfully seen as complementary approaches. In what follows, we outline a number of influential perspectives that have sought to explain child abuse, beginning with attachment theory. The names should be familiar from our discussion of child-developmental theorists in Chapter 2.

Attachment theory

Kempe, the American paediatrician credited with rediscovering child abuse (Kempe and Helfer, 1968; Kempe and Kempe, 1978), focused on the importance of the attachment between mother and child in explaining physical abuse. Kempe's approach was informed by the work of Bowlby (see 1953; 1969; 1973; 1985; 1988) on attachment and maternal deprivation. Kempe observed that mothers who abuse their children have themselves often suffered from poor attachment experiences and are thus unable to serve as good attachment figures for their own children. They expect their children to be naturally rewarding and, when this unrealistic expectation is not fulfilled, they frequently turn to physical abuse. In light of this, once steps had been taken to protect the child concerned, Kempe considered that treatment should focus on the parents through the provision of the supportive 'mothering' relationship that the parents themselves had missed as children. With respect to prevention, evidence of lack of bonding between mother and infant in the perinatal period could be taken as an indicator that the child was at risk of abuse.

A social-learning approach

Social learning theory, which has its origins in behaviourism, views child abuse as a consequence of poor learning experiences and inadequate controlling techniques. Parents who were themselves maltreated as children may not have learned how to control their children effectively using socially approved methods; instead, they adopt an abusive approach. Equally, parents who were overindulged as children are unable to establish appropriate limits and turn to violence when their own children go too far. Learning theorists have developed a range of behaviour-modification techniques. In the area of child abuse, attention has concentrated on supplanting inappropriate and ineffective approaches to parenting with those that are both effective and socially acceptable (McCauley, 1977).

Behavioural modification techniques have also been used with actual or potential offenders for some years now. The social-learning perspective views sexually abusive behaviour, for example, as behaviour that has been learned (Bandura, 1965). Abusers associate certain kinds of stimuli, such as sexual images of children, with sexual gratification, possibly as a result of sexual experiences during their own childhoods. This sexual orientation is reinforced through masturbation to fantasies of child abuse and reinforced by belief systems which provide a rationalisation for abusive behaviour. These belief systems challenge the sexual ethics and moral standards of the wider society, and include ideas such as: children can consent to and enjoy sex with adults; and, sex between children and adults is natural, healthy and positive. These views are reinforced through contact with other abusers who have similar beliefs, and may be used by abusers not only to justify their behaviour but also to minimise any guilt they might experience (Sampson, 1994).

This perspective on how sexually abusive behaviour develops helps to explain why some adults are sexually attracted to children, and suggests that abusive behaviour can be changed; that what has been learned can be unlearned.

Family dysfunction theory

A more recent perspective that has been applied to both physical and sexual abuse is family dysfunction theory and its associated method of therapeutic intervention, family therapy. In the 1960s, the majority of family therapists operated from a psychodynamic perspective and adopted a fairly passive role. However, a more directive approach has been advocated by Minuchin (1974), who employs systems theory as an aid to understanding and intervening with families.

Minuchin sees the family as comprised of parent–parent, parent–child and child–child subsystems. In his view, it is important to maintain clear distinctions between these subsystems. He argues that families can become 'enmeshed': a state where the roles and behaviours expected of 'mother', 'father' and 'child' are blurred and a child might assume a parental role, or vice versa. Alternatively, family members can become 'disengaged' from each other and interact barely at all, either within or between subsystems. Enmeshment and disengagement lie at extreme ends of a continuum of family interaction. For Minuchin, both extremes are dysfunctional, and the therapist's task is to achieve a healthy balance between too much and too little family interaction. Interaction between the family and wider systems such as schools is also important and constitutes another continuum. A healthy family maintains boundaries around itself but also encourages its members to participate in activities outside the family. Closed families, where the family boundaries are rigid and there is minimal interaction with the outside world, lie at one end of the family–other system continuum and also tend towards enmeshment. At the other end of the continuum, the family boundaries may be so permeable that members are not sure who does and does not belong to the family, or even, since members often move in and out, who is supposed to be living in the house. This may occur, for example, when a parent frequently changes partners, or step-siblings move between parents and live in different houses for varying periods of time. Not surprisingly, these families tend towards disengagement.

The concept of 'scapegoating' is also important in family systems theory. Scapegoating refers to the process by which one family member, often a child, is blamed for all the family's problems and is physically or emotionally abused as punishment. Laying blame in this way allows family members to avoid looking at other reasons for their problems and enables them to survive as a unit. Since the scapegoated child is essential to family preservation, any attempt to make the family safe for the child requires that the therapist work with the whole family to identify and attempt to resolve family problems (Corby, 1989).

Families where sexual abuse occurs are usually enmeshed and isolated from the outside world. For example, where the sexual relationship between the parents is unsatisfactory and the boundaries between parents and children are blurred, the father may turn his attention to an adolescent daughter, who takes over the mother's role not only sexually but often also with respect to household chores. The therapist's task is to work with the whole family in an effort to disentangle poor communication patterns and relationships (Mrazek and Bentovim, 1981).

The feminist perspective

The feminist writer Dominelli takes a rather different view of why sexual abuse occurs from that advanced by family-dysfunction theorists. She states:

> abuse in the form of violence against women is a normal feature of patri-archal relations. It is a major vehicle men use in controlling women. The rising incidence of child sexual abuse reveals the extent to which men are prepared to wield sexual violence as a major weapon in asserting their authority over women. (Dominelli, 1986, p. 12)

From this perspective, sexual abuse represents an extreme manifestation of institutionalised male power over females, rather than family communication problems or individual pathology. Feminists argue that men sexually abuse children because of the power imbalance between the genders and the consequent differing patterns of socialisation experienced by males and females. The obvious policy implication of this is that sexual abuse has to be tackled at the societal as well as the individual level (Rush, 1980; Dominelli, 1986; Driver and Droisen, 1989).

The feminist philosophy has made an invaluable contribution to our understanding of why sexual abuse occurs. Analysing and challenging male–female power relations at an institutional level has provided very important insights for child-protection work. However, there is a danger that feminist theory can be used in a reductionist and exclusive way, whereby every social problem is attributed to patriarchy. Moreover, the diversity of human sexual desire, and the fact that some men are sexually aroused primarily by children or by other men, appear to pose a challenge to feminist theory. So too do the (comparatively rare) examples of sexual offending by women (except where women have been coerced into such behaviour by men), and those instances where females use positions of power in an abusive way (Colton and Vanstone, 1996). It might also be noted that, whereas females are more likely to suffer sexual-abuse than males, the discrepancy is less than was once thought. Finkelhor (1993) estimates that about 29 per cent of sexual abuse victims in the United States are male, though boys are less likely to be reported to child-protective services than girls.

Sociological viewpoints

Sociological perspectives were developed by theorists in the United States during the 1970s and 1980s. Corby (1989) distinguishes three main strands of such thought: ecological, social cultural, and social structural.

Ecological theories emphasise that the healthy development of children requires healthy living environments. Socially impoverished environments exacerbate, and even engender, psychological stress in disadvantaged families. Child abuse is seen as a consequence of poor parenting skills and social stress caused by lack of family and social supports. Thus, it is suggested that families at risk should not be grouped together into a single neighbourhood, and that services must be adequately resourced and sensitive to the needs of local communities (Garbarino and Gilliam, 1980).

Social cultural theory holds that the incidence of child abuse is related to cultural support for the physical punishment of children, and cultural discomfort with the idea of challenging the rights of parents and intruding upon the privacy of the home. Moreover, violence against children is much more widespread than official estimates of child physical abuse appear to indicate. The solution requires a wider societal approach to dealing with violence as a whole. Currently, although the official attitude towards child abuse is disapproval, violence towards children is, in fact, passively condoned by a lack of a determined attempt to eradicate it (Gelles and Cornell, 1985).

The social structural perspective is underpinned by research undertaken by Gil (1978) which shows that children on child protection registers in the United States in the late 1960s mainly came from the lower social classes. According to this perspective, society establishes the preconditions for child abuse by condoning structural inequalities; that is to say, by allowing many families to live in acute poverty and social deprivation. Therefore, society must share the blame for child abuse, which should not be regarded as the result of individual failure. Child abuse is a political concern, and cannot be tackled by social workers alone. Rather than trying to change the behaviour of individuals and families by psychologically-oriented intervention, attention should focus on ameliorating the inequalities that result in impoverishment and poor living conditions (Gil, 1978).

Although sociological perspectives on child abuse were originally promulgated in the United States, many have expressed similar views in Britain (see, for example, Parton, 1985; Holman, 1988). Moreover, the report of the Rowntree Inquiry into Income and Wealth (Hills, 1995) documented a pattern of 'poor parenting' in the most disadvantaged council estates in Britain. However, it was argued that this did not result from poverty alone but from high rates of family break-up, lack of understanding of children's needs, social isolation and universally high rates of unemployment among young people – many of whom were already parents themselves. Around five times the number of children were on the 'at risk' registers from the poorest estates as from other areas of the same city. Similar findings have been reported by other studies (Waterhouse, 1997).

An integrated perspective on sexual abuse

With respect to child maltreatment in general, controversy has raged for years over whether the basic cause lies in the psychopathology of parents or in social, economic and cultural factors. We might remember that child maltreatment is a very complex phenomenon and is likely to be diverse in causation: in short, all of the opposing schools are likely to be right in some respect at least part of the time. With respect to physical abuse, Belsky and Vondra (1989) put forward an integrated model that emphasises the following determinants of parenting: developmental history, personality, work, marital relations, parenting experienced by the parents when they were children, social networks, the child's characteristics, and the child's development.

With respect to sexual abuse in particular, recent years have seen the development of approaches which seek to combine elements from different schools to provide a more powerful explanatory theory of child sexual abuse (Finkelhor, 1984; Marshall and Barbaree, 1990). These theories directly inform most of the work undertaken with sex offenders in Britain and suggest that a range of psychological and socio-structural factors contribute to child sexual abuse (Colton and Vanstone, 1996).

For example, Finkelhor (1984) suggests a four-stage process through which offenders pass when committing acts of abuse. First, the offender must be motivated to abuse a child. There are three components to the source of this motivation:

  (i) emotional congruence – relating sexually to the child satisfies some important sexual need;
 (ii) sexual arousal – the child comes to be the potential source of sexual gratification;
(iii) alternative sources of sexual gratification are not available, or are less satisfying.

Secondly, the offender must overcome his internal inhibitions against acting on his motivation. Abusers' own moral scruples can be overcome through alcohol or drugs, or may be undermined by psychosis, impulse disorder, senility, stress, or a failure of the incest-inhibition mechanism in family dynamics. Internal inhibitors may also be undermined by wider social factors such as apparent toleration of sexual interest in children, weak criminal sanctions against offenders, the ideology of the patriarchal prerogatives of fathers, and social toleration of deviant acts committed while intoxicated.

Thirdly, the offender must overcome external impediments to committing abuse. He must gain access to a victim and also have the opportunity to abuse. Both conditions can be easily met in the case of incest or intra-familial abuse. However, opportunities for non-familial (or extra-familial) abuse must be more actively sought. Thus, many abusers consciously plan opportunities to gain access to children. They seek out places where children are gathered, and cultivate acquaintance with those who have children. Many of those convicted of child sexual abuse committed their offences while employed as teachers, social workers, youth leaders and members of the clergy. Some such individuals deliberately seek positions with children so that they can engage in sexual abuse.

Finally, the child's resistance to sexual abuse must be overcome. Many abusers are in positions of power or trust in relation to their victims, which makes it easier to overcome such resistance. Abusers may use threats, coercion, violence, bribery, or reward to gain the compliance of their victims. Resistance will also be easier to overcome where the child is isolated or deprived, ignorant of sexual matters, and lacking the requisite knowledge or confidence to resist. Many abusers report 'grooming' their victims and may be very adept at obtaining compliance and ensuring that the child stays silent later on (Colton and Vanstone, 1996).

Colton and Vanstone (1996, p. 21) report that the strengths of Finkelhor's four-preconditions model include the following:

1. It combines psychological and sociological explanations of child sexual abuse.
2. It is at a sufficiently general level to integrate all forms of intra- and extra-familial abuse.
3. It suggests that abuse by both fathers and paedophiles require an explanation of how the sexual interest in the child arose, why there were no effective inhibitors, and why the child's resistance was either absent or insufficient.
4. It applies both to offenders whose deviant behaviour results from deviant sexual preference for children ('fixated' offenders) and to those whose behaviour is situationally induced and occurs in the context of a normal sexual preference structure ('regressed' offenders).

5. It puts responsibility for abuse in perspective and, unlike some explanations, does not remove responsibility from the offender and displace it onto victims, third parties or society as a whole.
6. It has direct implications for working with abusive families and individuals because it shows that evaluation and intervention can operate at four separate sites to prevent sexual abuse from re-occurring.

In conclusion, it is clear that child abuse is a product of an interplay between multiple factors: psychological, cultural and social. The influence of this viewpoint is evidenced in the broad definition of child abuse adopted by the report of the National Commission of Inquiry into the Prevention of Child Abuse (1996).

The consequences of child abuse

Physical abuse and neglect

The physical abuse of children and young people spans a range of actions from what some would see as 'justifiable chastisement' (for example, slapping or caning), to what most would agree constitute premeditated acts of sadistic cruelty against children. The immediate effects of physical abuse reflect the nature and severity of the injuries inflicted. They range from minor bruising and abrasions to fractured bones. In exceptional cases, severe internal injuries such as damage to the spleen, liver and kidney, which may result from punching and kicking, can prove fatal if left untreated.

The commoner non-accidental injuries in babies and young children include fractured ribs caused by excessive squeezing, and twisting fractures of the long bones of the arms and legs. In a young child, a bone may crack and distort, rather than break, resulting in a greenstick fracture. Fortunately, most such injuries heal over time without leaving permanent damage. But this is not the case in relation to the effect of subdural haematoma (bleeding into the membranes surrounding the brain) and retinal haemorrhage (bleeding in the back of the eye). Both can be caused by blows to the head or can be associated with a fractured skull; they can also result from violent shaking, which leaves minimal superficial evidence – for example, grip marks on the chest or upper arms. Retinal haemorrhage may result in blindness, and the unrelieved pressure on the brain from a subdural haematoma can cause permanent brain damage and mental retardation (Kenward and Hevey, 1989).

Besharov (1990, pp. 70–1) has identified a number of factors which might lead to the suspicion that an injury was caused by abuse. These factors include the following:

- *The child's level of development.* Given the limited capacity of infants to move about and injure themselves, any injury to an infant is considered suspicious.
- *The shape of the injury.* The child's body may show the shape of the object used to inflict the injury: for example, a belt buckle or a hot iron.
- *The location of the injury.* Children falling by accident tend to injure their chins, foreheads, hands, elbows, knees and shins. Injuries to other areas – thighs, upper arms, genital and rectal areas, buttocks and the back of the legs or torso – are rarely caused by anything other than a physical assault.
- *The type of injury.* It is almost impossible for some injuries to be self-inflicted. Some types of fractures, for example, can only be caused by pulling, jerking or twisting the long bones in the arms or legs.
- *The number of old and new injuries.* Although physical abuse can be an isolated event, it more usually consists of a pattern of repeated assaults. Multiple injuries in various stages of healing are not signs of an accident-prone child but of physical abuse.

Research indicates that children who suffer abuse, including those who experience emotional deprivation, show delays in their physical growth and mental development. It is also well established that social disadvantage *per se* can seriously damage the life chances of children. Sadly, for many socially disadvantaged children, neglect or active abuse by their parents is just one more factor in a generally abusive environment (Kenward and Hevey, 1989). However, it is also clear that good care and educational opportunities can compensate for bad experience irrespective of the child's age.

The behavioural characteristics of physically abused and neglected children include: an impaired capacity to enjoy life (often sad, preoccupied or listless); psychiatric or psychosomatic stress symptoms (such as bedwetting, bizarre behaviour, and eating problems); low self-esteem and feelings of worthlessness; learning problems at school (for example, lack of concentration); withdrawal; opposition defiance; hypervigilance (an expression of 'frozen watchfulness'); compulsivity and pseudo-mature behaviour (a false appearance of independence or of always being excessively 'good' or offering indiscriminate affection to all adults who show an interest) (Kenward and Hevey, 1989).

None of the behaviours listed above are exclusive to abused children; nor are they manifested by all those who suffer abuse. How children react depends on a complex interplay between a number of factors: the child's personality, particular family circumstances and relationships, and the nature, severity and duration of the abuse inflicted. Whilst it appears that adults who were abused in childhood are at higher risk of abusing their own children, by no means all abused children develop into abusive adults. As Kenward and Hevey (1989) state:

> Children have proved remarkably resilient to all forms of maltreatment and many thousands who have experienced what would be considered abusive childhoods by contemporary standards have become affectionate, caring and sensitive parents.

In recent years, there has been increased interest in resilient children who transcend abusive childhoods to become successful adults. It seems likely that both personal and environmental factors contribute to resiliency. Personal qualities of resilient children are thought to include good intellectual ability, a positive attitude towards others, physical attractiveness, enthusiasm, and an internal locus of control. External factors are the presence of caring adults outside the abusive family who take a strong interest in the child, and parents who, despite being abusive, are able to offer some family stability, an expectation of academic performance, and a home atmosphere in which the abuse is sporadic rather than a constant, pervasive element.

Sexual abuse

Sexual abuse has been defined as 'any act occurring between people who are at different developmental stages which is for the sexual gratification of the person at the more advanced developmental stage' (Coulborn Faller, 1988, p. 11). This definition includes sexual acts between children, provided that the perpetrator and the victim are at different developmental stages. For example, an adolescent may abuse a younger child, or one child may abuse another of the same age who is mentally disadvantaged.

Risk factors

Before looking at the consequences of child sexual abuse, it is worth considering who is abused, or so-called 'risk factors'. It is clear that girls are more likely to be sexually victimised than boys although, as previously mentioned, the discrepancy is less than was once thought. Research by Russell (1984) suggests that over half of all women are subject to some form of sexual abuse prior to reaching the age of 18. Although by no means all such cases would require intervention from child-protection agencies, Russell also found that around 16 per cent of women experience some form of incestuous abuse, two-thirds of which can be regarded as serious or very serious. Russell's work indicates that official incidence rates represent the tip of the iceberg of child sexual abuse cases (Colton and Vanstone, 1996).

Finkelhor (1986) and his associates discovered that the most common age at which both boys and girls begin to experience abuse is between 8 and 12 years of age. However, we should not overlook the fact that much younger children may be subjected to child sexual abuse (Colton and Vanstone, 1996).

Finkelhor (1984) has also explored the question of why some children experience abuse while others do not. He reports that eight of the strongest independent predictors of sexual victimisation among girls and young women are:

- *Having a stepfather.* Most stepfathers do not abuse their stepchildren. However, having a stepfather in the home does somewhat increase the risk of sexual abuse for girls, particularly if the stepfather offers an affection which the child did not receive from her natural father.
- *Living in a single-parent family.* Children from single-parent families or children whose mothers are disabled or out of the home for extensive periods are at somewhat higher risk than other children.
- *Having a poor relationship with the mother.* Children who are not close to their mothers tend to be more vulnerable to sexual abuse and are also more likely to 'keep it secret' when initial sexual advances are made.
- *Mother did not finish high school.* Higher risk of abuse has been found to correlate with low educational achievement by parents, particularly by mothers because they tend to have more contact with children.
- *Certain parental characteristics.* Parental characteristics associated with increased risk for children include poor supervision of children, punitive discipline, extreme marital conflict, parental violence, substance abuse, and depression.
- *A punitive attitude with respect to sexual matters on the part of the mother.* Children are less likely to confide in mothers who are blaming and punitive with respect to sexual matters.
- *Household with low income.* As ecological theory tells us, an impoverished environment increases the risk of all forms of abuse. However, it should be emphasised that abuse occurs at every socio-economic level.
- *Having only two friends or less in childhood.* Isolated children tend to be more susceptible to the ploys of child molesters who offer attention and affection.

Obviously, the risk factors listed above are too general to be of use in identifying specific cases of sexual abuse. They are perhaps more useful in enabling social workers to select groups of children for prevention programmes.

Consequences of sexual abuse

The harrowing accounts of women who were sexually victimised during childhood (e.g., Rush, 1980; Spring, 1987) have not only increased awareness and sensitivity about the adverse consequences of sexual abuse but have also fuelled a growing body of research into the short- and long-term effects of abuse. The short-term effects include a range of emotional and behavioural problems, including: general psychopathology, fearfulness, depression, withdrawal and suicide, hostility and aggression, low self-esteem, guilt and shame. Other short-term effects include physical symptoms, running away and other 'acting out' disorders, cognitive disability, developmental delay and poor school performance, as well as inappropriate sexual behaviour (Colton and Vanstone, 1996).

However, Corby (1993) argues that the only clear and direct initial outcome of sexual abuse appears to be the inappropriately sexualised behaviour that occurs in up to a third of all sexually victimised children. He also maintains that sexual abuse, in itself, does not appear to have an incapacitating effect in the short term for most children.

Corby (1993) states that the links between sexual abuse and emotional and behavioural difficulties are even more problematic in relation to long-term effects. This is partly because of the much greater length of time between the abuse and the observed behaviour problems, and also because of the possible effects of a much larger number of intervening variables. Even so, research does indicate that women who have been sexually abused as children are more likely than other women to encounter difficulties in relation to fear, anxiety, self-esteem, depression, and sexual satisfaction; they are also more vulnerable to further abuse. It may be concluded, therefore, that child sexual abuse can have a serious adverse effect on long-term mental health (Colton and Vanstone, 1996).

Research indicates that sexual abuse is likely to be most harmful in cases where the abusive act involved penetration, the abuse has persisted for some time, the abuser is a father figure, the abuse is accompanied by violence, force and/or the threat of it, and the response of the child's family to disclosure is negative (for example, the child is not believed or is blamed for the abuse).

The age and sex of victims may also have an impact on the outcome, but the nature of these relationships is not clear. Neither is it always clear whether intervention by child protection agencies has a positive or negative effect on the outcome for victims (Colton and Vanstone, 1996). Intervention possibilities may include removing the perpetrator from the home, removing the child if the mother is unable or unwilling to prevent continued access to the child by the perpetrator, and criminal prosecution of the perpetrator. All of these possibilities involve emotional trauma to the family and possibly financial deprivation as well if the perpetrator was also the breadwinner. Even if the child is not blamed for the situation, the family will have mixed feelings about criminally prosecuting a father or father figure. In addition, the child may be further traumatised by having to describe the circumstances of the abuse many times to many different investigators. If the case is criminally prosecuted, the child faces public court appearances, sometimes delayed for as long as two years after the initial disclosure was made. Duquette (1988, pp. 399–403) has identified several procedures which may serve to reduce trauma to the child during the investigative phase:

- Reduce the number of interviews and interviewers the child must endure by coordinating the procedures of different agencies: for example, child protection, the police, and the juvenile and criminal courts.
- Employ 'vertical prosecution' in which a single prosecutor is assigned to the case through all stages of the proceedings.
- Videotape the initial interview so that those who need to know the child's story can watch the videotape. Videotapes may be able to substitute for the child's testimony in some courts.
- Allow an emotionally supportive adult, such as a relative or victim-advocate, to accompany the child through all stages of the legal process. It will also be helpful if the child, and the mother if she is supportive, have been prepared for what will happen in court through participation in a victim-witness programme.
- Allow children with limited vocabularies to use anatomically correct dolls and drawings with which they can demonstrate what happened to them.
- Expedite the legal process.

Despite our best efforts, child-welfare intervention is bound to be traumatic, but the alternative to intervention is that the abuse will continue and therapeutic services will not be offered. Treatment programmes for sexual-abuse victims and their non-offending parents (usually the mother) vary widely with respect to both philosophy and structure. As previously mentioned, the feminist perspective views sexual abuse as a demonstration of institutionalised male power over women: programmes offered from this perspective often work towards permanent exclusion of the perpetrator from the family unit and focus on promoting healing and independence in the victim, her mother and siblings. Conversely, systems theorists may work towards reunification of the perpetrator with the family, provided that this does not compromise the future safety of the child. Some programmes offer only group therapy for 2–3 hours a week over 10–14 weeks, while others offer a progression of individual, couple, group and family therapy for periods up to two years or even longer.

The child-protection system

No aspect of the social-work task is more challenging or has aroused more concern than child protection. In the UK, the tragic death of Maria Colwell in 1973, and the public inquiry that followed, marked the beginning of the contemporary political, public and professional interest in the issue of child abuse (Parton, 1985; Parton and Parton, 1989). Following the recommendations of the inquiry (DHSS, 1974, 1982), a nationally coordinated child-protection system has evolved (Waterhouse, 1997). This system requires the effective coordination of child-protection agencies, and it also involves communication and cooperation between a number of professionals from other agencies (Hallett and Stevenson, 1980; Home Office et al., 1991; Hallett and Birchall, 1992; Hallett, 1995; Birchall and Hallett, 1995; Colton et al., 1996; Sanders et al., 1997; Sanders and Thomas, 1997; Sanders, 1999).

Those particularly involved in the process of gathering relevant information and working with the child and family include: social workers, health visitors, general practitioners, paediatricians, police officers, and representatives of the NSPCC (National Society for the Prevention of Cruelty to Children). Probation officers, teachers and psychiatrists may also make an important contribution. In addition, expert advice may be needed in a number of areas, including issues associated with race, culture, and disability. Such advice may be obtained from professionals like medical specialists, psychologists and lawyers and from members of ethnic communities, particularly those skilled in the translation of languages and cultural value systems.

Work on individual child-protection cases follows the basic principles of the Children Act 1989. These principles include a focus on the welfare of the child (taking into account the child's views in the light of his or her age and understanding), partnership with parents and other family members, the concept of parental responsibility, sensitivity to issues of gender, race, culture and disability, and a shared mutual understanding of the goals of child-protection work and of what constitutes good practice.

It is essential that all stages of the child-protection process are recorded. All agencies must have clear policies to ensure good record keeping, which should include giving children and parents access to records. Records must be accurate and clear; they should include all the information that is known to the agency about the child and family; and should reflect all the work undertaken with the agency and working arrangements with staff in other agencies (Home Office et al., 1991).

In the last five years there has been a radical rethinking about the role of child protection in promoting the welfare of children who are vulnerable to abuse, and this has been reflected in the way the government has responded to the themes from *Child Protection: Messages from Research* (Department of Health, 1995) by revising *Working Together under the Children Act 1989* (Home Office et al., 1991) to produce *Working Together to Safeguard Children* (Department of Health et al., 1999). The reason for the production of the revised guidance was to develop a child-protection service that was more integrated with services for children in need: in other words, to integrate protection with prevention. The main means to achieve this was the production of a unified framework for assessment (Department of Health et al., 2000), which is to be used both for children in need and for abused and neglected children.

Under the original guidance (Home Office et al., 1991), the stages of work with individual cases were described as referral and recognition; immediate protection and planning the investigation; investigation and initial assessment; child-protection conference and decision-making about the need for registration; comprehensive assessment and planning; and implementation, review and, where appropriate, de-registration. Under the new guidance, all referrals concerning the welfare of a child will begin by being processed in the same way, but will have differential outcomes (and different exit points from the process) depending upon how the information and assessments unfold.

The new guidance indicates that everybody who works with children should be aware of indicators that a child's welfare may be at risk. They should be mindful of this whether they are working directly with children, with parents or caregivers (who may need help in promoting and safeguarding the welfare of their children), or with family members, employees, or others who have contact with children. Professionals from specific disciplines should have particular arrangements for ensuring that those who have less contact with the child-protection system are still sufficiently knowledgeable to know what kinds of issues should raise concerns, and to whom those concerns should be passed when they arise.

All schools and colleges should have a designated member of staff with special knowledge and skills in recognising abuse. The designated person will also have knowledge of the local child-protection procedures and know what to do when concerns about a particular child or young person arise. Likewise, health services should have their own arrangements. Health authorities will have a senior paediatrician and a senior nurse (with health visiting qualification) to act as 'designated senior professional'. This 'senior professional' will not necessarily become professionally involved in every locally referred child-protection case, but will certainly have a role as coordinator of information about child protection, and may well be involved in training and professional development concerning child abuse and child protection. The NHS Trusts as well should have specific professionals (doctor, nurse, midwife) with responsibility for child protection, referred to as 'named' professionals.

The process of handling individual cases is summarised in Table 5.1. Referrals to social services should normally have a decision made within 24 hours. That decision can be that no further action is necessary, or that services should be provided by another agency, or that further action (e.g., initial assessment) is needed. Under normal circumstances, agencies referring a family to social services should discuss the referral with the family first (unless seeking the family's agreement would place the child at increased risk). Members of the public making referrals should be able to be assured that personal information about them will not be disclosed to anyone without their consent. Referrers (both agency and members of the public) should have information about what has happened in respect of the referral made, but where the information is given to members of the public it must be done in a manner respecting the confidentiality of the child and family.

Table 5.1 *Referrals to social services departments where there are child-welfare concerns*

Referral (to be decided within 24 hours)	Initial assessment (not later than 7 working days)	Core assessment (not later than 35 working days)
• no further action	• involves seeing and speaking to the child, and family	• if child is in need, a core assessment
• provision of services or other help (from own or other agencies)	• obtaining information from sources and other professionals	• if significant harm, make inquiries under Section 47
• an initial assessment is required	• is this a child in need? (Section 17)	
	• is there reasonable cause to suspect that this child is suffering, or is likely to suffer, significant harm? (Section 47)	
	• decisions should be endorsed at managerial level and recorded	

If it is decided that further assessment is necessary, then the new *Frame-work for the Assessment of Children in Need and their Families* (Department of Health et al., 2000) comes into play. The broad outline of the frame-work is three major headings with six or seven subheadings under each heading:

1. **Dimensions of the child's developmental needs**
   Health
   Education
   Emotional and behavioural development
   Identity
   Family and social relationships
   Social presentation
   Self-care skills

2. **Dimensions of parenting capacity**
   Basic care
   Ensuring safety
   Emotional warmth
   Stimulation
   Guidance and boundaries
   Stability

3. **Family and environmental factors**
   Family history and functioning
   Wider family
   Housing
   Employment
   Income
   Family's social integration
   Community resources

Using the three dimensions (and the subheadings) the initial assessment should address the following three questions (Department of Health et al., 2000, p. 41):

- What are the needs of the child?
- Are the parents able to respond appropriately to the child's needs? Is the child being adequately safeguarded from significant harm, and are the parents able to promote the child's health and development?
- Is action required to safeguard and promote the child's welfare?

This assessment should involve direct contact with the child and the family, the compilation of all available information about the child and the family, and information from other professionals. It is during this initial assessment that a decision may be made about whether the situation concerns a child in need (Section 17) requiring a family-support response, or whether it is a situation involving actual or potential significant harm requiring a child-protection response (Section 47 – see below).

The guidance draws on research (Cleaver et al., 1998) to emphasise pitfalls that may occur during an initial assessment. These include: not giving enough weight to information from family, friends and neighbours; not giving enough attention to what children say, and how they look and behave; focusing attention too narrowly on the most pressing or visible problem; over-precipitate action (based on media or senior management concerns); failing to check out the understanding of family members; basing conclusions on assumptions and pre-judgements; misinterpreting parental behaviour; failing to redirect families to other services (when the risk of significant harm is not established); reluctance of workers to assess the risk to personal safety (or to ask for help when concerned); and lack of recording. With so many potential pitfalls, it is indeed a wonder that an adequate initial assessment is ever achieved.

Where there is no concern about actual or potential significant harm, there may still be 'child in need' concerns, and the initial assessment should proceed to a core assessment as a basis for the provision of family-support services. Interestingly, the guidance discusses the role of Family Group Conferences (normally applied in contexts of child protection and/or youth offending) as a means of taking forward the work with families of children in need.

Where there is a concern about actual or likely significant harm, then a 'Section 47 inquiry' must be undertaken. Section 47 of the Act states:

> Where a local authority (a) are informed that a child who lives, or is found, in their area (i) is the subject of an emergency protection order; or (ii) is in police protection; or (b) have reasonable cause to suspect that a child who lives, or is found, in their area is suffering, or is likely to suffer significant harm, the authority shall make, or cause to be made, such enquiries as they consider necessary to enable them to decide whether they should take any action to safeguard or promote the child's welfare.

Where there is risk of immediate harm to the child, then an agency with statutory powers (for example, police, NSPCC, social services) should act without delay to ensure the child's immediate safety. Even under such circumstances there should be a preliminary 'strategy discussion' between the relevant agencies, but the guidance anticipates that sometimes even this may not be possible, in which case such a discussion should take place as soon as possible afterwards. There is a range of methods for securing a child's immediate safety. In recent years protection agencies have had legal options requiring the removal of the perpetrator (under the Family

Law Act 1996) rather than removing the child. Other options can include orders to keep a child where he or she is, thus preventing removal from a safe environment. Some of these options are discussed below in 'The legal framework'.

The 'strategy discussion' (which may or may not be a meeting) should involve social services, police, a senior doctor (where a medical examination may be needed), and other relevant agencies (and in particular the agency making the referral). The purpose of the strategy discussion is primarily to plan how the inquiries should be handled (once it is established that an inquiry should be begun, or continued). The agencies will develop an immediate action plan to protect the child, and will decide on what information arising from the strategy discussion should be shared with the family. Information that is shared, and decisions that are reached about action to be taken, should be recorded.

Where a core assessment is required as part of Section 47 inquiries, the framework again provides the structure for pulling together all of the necessary information to enable decision-making. However, the timing of the subsequent child-protection action (child protection conference) means that the full core assessment will not be completed by the time of the conference. It is at this very early stage that the child and family should be prepared for participation in the inquiry process. Obstacles to their full participation (young age of child, communication difficulties, ethnicity) should be addressed. The parents would normally be involved and their consent requested for an inquiry in relation to the child. There may, however, be some circumstances when such consent may not be sought, and indeed some circumstances where the parent would not be informed about the inquiry, because to do so would place the child at greater risk.

Videotaped interviews may be conducted as part of the inquiry process. There is now a legal presumption that children under the age of 17 years will give evidence through pre-recorded videotaped interviews (Youth and Criminal Justice Act 1999).

Families should be provided with a written record of the outcome of a Section 47 inquiry. There are basically three possible outcomes: the concerns are not substantiated; the concerns are substantiated, but the child is not considered to be at *continuing* risk of significant harm; or the concerns are substantiated and the child is considered to be at continued risk of significant harm.

In the first case, it is important that the family be offered the opportunity of family-support services if the child is considered to be a child in need. It may be that the concerns about the risk of significant harm were not completely allayed by the inquiry, but there is insufficient evidence upon which to base any other decision. In such a case, agencies may want to monitor the situation, but the guidance is quite clear that such monitoring should not be used as a means of avoiding or delaying making a difficult decision.

In the second case, where there clearly was a risk of significant harm to the child, but that risk is not seen as continuing, it is possible for the agencies to decide not to convene a child-protection conference (because an inter-agency plan is not seen as necessary). It is specifically in this provision that we can see the attempt of the government, with caution, to introduce the 'lighter touch' in child protection that seemed to be such a clear message from the research summarised in 1995 (Department of Health, 1995). It is perhaps specifically this type of situation, in which harm had been established, where agencies previously may have felt obliged to put the child's name on the register.

However, the examples provided by the government in the present guidance (the abuser has left home, isolated instance of abuse by a stranger), when combined with the cautionary notes about the 'dangers of misplaced professional optimism' (p. 51), do not encourage agencies to dispense with a child-protection conference. The guidance also requires that a decision not to hold a conference be endorsed by 'a suitably qualified and designated person within the social services department' (p. 51). Research into the percentage of cases in which a conference is held and under what circumstances could be very illuminating.

Child-protection conference

In the third case, where the risk of significant harm continues, there should be a child-protection conference. The purpose of the initial child-protection conference (which should be held within 15 working days of the strategy meeting) is to bring together the information about the child's health, development and functioning and the parent's (or carer's) capacity, assess the likelihood of future significant harm, and decide on what action is needed, how that action will be undertaken, and what the objectives of that action are. Initial child-protection conferences are generally quite large, and include professionals who have a contribution to make by virtue of either their expertise or their knowledge of the family (or both). The person chairing the conference will be someone who does not have operational line management for the case. A quorum for attendance is the social services department plus at least two other agencies, although in exceptional circumstances a conference may proceed without this quorum.

Over the last ten years there has been a gradual transition from parental attendance being the exception to parental attendance being the norm – though the transition has not been without difficulties (Cleaver and Freeman, 1995; Thoburn et al., 1995). More recently, attention has been given to the involvement of young people in the child-protection process. The young person may appear himself or an advocate may appear on his behalf. However, as noted in the guidance: 'Adults and any children who wish to make representations to the conference may not wish to speak in front of one another' (Department of Health et al., 1999, p. 53). Therefore, it may be necessary to do a bit of shuffling during conferences to allow the direct but separate input of both the parents and the child. It is important that parents and children are prepared for attendance at the conference, and are helped to formulate the main points that they would like to convey. There are times when parents will be excluded from attending part or even all of a conference. The main criterion for this is when the presence of the parent (perhaps because of the threat of violence or intimidation) would interfere with the process. The guidance points out, however, that the fact that a parent is being prosecuted is not in itself a reason for exclusion, although there may need to be some discussions with the police and the Crown Prosecution Service about this.

Reports will normally be prepared for the child-protection conference; a copy of the social services report should be given to the parent (and child if appropriate) beforehand, and they should have the opportunity to discuss the contents of the report before the conference. The report should contain a chronology of significant events, information about the child's health and development, information on the parenting capacity of the parents, the direct views, wishes and feelings of the parents and the child, and an analysis of the above and consideration of the implications for the future.

The main task of the conference is to address the continuing risk of significant harm to the child. The main decision of the conference is whether or not to add the child's name to the child protection register: and, if the decision is to register the child, then certain other actions need to be taken. However, these other actions – deciding whether to implement care proceedings in respect of one or more of the children in the family, and deciding whether to prosecute the abuser – are not the business of the child protection conference. The input of the conference may be influential in making the decisions but the decisions themselves are made by the agency concerned: social services and the police respectively.

An important principle of child protection is that the act of registration in itself confers no protection on the child; it is the concerted and coordinated actions of the agencies that will serve to protect the child from future harm. Therefore, if the conference decides that the risk is continuing, it should do the following things: appoint a key worker; identify a 'core group' (professionals and family members who will work together to take the plan forward); decide how family and children are to be involved in the plan; establish a timescale for core group meetings (the first one should be within 10 working days); consider future assessments required; outline a child-protection plan (with a contingency plan); and ensure participants are aware of the different purposes of the initial conference, core group, and review conference. A date for the first review conference (no longer than three months away) should be set.

The key worker is the central coordinating link of the child-protection plan. He or she is responsible for completing the core assessment; for ensuring that a detailed child-protection plan develops from the conference plan, and that the plan is reviewed; and for leading the core group. Although the guidance does not say so explicitly, it is implicit in the key-worker role that he or she will be the one to act as the hub of the wheel of communication, informing agencies of developments, and serving as a central communication point for agencies to share their information. There should also be a written agreement drawn up with the family.

The need for an inter-agency plan has, in the past, been the criterion (along with the continuation of significant harm) for the inclusion of the child's name on the register. The child-protection plan is an action plan that indicates who will do what, by when, and why. The core assessment, begun as part of the information for the child-protection conference, will need to be completed as part of the plan; it should be completed 42 (7 + 35) working days from the beginning of the initial assessment. Where specialist assessments are required as part of the core assessment, the bringing together of the core assessment findings should not be delayed pending the result of a specialist assessment.

After the decision to register has been made, a review conference will be required. The first one should be within three months of the initial child protection conference, and thereafter review conferences should be no longer than six months apart. Review conferences, however, can be convened earlier if there are concerns warranting an earlier review. The review will consider whether or not the child's name can be removed from the register. There are three circumstances permitting this. First, if there is no longer a risk to the child. Secondly, if the child has moved permanently to the area of another authority. Thirdly, if the child becomes 18, dies, or permanently leaves the UK, then the name will be removed from the register.

Government policy states that access to services should never be a reason for a child's name to be added to the child-protection register. Likewise, when a child's name is removed from the register, the child and the family should continue to receive whatever services they have been receiving, for as long as is necessary, whilst the child continues to be a child in need.

Having outlined the child-protection procedures under the new guidance, it may be useful to look backwards a little at the findings of Gibbons et al. (1995), who investigated the matter of filtering in the child-protection system. That is, how many cases are stopped at each of the three stages of the child-protection process: referral, conference, and registration. They found the following:

First filter: initial decision by duty social worker whether to investigate
Investigated (3/4 of referrals)
Not investigated (1/4 of referrals)

Second filter: decision by manager whether to call conference
Conferenced (1/3 of cases investigated)
Not conferenced (2/3 of cases investigated)

Third filter: decision by case conference whether to register
Registered (2/3 of cases conferenced)
Not registered (1/3 of cases conferenced)

As a result therefore of 100 referrals to the child-welfare services, only 16 would actually end up with their names on the child-protection register. The results of this filtering process have been used as an argument to suggest that too many children are being brought into the child-protection system who perhaps need not be. If it is effective, the new guidance should have an impact on that.

The legal framework

The Children Act heralded a shift towards the use of voluntary arrangements rather than compulsory intervention in efforts to protect children. Nevertheless, in cases where parental cooperation is not forthcoming or is insufficient to protect the child, compulsory measures are still required. The powers to intervene, together with the statutory controls on those powers, are contained in Parts IV and V of the Children Act 1989 and include the following orders and provisions.

Court-ordered investigations

When a court becomes sufficiently concerned about a child who is before it in connection with any family proceedings, the court may order the local authority to investigate the child's circumstances under Section 37 of the 1989 Act. To ensure the child's protection while the investigation is proceeding, the court may also, at the same time, make an interim care or supervision order and appoint a guardian *ad litem* for the child. Whether the order is sought through the court's own initiative or because of an application by a local authority, under Section 31(2) of the Act, the court may only make a care order or supervision order if the threshold conditions (see below: 'Care order') are satisfied.

If an interim care or supervision order is made, the local authority must report back to the court within 8 weeks and notify the court of any action it proposes to take, or justify a decision to take no action.

If the threshold conditions are not satisfied the court could, either on application or on its own initiative, make any Section 8 order. There are four such orders: residence order, contact order, prohibited steps order, and specific issues order.

The orders are defined in the Act. A *residence order* is 'an order settling the arrangements to be made as to the person with whom a child is to live'. A *contact order* is 'an order requiring the person with whom a child lives, or is to live, to allow the child to visit or stay with the person named in the order, or for that person and the child otherwise to have contact with each other'. A *prohibited steps order* ('things that must not be done') is 'an order that no step which could be taken by a parent in meeting his parental responsibility for a child, and which is of a kind specified in the order, shall be taken by any person without the consent of the court'. A *specific issue order* ('things that must be done') is 'an order giving directions for the purpose of determining a specific question which has arisen, or may arise, in connection with any aspect of parental responsibility for a child'.

Care order

A care order is the only means, apart from an emergency protection order, whereby a local authority acquires parental authority for a child. Unless discharged, the order lasts until the child is 18. A care order can only be made if the conditions contained in Section 31 are satisfied: that is, if the court believes:

(a) that the child concerned is suffering, or is likely to suffer, significant harm; and
(b) that the harm, or likelihood of harm, is attributable to:
    (i) the care given to the child, or likely to be given to him if the order were not made, not being what it would be reasonable to expect a parent to give him; or
    (ii) the child being beyond parental control.

Courts are not permitted to add any conditions or requirements to a care order, with the exception of the contact that a child in care may have with parents and others under Section 34 of the Children Act 1989. Parents whose children are in care retain the right to exercise any aspect of their parental responsibility which is not in conflict with local authority decisions regarding the child's upbringing. Under Section 34(1), local authorities have a duty to allow reasonable contact between a child who is the subject of a care order and parents, guardians and others with parental responsibility, or anyone who has had care of the child immediately before the order was made. This provision is a major reform since, prior to the Children Act 1989, parental access to children who were the subject of care orders was entirely at the discretion of the local authority. Now, however, when a care order is made, the court must satisfy itself as to the arrangements that will be made for contact and must invite comment from any interested party. Any later variation of contact which is not agreed by the parents can become the subject of an application to court (Ball, 1996).

Once the application is made and the trial venue has been decided, a guardian *ad litem* (GAL) will be appointed and a directions hearing will be arranged. The latter will usually be before a district judge at the care centre or a justice's clerk at the family proceedings court (Ball, 1996). Parties will either be present or represented, and the GAL can advise the court on matters pertaining to the child's welfare. The over-arching aim of the directions hearing is to avoid unnecessary delay prior to the matter coming to a final hearing for resolution. Thus, decisions are made about the parties to the proceedings, the expected length and timetable of the final hearing, deadlines for witness statements and the report of the GAL, the commissioning of expert medical reports, and so forth.

All reports and witnesses' statements must be exchanged in advance of the final hearing. The court must give reasons for its decision. All parties have a right of appeal. Before making an order the court must be satisfied that such a course would be better for the child than making no order at all.

Supervision order

A supervision order does not give the local authority parental responsibility but puts the child under the supervision of a designated local authority or probation officer for up to one year. The order may be discharged by the court at an earlier date or extended for up to a maximum of three years. It may contain directions that the child reside in a particular place or participate in particular activities or receive medical or psychiatric treatment.

Emergency protection order

Emergencies present a dilemma in that wide powers, available without delay, are needed to protect children in crisis situations. Someone must have the authority to immediately insist that the child is removed from a dangerous place, or remains in a safe place if threatened with removal.

On the other hand, wide powers, immediately available, are obviously open to abuse. The broadly-framed and somewhat imprecise emergency provisions contained in previous legislation (Children and Young Persons Act 1969) did allow discrepant and sometimes abusive social-work practice. As a result, the emergency provisions contained in Part V of the current legislation (Children Act 1989) are detailed and specific.

The emergency protection order (EPO) is intended for use only in real emergencies where the immediate protection of the child cannot be secured in any other way. It is intended to last for the minimum necessary time, and to be open to challenge at the earliest opportunity. Anyone (not just a statutory agency) may apply for an EPO. Application is made to a court or, with leave of the justices' clerk, to a single justice who is a member of the family proceedings panel. The order may be granted *ex parte* (without anyone who might oppose the application being either present or served notice). The grounds for an EPO are that

> there is reasonable cause to believe that the child is likely to suffer significant harm if … he is not removed to accommodation provided by or on behalf of the applicant; or … he does not remain in the place in which he is then being accommodated, or where enquiries are being made by a local authority, anyone authorized by them, or by the NSPCC, and they are denied access to the child. (Section 44)

An EPO may be made for up to eight days. After 72 hours, the child or anyone with parental responsibility may apply to a court for discharge of the order, provided that they were not served notice and were not present when the order was made. An EPO:

(a) operates as a direction to any person who is in a position to do so to comply with any request to produce the child to the applicant;
(b) authorises:
   (i) the removal of the child at any time to accommodation provided by or on behalf of the applicant and his being kept there; or
   (ii) the prevention of the child's removal from any hospital, or other place, in which he was being accommodated immediately before the making of the order; and
(c) gives the applicant parental responsibility for the child. (Section 44(4))

The court or justice making the EPO may add a direction requiring any other person to provide information about the child's whereabouts (Section 48(1)). An EPO may be extended once for up to seven days. It gives the local authority limited parental authority, which allows for the making of day-to-day decisions concerning the child though parents do retain their parental responsibility subject to the EPO. There is a presumption of reasonable contact between parents and child. However, the court may set conditions about such contact and about medical treatment investigation. Children who are old enough may refuse such treatment, although in extreme cases the High Court may override the child's refusal (Ball, 1996).

Police powers

If a constable has reasonable cause to believe that a child would be likely to suffer significant harm, he or she may remove a child to suitable accommodation or take reasonable steps to ensure that the child remain where he or she is. The constable must consider the child's wishes and feelings. In addition, the constable must inform the parents, the local authority and a designated police officer inquiring into the case. Police protection lasts for a maximum of 72 hours, but during that period the designated officer may apply for an EPO, which, if granted, begins on the day that the child was taken into police protection (Section 44).

Under Section 48(9) of the 1989 Act, where it is clear that anyone attempting to exercise power under an EPO is being denied, or is likely to be denied, entry to premises or access to the child, a court or a single justice may issue a warrant authorising a police constable to exercise those powers by force if necessary.

In addition, the police have the power to enter and search any premises for the purpose of 'saving life and limb'. Where appropriate, the child could then be taken into police protection (Ball, 1996).

Recovery order

The court may issue a recovery order under Section 50 of the 1989 Act where a child who is (a) in care, or (b) the subject of an emergency protection order, or (c) in police protection, has been removed or run away from care, or is being kept away from any person who has care of them as a result of that order. The order serves as a directive to produce the child; it also authorises the child's removal by any authorised person, and permits a police constable to enter and search specified premises.

Child assessment order

The 1989 Act introduced an entirely new order concerning the assessment of a child's health and development. The child assessment order (CAO) can only be applied for in court, on notice, by a local authority or the NSPCC where there is reasonable cause to believe: that the child is suffering, or is likely to suffer, significant harm; that an assessment of the child's health and development are necessary; and that it is unlikely that a satisfactory assessment will be made if a CAO is not made. However, if the court considers that an EPO is justified it should make such an order instead. CAOs are deemed appropriate only in those infrequent cases where a decisive step to obtain an assessment is required and informal attempts to carry out an assessment have been unsuccessful. In 1994 only 82 CAOs were made (Ball, 1996).

Having looked at some of the orders which comprise compulsory intervention it is important to stress once again that compulsory intervention is a last resort and should be undertaken only when voluntary arrangements have failed or are manifestly inappropriate (Ball, 1996).

However, research into child protection funded by the Department of Health indicates that, generally speaking, this last-resort philosophy was not put into practice. Contrary to the intentions of the 1989 Act, it seems that local authorities were initiating child-protection procedures on the basis of injuries to children, thus failing to fully consider the child's wider situation. It also appears that vital family-support services under Part III were often overlooked, with social workers instead focusing on a bureaucratic response to identified injuries. This suggests that large numbers of children were inappropriately drawn into the child-protection system. Even after it was clear that protective measures were unnecessary, the needs of such children for *services* were often left unmet (Department of Health, 1995).

Guardian ad litem

To safeguard the interests of the child a guardian *ad litem* will usually be appointed by the court. The guardian *ad litem* (GAL) is an independent social worker drawn from a panel of GALs and reporting officers administered by the local authority. The GAL is responsible for ascertaining the child's wishes and feelings and instructing the child's solicitor. In addition, the GAL advises the court on the identification of involved parties, the timetable for proceedings, and the making of interim orders. The latter includes the possible discharge of an emergency protection order. Finally, the GAL prepares a report for the court.

In cases where the child and the GAL hold differing views about the child's need, a child of sufficient age and understanding may give his or her own instructions to the solicitor. The child's solicitor then presents the child's view to the court and the GAL presents his or her own view, with legal representation where required.

The GAL's role is to provide an independent assessment of the work of local authority social workers and to make recommendations to the court, which may or may not agree with those of the local authority. Given that it is this same authority that pays the GAL's fee, it is hardly surprising that the independence of GALs has been questioned. The obvious remedy is to remove responsibility for managing the GAL service from local authorities (Ball, 1996). At present, the GAL service faces the prospect of reorganisation and integration with the divorce court welfare service.

Messages from research

A substantial body of reliable evidence on child protection and child abuse has been established over recent years. Much of this research has direct implications for policy and practice. Of particular importance are the 20 studies summarised by the Dartington Social Research Unit and published in an overview entitled *Child Protection: Messages from Research* (Department of Health, 1995). Here, we will look very briefly at those parts of the summary which shed light on the following key questions: What does the child-protection process entail? How effective is it? How can professionals best protect children?

The child-protection process

Around 160,000 children are subject to Section 47 inquiries each year. Most of the families involved in the child-protection process are multiply disadvantaged. Some 96 per cent of the children concerned remain at home, while most of those who are removed are quickly reunited with their families.

The purpose of child-protection inquiries is twofold: (a) to determine whether child abuse has occurred; and (b) to determine whether the family can benefit from support services. Unfortunately, however, inquiries usually turn into investigations, and the majority of families do not receive any services that might justify the intrusion by professionals into their lives.

Undue emphasis is placed on decisions about whether to place the child's name on the child protection register, or to remove the child's name, with insufficient attention given to supporting the child and family in the months following the case conference.

> Professionals are far less concerned with the way families are left when the enquiry is complete and concerns subside than they are with the way children enter the protection process.   (Department of Health, 1995, p. 39)

Given that virtually all the children involved remain at home, it makes sense to involve the family in the child-protection process. However, the research evidence shows that professionals could do more to achieve a partnership with parents and children. For example, many investigations take place without the parents' knowledge.

How effective is the child-protection process?

The studies offer mixed findings with regard to the effectiveness of the child-protection process. There is a wide range of services for children in need. However, the authors of the overview state that: 'these should not be deployed in a way that overwhelms clients or greatly circumscribes parental responsibility or autonomy' (Department of Health, 1995, p. 44). Disturbingly, it was found that between a quarter and a third of the children studied were re-abused after child-welfare intervention, although the incidence of 'severe maltreatment' was low.

How can professionals best protect children?

Families are traumatised by a suspicion of child abuse. Therefore, good professional practice is required to alleviate the anxiety of parents and to facilitate the cooperation necessary to protect the child. The studies identify the following five pre-requisites of effective practice in protecting children and promoting their welfare:

- sensitive and informed professional/client relationships;
- an appropriate balance of power between participants;
- a wide perspective on child protection (i.e., a perspective which views cases as *children in need in circumstances where there may be a protection problem*);
- effective supervision and training of social workers;
- services which enhance children's general quality of life.

The studies found that parents were often insufficiently informed and their lack of participation (from the point of view of the social worker) frequently undermined relations between parents and social workers. Moreover, the narrowness of the social-work approach to child abuse, which reflects poor training and supervision, meant that the wider needs of children and families were overlooked.

Clients in the studies were adversely affected when professionals became preoccupied with a specific event, ignored the wider context, made the wrong 'career avenue' choice for the child, and excluded the family from the inquiry. In the rare cases when appropriate attention was given to the 'secondary adjustment' needs of children and their families, all benefited.

Building on the existing strengths of a child's living situation is more likely to ensure effective prevention than the current approach in which 'miracles' are expected from 'isolated and spasmodic interventions'.

Effective child protection also necessitates respect for family rights. Further, basic child-care principles must be combined with specialist work to safeguard the long-term welfare of children.

In this chapter we have discussed various definitions of abuse and neglect, the causes and consequences of different types of abuse, and the child-protection system, (including the legal context). Let us now go on to explore provisions for children who are being looked after by a local authority.

Case examples

Case example 5.1   Paula Hislop

Paula Hislop is the single parent of three children, Paul James (8), Melanie James (5) and Jessica Thomas (2½). Jessica has a different father from Paul and Melanie. Paul and Melanie's dad left when Melanie was one year old, because he became involved with another woman. Jessica's dad had a very violent temper and used to be violent towards Paula, until she left, taking the children with her to a Women's Aid Refuge. She was there for six months before being rehoused into an area very far from her friends and relations. Paul appears to be a very slow learner, and the school is worried that he does not appear able to keep up with the other children. Jessica's speech has been slow to develop and she is being referred for further investigation. Her hearing appears to be normal.

After she had been in the new home for three months, Paula's neighbours became concerned because it appeared that at weekends she would go out early in the evening, and not come home until very late, leaving the children unattended. The matter has been referred to the social services.

1. Should this case be treated as one where there are children in need, requiring family-support services, or as a child-protection case? Why?
2. Regardless of whether it is a family-support case or a child-protection case, who needs to be involved and why?
3. When all professionals have been identified, consider 'How are these different agencies to be coordinated to work together?'

Case example 5.2   Jean and Paula M

Jean M (3 years, 10 months)
Paula M (2 years, 6 months)

Jean and Paula are the children of Jane M (22) and Tom M (28). They live in a private flat in the centre of a small city. Neither of them are from the area where they now live, having come here about four years ago, shortly after the birth of Jean. All of their family relations are in the area the family have come from. They have not made many friends locally, tending to keep very much to themselves. Tom moved here because of relocation with his work, but shortly after, the firm went bankrupt, and all the workers were laid off. Tom has been unemployed ever since. There are no immediate prospects for employment. The family are worried about finances because Jane is six months pregnant, but nevertheless Jane says that she and Tom are looking forward to another child. The health visitor is not sure that that is Tom's view, a result of impressions gained from the one time she met him.

Because of the relocation, Jane and Tom have no family in the area, and they have only formed friendships with two families near to them. Both of these are families being worked with by social services because of parenting difficulties. Tom has a fairly good relationship with his parents and brother, although rarely gets to see them. Jane describes there being no love lost between her and her mother, and even less between her and her stepfather.

The health visitor visits the family fairly often because she is worried about the development of the two girls, and also because she is concerned about the condition of the home. Both children are extremely low in weight and height; so low, that more than 97 per cent of children of their respective ages are taller and weigh more than they do (they are below the '3rd centile' of development for height and weight). Jane says that both of the children are difficult feeders, but that they do eat what is put before them. Tom was present when the health visitor first expressed her concerns to Jane and Tom. He reacted very angrily, saying 'Are you trying to say I'm starving my kids?' He demanded that the health visitor leave. Nevertheless, the health visitor has remained in contact with Jane and the two girls, despite Jane being a poor attender at clinic.

The home is kept in a very unhygienic and untidy state. The floors are sticky from grime and dirt. Kitchen refuse is piled in a corner of the kitchen, not in a container. Dirty clothes are littered everywhere around the house. There is often dog mess in the house caused by one of the two Alsatians that the family keep; the dogs are rarely exercised. Dirty dishes from meals are left lying around in various rooms of the house. There is no dining table *per se*, but the family eat in the sitting room, usually watching television. Generally there is an unpleasant smell within the house. There are few toys around the house or in the children's bedroom, and those that are there are not age appropriate, being more suitable for older children.

On two occasions neighbours have complained to the local authority, because of concern that the conditions might be the cause of an increased occurrence of rats in the vicinity. An officer from the local authority visited, and confirmed that the conditions could be an attraction to rats. A specific list of recommendations/requirements was drawn up, and the family obliged ... but the improvement on both occasions was short lived, before relapsing into the same conditions as before.

As regards the children's eating pattern, Jean says that she gives them their meals at set times of the day, and has described in detail to the health visitor the content of meals. The health visitor feels that if the children were actually eating everything that was described by their mother, then they would be growing better. Both Mr and Mrs M are on the slightly stout side, but not so much that one would describe them as obese.

Paula is an active, inquiring toddler, who seems to be developing normally apart from the lack of weight and height gain. She is very comfortable around people, and indeed will go to be picked up by nearly anyone who comes to the door of the home. Jean spends two mornings a week at playgroup. Unlike her sister, she is more reserved in temperament. The playgroup supervisor has observed that she is a bit behind in some things that the other children can do easily (colour and shape recognition, counting, etc.), but when given individual attention, can usually learn fairly rapidly. She loves being told stories. The supervisor has observed that she comes to playgroup in dirty clothes, has an unpleasant odour, and is always asking for food, even when she first arrives at the playgroup.

Jane and Tom have a fairly good relationship with each other, although Jane does say that Tom will go off, often for a few days at a time, without her knowing where he has gone. She tends to look up to him. Tom has never been married before, but a long-term relationship ended just prior to his meeting Jane.

The health visitor has discussed the case with the consultant paediatrician, because of the low height and weight gain, and because of concern about how the family will cope when the new baby arrives. They have decided to make a referral to social services.

- Consider what will happen next in accordance with the new government guidance.

Looking after children

In the previous chapter, we talked about protecting children and we discussed the types and theories of child abuse. In this chapter, we will consider the various alternatives open to a child who is being 'looked after' by a local authority.

Objectives

When you have read this chapter, you should know what the term 'looked after' means. You should understand recent trends in the numbers of children being looked after, principles underlying good practice in working with looked-after children, and the advantages and disadvantages of using the government-produced Looking After Children (LAC) materials when working with children living away from their families. You should have a better understanding of kinship care, foster care and residential care as ways of providing for children needing to be looked after. The chapter will also cover secure accommodation and adoption practice, including a consideration of 'open adoptions'.

Children who are 'looked after'

Before we discuss the various alternatives open to children who are being 'looked after', it will be as well to note briefly a few facts about them – including what exactly is meant by the term 'looked after'.

What does the term 'looked-after' denote?

In England and Wales, social services for children and young people are provided under the Children Act 1989. Under the Act, the term 'looked after' denotes all children subject to a care order or who are provided with accommodation on a voluntary basis for more than 24 hours. This includes those children who are the subject of an emergency protection order, police protection powers, or an interim or full care order. It includes children and young people committed or remanded to local authority accommodation, or made the subject of a residence requirement of a supervision order in criminal proceedings, and those transferred to local authority accommodation under the provisions of the Police and Criminal Evidence Act 1984. Finally, it includes those accommodated in community homes following sentence under Section 33 of the Children and Young Persons Act 1963 (NCH Action for Children, 1996).

In Scotland, social-work services are provided under the children (Scotland) Act 1995. The 'looked after' and 'accommodation' provision are similar to those of the Children Act 1989.

How many 'looked-after' children are there?

The number of children looked after in England decreased steadily from over 90,000 in the late 1970s, to 60,000 in 1985 and 48,000 by 1995 (Department of Health, 1995). As a consequence of the implementation of the Children Act 1989, the number of children under care orders fell from 36,600 in 1992 to 26,800 – or 55 per cent of children looked after – in 1995. Before the Act came into force, some 59,834 children and young people were under care orders. In addition there has been a rise in the proportion of children looked after by voluntary agreement from 17,300 in 1991 to 20,600 in 1995 (NCH Action for Children, 1996).

What are the general characteristics of 'looked-after' children?

Deprivation is a common condition among young people who are being looked after. A study of 2,500 children found that before entering the care system, only a quarter were living with both parents. Around three-quarters of their families received income support. Only one in five lived in owner-occupied housing, and over half were living in poor neighbourhoods (NCH Action for Children, 1996).

The study found that additional factors which increased children's chances of admission were: overcrowding, linked with large families; having a young, often a teenage, mother; and having parents who came from different racial backgrounds from each other.

The study's authors argue that it is probably not just the poverty of single parents but also their lack of available social supports that increases the likelihood that their children will be placed away from home. Also highlighted is the interaction of environmental problems or disability and family stress, with breakdown. Indeed, a 'broken family' was found to be the factor most highly correlated with entry to care (Bebbington and Miles, 1987).

More recently, Jackson (1998, p. 47) has argued that:

> even when all the factors contributing to a likelihood of material disadvantage are combined, the chances are only one in ten that a child will enter the care system. ... For this to happen ... there have to be other factors, most commonly the mental illness of a parent, domestic violence, or the physical and/or sexual abuse of the child. The family has probably become isolated or alienated from friends and relatives or someone would

have stepped in to care for the children. Of course, there are exceptions. Parents still fall ill and die; they may lack an extended family network, their coping capacities may have been overwhelmed by a series of catastrophes. But, in general, children within the care system are most unlikely to come from 'ordinary' working class families, that is, those which simply lack material resources.

Age is also a factor. Approximately two-thirds (63 per cent) of children accommodated are aged over 10 years. Between 1992 and 1995 the proportion of children aged 10 to 15 looked after in England rose from 39 per cent of the total to 43 per cent (NCH Action for Children, 1996).

Where are 'looked-after' children placed?

Almost two-thirds of children (65 per cent) looked after in England on 31 March 1995 had been placed with foster carers, while 17 per cent (8,200) were in residential homes. Most of these youngsters (5,700) were placed in local authority community homes. In addition, an estimated 2,100 were placed for adoption and 4,300 were placed with their parents (NCH Action for Children, 1996). The proportion of looked-after children fostered rose from 50 per cent in 1985 to 58 per cent by 1991, although the *number* of children fostered fell by 2,000 during the same period. The number of these children in community homes fell from 23 per cent in 1985 to 14 per cent by March 1995 (NCH Action for Children, 1996).

Principles of child placement

Principles and philosophies in child placement, as in anything else, evolve over time. For example, Table 6.1 depicts trends in child welfare during the latter part of the twentieth century. As the table shows, the progression has moved quite swiftly from the idea that children ought to be brought up as normally as possible within a family rather than an institution, to the idea that it ought to be a permanent family, to the idea that preferably it should be their own family. With the diversification of the nuclear family (two biological parents bringing up their mutual children) into an increasing number of alternative family forms (for example, blended or reconstituted or step-families, and single-parent families), the focus has shifted to maintaining the child's ties with the family over time whether that family consists of parents and siblings or the extended family network.

However, the Children Act 1989 supports the principle that, if at all possible, children should still be cared for by their own biological families. The primary goal of child welfare is therefore to prevent removal of the

Table 6.1 *Trends in child welfare in the twentieth century*

Time	Reform	Focus	Philosophy
Before 1970	Family foster care	Foster family	Children belong in a family rather than an institution.
1970s	Permanency planning	Adoptive family	Children belong in a permanent family: no child is unadoptable.
1980s	Family preservation	Biological parents	Children belong with their biological parents: reasonable efforts must be made to maintain the family.
1990s	Family continuity	Extended family	Children belong in a family network that continues relations over time.

child from the home, if this is consistent with the child's best interests, by offering appropriate services to the family. This is *family preservation*. If the child must be removed, the goal is then to reunite the child with the family as rapidly as possible, again consistent with the child's best interests. This is *family reunification*.

Family reunification, usually the preferred goal for permanency planning, is defined by Pine, Krieger and Maluccio (1993, p. 6) as:

the planned process of reconnecting children in out-of-home care with their families by means of a variety of services and supports to the children, their families and their foster parents or other service providers. It aims to help each child and family to achieve and maintain, at any given time, their optimal level of reconnection – from full re-entry of the child into the family system to other forms of contact such as visiting – that affirms the child's membership in the family.

In earlier years, family reunification was viewed *only* as the physical return of the child to parental care, with full parental rights returned, after a limited period of supervision. It is now seen as a continuum of relationship and reconnection, an acknowledgement of the importance of family continuity. A child may remain, for compelling reasons, in planned long-term care but may still be reconnected to his or her parents.

Given these basic principles, we can also identify a number of other guidelines for child-placement practice which are drawn from research. In 1991, the Department of Health published *Patterns and Outcomes in Child Placement* (Department of Health, 1991d). This was intended as a sequel to the 'Pink Book', *Social Work Decisions in Child Care* (Department of

Health and Social Security, 1985a). As with the earlier volume, the purpose of *Patterns and Outcomes*, as it came to be known, was to make recent research findings accessible to social workers and demonstrate their relevance to day-to-day practice. The review that follows is based on major research studies funded by the Department of Health, together with other national and local studies concerning child-care placements. Although this research was carried out some ten years ago, it is of continuing relevance. The findings of the studies and their implications for policy and practice are presented in terms of four themes: promotion of the child's welfare; partnership with parents and carers; policies, planning and decision-making; and evidence-based practice. These findings constitute principles on which effective child-welfare practice should be based.

Promotion of the child's welfare

For the sake of brevity and clarity the principles drawn from the research findings are presented below in point form.

- Preventative services, geared to family preservation, must involve a combination of practical services and help with family relationships, and should focus on the functioning of family and social networks.

- Notwithstanding the need for prevention, short, medium and even lengthy periods in care or accommodation can be beneficial and appropriate, and least detrimental for particular children. Thus, there is no room for inflexible policies regarding admission and the timing of 'permanency' plans.

- Greater attention must be given to the health and educational needs of looked-after children. Many children placed away from home require remedial help and treatment to overcome the adverse effects of deprivation and abuse.

- Changes in placements, resulting in a breakdown and discontinuity of relationships, are a persisting problem. Children of families under stress may need frequent or regular periods in accommodation. They must be able to return to the same respite-care placement and the supply of such placements must be increased to meet such demand. Innovative provision such as a small network of carers known to vulnerable families, and perhaps linked with residential provision, may be required. Special consideration should be given to the needs of socially disadvantaged families who find it difficult to use respite services.

- Ideas about permanence should be expanded to embrace continued family contact through open adoption or permanent fostering. Premature or routine termination of contact when a permanent placement is made is usually inappropriate.

- Attempts to rehabilitate children with their families should begin immediately after admission in view of the finding that the period after which children are likely to have a long stay in care can be measured in weeks rather than months.

- The key to discharge is visiting; contact is highly beneficial for children's welfare and does not increase the risk of placement breakdown. Informal barriers to contact, such as the attitudes of foster carers and residential staff, should be addressed through training.

- Relatives can offer stable placements, particularly in relation to long-term placements; they are also a major source of family contact, and visits by grandparents, aunts and uncles can often be encouraged.

- Too little attention has been given to the role of siblings and other children despite the fact that this factor is known to affect the outcome of placement. For example, the presence of 'own' children close in age to a foster child is associated with negative outcome. In contrast, placement with siblings is usually beneficial and highly valued by the children concerned. Equally, it is clear that other youngsters can be a source of stress rather than support. Thus, caregivers must be aware of the need to protect children and not leave them to 'fight their own battles'.

- Ethnic monitoring should be routinely carried out with regard to services for black and ethnic minorities; the findings should be translated into policy, service design and practice; the outcome of this process should be monitored. In addition, special attention should be given to children of mixed parentage or heritage who are placed away from home in disproportionate numbers. More attention must be given to what the phrase 'cultural issues' means in relation to direct work with children and families and the provision of services.

Partnership with parents and carers

The importance of partnership with parents and carers is another primary thrust of the Children Act 1989. Unfortunately, the studies discussed in *Patterns and Outcomes* revealed that major changes in the attitude of social workers towards parents would be necessary to make partnership with parents an integral feature of social-work practice. Real partnership requires self-awareness on the part of practitioners and the ability to empathise with parents' feelings and concerns, skills in the use of written agreements, and the attendance of parents at reviews, case conferences and planning meetings.

With regard to looked-after children, it was evident that a fundamental reappraisal of roles and expectations would be required before social workers and agencies could serve as parents' agents when providing accommodation. However, it was noted that partnership models had already been used successfully in respite-care schemes and in adoption. Finally, as mentioned above, it was clear from the research that more attention should be given to the needs and feelings of carers' own children; a factor which is known to play a part in the success or otherwise of foster-care placements, but which has received surprisingly little attention from researchers.

Policies, planning and decision-making

The research findings with respect to policies, planning and decision-making are presented in point form here for the sake of brevity and clarity.

- The studies highlighted the need for improved national and local child-care statistics that will provide detailed information about the turnover of children and their care careers, allowing changes to be monitored.

- Managers should be aware that the fall in numbers of children placed away from home masks the workload caused by more frequent admission, discharges and changes in placement; it also hides the fact that many young children continue to be placed away from home for short periods.

- Residential care still plays an important role in child care. It must be adapted to current use, and the purpose and facilities of each establishment should be matched to the needs of the young people looked after.

- The central role of foster care continues to be that of providing short-term care for younger children. More resources for recruiting will be required to substantially increase short-term and/or task-centred placements for teenagers. The success of such placements depends in large part on the effective recruitment, preparation and support of foster carers.

- There is a need for more precise classification and differentiation of children and types of placement. This would assist appropriate allocation of resources and social-work input. Priority should be given to identifying racial and cultural differences.

- There are wide differences between authorities, which should lead managers to question their own priorities, and admission and placement patterns. If the differences are not identified and taken into account, they can lead to false conclusions being drawn from comparisons of numbers of foster placements, breakdown rates, and so forth.

■ Studies of departmental structures suggest that improvements in practice are unlikely to flow from organisational changes. However, it is vital to ensure that policies, directives and guidance are known and understood by practitioners. It appears that staff are often unaware of policies and regulations. Channels of communication must flow freely to avoid the danger of far-reaching misunderstanding and errors.

■ Planning for individual children is essential, and the needs of individual children should be aggregated into departmental policies. Effective planning requires:
  - written specification of what should be done, by whom and when;
  - long- and short-term goals for each child;
  - a contingency plan to cover crises.

It is vital that social workers involved in planning decisions have a sound knowledge of the research evidence on placement outcomes. Further, placement panels should specify the risks and countervailing factors and the reason for any placement which is made despite the presence of factors known to be linked with placement breakdown – for example, an 'own' child close in age to a young child being placed in a foster or adoptive home; or placement at home when changes in family composition have occurred during the child's absence. Finally, planning decisions must be informed by detailed knowledge about the history of both child and family.

Evidence-based practice

Despite the variety and differences in scope of the research studies, they were linked by a recurrent theme of profound importance: 'the whole question of evidence – how to gather, test, record and weigh it' (Department of Health, 1991d, p. 77).

The studies indicated that 'all the professionals involved in child care decisions would benefit from some rigorous training in the collection and use of evidence and should be challenged to examine the values on which their views are based' (Department of Health, 1991d, p. 76). Moreover:

> Without adequate evidence about existing needs and resources, strategic planning is a waste of time. Sound assessment of the problems and strengths of individual children and families must be based on clear, sufficient and well-recorded evidence about past and present functioning. Decisions can only be as good as the evidence on which they are based, and if evidence is distorted, ignored or not weighed up carefully, the

decisions will be flawed. They may even be dangerous if risks and benefits are not analysed and balanced objectively.

(Department of Health, 1991d, p. 78)

To be sure, social work is more than a science; it inevitably involves an
emphasis on empathy, negotiation and building relationships. However,
'perhaps the most important message from recent research is that if
progress is to be made in developing professional standards in the care of
children, then more attention must be given to scientific disciplines in
dealing with evidence' (Department of Health, 1991d, p. 78).

We come now to a discussion of the Looking After Children materials,
which are designed to improve the parenting experiences of children
looked after by local authorities and which identify a number of pointers for
practice.

The Looking After Children project

The extensive child-care research undertaken in the 1980s and summarised
in *Patterns and Outcomes* (Department of Health, 1991d) showed that the
child-care system was failing badly when judged by the outcomes for children and young people. All aspects of their development – education,
health, relationships, employment and identity – were found to be more
problematic than those of children cared for by their own families or
adopted at a young age.

A number of studies have since highlighted the extremely poor prospects
of care leavers, 'who are many times more likely than their peers to experience illiteracy, homelessness, unemployment, early parenthood, problems
with drugs and alcohol and imprisonment'. It may be further noted that the
Education Reform Acts of the Conservative government mean that many
looked-after children are in danger of being excluded altogether from the
educational process (Jackson, 1998, p. 48). One research study showed
that children usually bring their educational problems with them when they
enter care or accommodation. Unfortunately, the experience of being
looked after away from home all too frequently does little to ameliorate
these deficits (Heath, Colton and Aldgate, 1989 and 1994).

Towards the end of the 1980s, the Department of Health and Social
Security suggested that an independent working party be set up to consider
the question of outcomes in child care (Parker et al., 1991). Specifically,
the working party was asked to consider how the experience of being
looked after in the public care system affects the quality of life and life
chances of children and young people.

The working party identified the failure to specify outcomes as a significant weakness of the child-welfare system. As one member of the working party, Sonia Jackson (1998, pp. 48–9), succinctly puts it: 'there is no way of assessing outcomes if you do not know what you are aiming at'. Moreover, 'assessment of outcomes can only occur in relation to some kind of standard and someone has to set the standard'. The working party came to the conclusion that many of the shortcomings of the system were attributable to the fact that, in the majority of child-care cases,

> there was no one person monitoring the developmental process of the child in the informal and perhaps hardly conscious way that most parents do and taking corrective action if necessary. In devising the assessment scheme, therefore, we decided to base it on the aspirations and behaviour of 'ordinary' parents. What aspects of development are considered important by parents bringing up their own children? What do they do to try to promote good outcomes for their children?

The working party's deliberations resulted in the production of the Looking After Children (LAC) materials, which are designed to improve the parenting experience of children looked after by local authorities and other agencies. The first stage of the LAC project is reported in *Looking After Children: Assessing Outcome in Child Care* (Parker et al., 1991). This package of materials attracted widespread interest, which encouraged the Department of Health to engage in a programme of research and development into the application of the LAC materials to social-work practice and issues surrounding their use. This work is reported in full in *Looking After Children: Research into Practice* (Ward, 1995).

The research and development work included testing the materials with a group of 379 children living at home to establish whether the forms reflect the expectations held by families in the community for their own children. The acceptability and usefulness of the materials to social workers, caregivers, children and young people looked after away from home was also evaluated using a group of 204 children in care or in accommodation in five local authorities.

In the light of the results of research and development work, the original LAC materials were significantly revised. They were then launched by the Secretary of State for Health in May 1995. This heralded the start of a highly effective dissemination and implementation programme. Thirty-nine local authorities in England agreed to implement the LAC materials in 1995/96 with support from the Department of Health.

The materials have been widely adopted throughout the UK. It is estimated that by the end of 1998 the system was being operated by 90 per cent of English authorities and the majority of those in Wales, Scotland,

and Northern Ireland. The Central Council for Education and Training in Social work has promoted the use of the LAC material in Diploma in Social Work programmes and at post-qualifying levels. In addition, the LAC materials have been adapted or translated for use in many other countries (Jackson, 1998).

The LAC materials promote good parental care by identifying the experiences, concerns and expectations of children at different ages and stages through highlighting the likely impact of different actions. In a nutshell, they introduce ideas about the outcome of social-work practice.

They also facilitate discussion of the difficulties as well as successes in the lives of looked-after children and young people. The Assessment and Action Records (see below) assist with the planning of improvements to the quality of care that children receive, and with monitoring the extent to which these are carried out. However, the Records must be set within an overall framework of information-gathering, planning and review. Their purpose is to reinforce working partnerships between key people in the child's life and improve the allocation and clarification of professional responsibilities. This is particularly important in relation to multi-disciplinary work with health and education, where it is vital to improve current poor outcomes for children.

The materials are an integrated package which helps social workers and caregivers to set an agenda for work with children and young people, and ensure that these plans are acted upon. By assessing children's progress across a range of developmental dimensions including health and education, they direct attention to the ordinary everyday goals of parenting, and ensure that all essential information is recorded in one accessible place and is regularly updated. They encourage workers to listen attentively to children and young people and reflect on their successes as well as their problems and they strengthen partnerships between children and young people, parents, teachers and others. They rationalise documentation and create consistency across agencies, thereby facilitating improvements in the quality of care provided.

The LAC materials include *Planning and Review Forms* and *Assessment and Action Records*. The Planning and Review Forms are records which hold the essential information that is too often lost, for children who spend time in public care. They contain key details about the child's health and educational achievements, and his or her family. They also record formal agreements about placements and other issues appropriate to short- and long-term planning.

The Assessment and Action Records centre on the child's developmental needs, the quality of day-to-day care and the actions necessary to promote good outcomes. When used over time they enable agencies to assess outcomes for children. They are designed around seven dimensions: health, education, identity, family and social relationships, social presentation, emotional and behavioural development, and self-care skills. It will be observed that these are the same seven dimensions as in the Child's Development Needs component of the *Framework for the Assessment of Children in Need and their Families* (Department of Health et al., 2000).

Clearly, use of the LAC materials will help local authorities fulfil their responsibilities under the Children Act 1989. They set out explicitly what good parental care means in practice, listing the aims that any reasonable parents might be expected to hold for any child. Thus, they require those responsible to consider all aspects of children's lives, not only those that have resulted in the child's placement away from home. The materials rightly encourage partnerships between key people involved in the child's care, such as carers, social workers, families and others; they also promote continuity in the lives of looked-after children to avoid the damaging levels of disruption highlighted by previous research.

A new research programme, funded by the Department of Health, has been set up to show how 'the data contained in Assessment and Action Records can be aggregated and analysed to provide an overall profile of looked after children compared with their peers, and to reveal organisational risk factors which get in the way of effective service delivery' (Jackson, 1998, p. 53).

The LAC materials have been widely acclaimed and now appear to represent the mainstream of child-care practice. Although the field trials encountered some resistance from social workers, mainly on the practical grounds that the Assessment and Action Records were too time-consuming, there has been no serious challenge to the theoretical basis of the LAC model (Jackson, 1998).

However, Knight and Caveney (1998) have recently criticised the Assessment and Action Records for imposing white middle-class assumptions about child development, for undermining the principle of partnership underpinning the Children Act 1989, and for blaming individuals rather than structural factors for deficiencies in the care system and poor outcomes. In reply, Jackson (1998, p. 45) welcomes critical scrutiny of the Looking After Children model. However, she contends that Knight and Caveney's views reflect a misunderstanding of the LAC approach and 'a classbound view of parenting which would deny looked after children the chance of a better quality of adult life than their families' experience'. Jackson accepts that implementing LAC is not an alternative to tackling widespread inequality and discrimination, but argues that the Assessment and Action Records increase the likelihood that social workers and caregivers will address key aspects of children's development; they also help those responsible to understand better how their actions or inactions contribute to child-care outcomes.

Other principles of practice include attention to anti-oppression, not least in relation to race, sexual orientation and disability. These principles are discussed in Chapter 7.

Having discussed the principles underlying work with looked-after children, we come now to the selection of appropriate care options for them.

Selection of appropriate care options

A number of options are available to serve young people being looked after and few empirical data exist to help decide which option would best suit a particular child. Nevertheless, there are certain guidelines to aid in selecting a placement. One of these is the degree of restrictiveness or control which it is felt the child needs at that particular time. For example, living at home or with a relative is the least restrictive while being kept in secure accommodation is most restrictive. Other options, such as foster care and residential care, fall between the extremes on the restrictiveness continuum. In order, from least to most restrictive, placement options might be rated as follows:

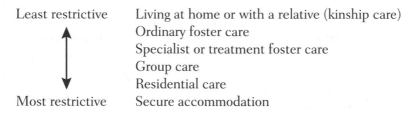

Least restrictive Living at home or with a relative (kinship care)

Ordinary foster care

Specialist or treatment foster care

Group care

Residential care

Most restrictive Secure accommodation

Apart from restrictiveness, other guidelines focus on the best fit between the child's needs and the characteristics of the placement, taking into account the principle of family continuity.

Kinship placements are often preferred as they promote the continuity of relationships for the child in a familiar environment. They provide a placement within the child's own ethnic/cultural group and are less likely to be disrupted than placements with non-relatives. They are not appropriate if the relative cannot establish boundaries with the parent or is afraid of the parent, or there is any indication that the relative may have abused the parent or child or supported the parent's maltreatment of the child.

Family foster homes are preferred over group homes for the majority of children. For infants and preschool-age children, a family setting is almost mandatory except for those with very severe problems who require specialised care. For children who are able to participate in family life, attend local schools and live in the community without danger to themselves or others, family foster care is preferred.

Treatment or specialist foster homes are appropriate for children with emotional or behavioural problems that can be handled in a family setting. Specialised, highly trained foster homes that take medically vulnerable children and work closely with the hospital and medical team are appropriate for children with severe or multiple needs who might otherwise be hospitalised.

Group care is generally considered appropriate for adolescents who are unable to tolerate the demands and intimacy of family life but are still able to function within the community in terms of school or work. For some adolescents, small or family-type group homes in which the caregivers act as parent figures to a number of young people are a good solution. For others, group homes or cottages, where the caregivers act more as role models than as parent figures, work best. A few group or residential settings will accept both child and parent in placement, as will some family foster homes.

Residential care is recommended for young people who display behaviour that a family or community would not usually tolerate, perhaps acting in an aggressive way or posing a danger to themselves or others. Youths who have difficulty forming relationships with parenting figures because of past negative experiences may do better in a residential setting. For some parents, it may be more comfortable to see their children placed in residential care because they do not have to watch other 'parents' succeeding where they could not. Residential care is more commonly preferred in Europe than it is in the United Kingdom where practice is toward moving young people back from institutional settings into the community.

Having briefly described the various options, we will now explore each in greater depth.

Kinship care

As we have seen, the focus in the 1990s has turned increasingly towards family continuity. This concept emphasises the necessity for continuing important relationships across the lifespan and acknowledges that children need to be embedded in family and community networks. Even when children cannot live with their biological families and must move away from familiar communities, continuity can be maintained by involving their families in alternative living situations such as foster care, residential care and adoption. The importance of the continuity of kinship ties was emphasised by Joan Laird when she said in 1979:

Human beings are profoundly affected by the family system of which they are a part. Kin ties are powerful and compelling, and the individual's

> sense of identity and continuity is formed not only by the significant attachments in his intimate environment but also is deeply rooted in the biological family – in the genetic link that reaches back into the past and ahead into the future. Ecologically oriented child welfare practice attends to, nurtures and supports the biological family. Furthermore, when it is necessary to substitute for the biological family, good practice dictates that every effort be made to preserve and protect important kinship ties.   (Laird, 1979, p. 175)

Nowadays, we tend not to talk about 'substitute' parents or families. Even the term 'foster parent' is being replaced by 'foster carer' in recognition of the belief that parents in the foster family do not, and should not be expected to, replace the child's own parents: they are complementary not substitute adult figures in the child's life.

Ideas about what constitutes a 'family' are also continuing to change. In social-work practice, 'family' has often been synonymous with 'household' and, in the high proportion of cases where the household is headed by a single female, has sometimes come to mean 'mother'. Social workers might consider involved step-parents as 'family' but wider patterns of kinship are often overlooked. A recent study by Peter Marsh (Marsh, 1999) explored the definition of 'family' by young people leaving care, and compared the family tree constructed by the young person with the same family tree constructed by the young person's social worker. Cousins were the largest group of relatives in the family tree drawn by the young person, followed by maternal and paternal uncles and aunts, who together accounted for nearly one-third of the relatives named. Full siblings and other siblings counted for another third. There were some interesting differences in maternal and paternal kin groups, as maternal uncles and aunts accounted for 20 per cent of relatives but paternal for only 10 per cent. This pattern was repeated in other areas: for example, three times as many maternal as paternal grandparents were named. Young people were obviously more familiar with their mother's side of the family. Step-parents accounted for only 6 per cent of the relatives listed and sometimes included previous step-parents, who continued to be important figures for the child even when they were no longer the parent's partner. Other examples of unrelated people still looked on as 'family' included previous foster parents and family friends who had achieved the status of honorary aunts or uncles.

On average, family trees constructed by social workers contained just 40 per cent of the relatives named by the child. Social workers showed good knowledge of parents and full siblings but knew less about grandparents and even less about aunts and uncles. They fell down, too, when it came to identifying the most influential person in a child's life. They and the care leaver identified the same person in only 17 of the 41 cases: and only 3 of the 41 people nominated as most influential had attended the young person's last formal review.

Marsh remarked that 'potential family support for young people leaving care resembles a target' (Marsh, 1999, p. 13). At the centre of the target are 'key kin' who are likely to be proactive about involving themselves in the young person's life and are very important both emotionally and practically. The next ring contains kin who are not proactive but are willing to become involved if approached; and the furthest ring contains kin who are known to the young person but are unlikely to want to become involved. Although Marsh was talking about kinship involvement with young people leaving care, his model of the kinship support system as a target with a centre and inner and outer rings would be just as applicable to young people in care or being looked after. If we accept that social workers are unlikely to be familiar with kin in the inner ring – that is, kin who are not proactive but would be willing if approached – then it seems that a potential source of valuable support for young people is being overlooked.

To what degree kin support should be extended to providing a home for the young person – to what degree, that is, kinship care should be an accepted part of the foster-care system – is still a matter for debate. Advocates of kinship care point out that the trauma of placement may be minimised if children can be placed with extended family members. Keeping the child 'in the family' is likely to ensure that cultural traditions are maintained, particularly if the child is a member of a minority ethnic group and could not otherwise be placed with foster carers of the same cultural background. Ties to relatives will be strengthened and will serve to reinforce the child's sense of belonging and identity. Moreover, some studies have shown that kinship homes are less likely than non-related placements to be disrupted and more likely to keep children until they reach majority (Berrick, Barth and Needell, 1993). Thus, kinship care can satisfy both proponents of permanency and those who believe that family preservation should be paramount.

However, kinship homes can also have their drawbacks. If the kin home is in the same, sometimes quite disadvantaged community as the parental home, children will maintain their ties not only with relatives but with peers who are still engaging in the kinds of negative activities the child is now trying to avoid. In the same vein, kin may have shared with the child's natural parent a disadvantaged upbringing and may be struggling with many of the same problems which afflict the biological home. In addition, where contact with the natural parent is not advised – where continuing abuse is a danger, for example – kin may have more difficulty in denying the parent access to the child than would a non-related caregiver. From the social worker's point of view, kin carers are less likely to see themselves as working for an agency. They are less aware of child-welfare policies and may be less interested in cooperating with agencies in the interests of the child. These characteristics make the home a more natural atmosphere for the child but may present difficulties for social workers. Thus, while kinship care is often a very appropriate placement option, safety and protection issues must be addressed through a careful assessment of the kinship home. In the United States, the Child Welfare League Kinship Care Policy and Practice Committee recommend consideration of the following factors in assessment (Child Welfare League of America, 1994, pp. 44–5):

- The nature and quality of the relationship between the child and the relative;
- The ability and desire of the kinship carer to protect the child from further maltreatment;
- The safety of the kinship home and the ability of kin to provide a nurturing environment for the child;
- The willingness of the kinship family to accept the child into the home;
- The ability of the kinship carer to meet the developmental needs of the child;
- The nature and quality of the relationship between the birth parent and the relative, including the birth parent's preference about the placement of the child with kin;
- Any family dynamics in the kinship home related to the abuse or neglect of the child;
- The presence of alcohol or other drug involvement in the kinship home.

When assessing kinship homes, social workers must be aware of their own biases. Kinship caregivers are typically grandparents or even great-grandparents, and while many are neither aged nor infirm, workers may feel that a home with a younger caregiver might be better. Kinship homes may involve predominantly members of ethnic minorities, who may be suspicious of 'the system', a situation requiring cultural competence on the part of the social worker in engagement and developing trust. Caregivers in kinship homes are often less well educated than unrelated foster carers and tend to have lower incomes. Workers may feel less comfortable with them than with foster carers who are known to the agency, have more financial resources and are better educated.

A genuine concern in placing children with relatives, particularly older relatives, is whether these adults have enough supports available in the community to help them in their efforts with the child. Use of an ecomap (see Chapter 4) can help to determine which supports are available and which need to be provided. Meeting with the entire kinship network in a family conference often provides evidence that, although the carer's resources are limited, there are others close by who will provide respite care, transportation or other forms of support.

Sometimes, a family conference can be used not just to explore supports but as a decision-making tool. The Family Decision-Making Model in New Zealand has evoked wide interest in those working in family-based services. Although the model was originally developed for use with the Maori people of New Zealand as a way to honour the Maori culture, it has been used with other ethnic-minority peoples – for example, Aboriginal bands in Canada and the United States – as well as with members of the dominant culture. The model involves holding a conference of extended-family members following an investigation of child abuse by a child-protection worker or the police. The conference is facilitated by a specialist chairperson, takes place in a comfortable setting and may last for several days. Involved professionals share information with the family about factors that place the child at risk. Then the professionals leave the room, although the facilitator may remain available in a nearby room for consultation. The family develops a plan for protecting the child and providing a home within the kinship network. The facilitator records the decisions and accesses the resources needed for implementing the family's plan (Smith and Featherstone, 1991).

Adapting the family decision-making model to a UK setting raises a number of issues, including legal constraints regarding confidentiality, court processes and liability. A major issue is control. Child-welfare practice has traditionally focused on control by the social worker and it may be difficult for some social workers to engage in a process that hands control back to the family. Although a major thrust of the Children Act 1989 is towards partnership with parents, parents still often feel that they do not have equal decision-making power with social workers (Colton et al., 1995a) and some social workers still feel that parents do not have the expertise necessary to make decisions in the best interests of their children. For example, there is some debate over whether a kinship home should be required to meet the same standards as any other foster home or whether the standards should be relaxed somewhat, particularly if the home is going to be approved for one particular child and not for foster children in general. A kinship home selected through a family conference may fall short of accepted standards in many respects; and social workers may be reluctant to implement a family decision that they personally do not agree with.

Accepted standards include not only the level of care provided to the child but the level of training achieved by the foster carer. A high proportion of kinship carers are grandparents who brought up their own children without any training in the art of parenthood and do not see why they should now need training to bring up their children's children – particularly as this training is likely to be provided by young professionals who have not themselves brought up children. The result is that kin carers are very often untrained and this leads to questions about the quality of care provided. After all, if training does not improve the quality of care, why are we spending money to train non-related foster carers?

Another controversy centres around financial support for kin carers. Some would argue that kin should not be paid for taking care of their own: they have a moral duty that does not apply to unrelated carers. In addition, fraudulent manipulation of the system may occur in cases where kin receive payment for children who are not really living with them and pass part of this payment on to the parents. On the other side of the debate, proponents of financial support point out that kin are often subject to the same economic conditions that affected the child's own parents and will probably need assistance with housing, respite care, support groups and special health and educational services to meet the needs of children. If they are not paid at the same rate and given the same support services as unrelated carers, it is the children who will suffer. Kin carers should not be used as a cheap substitute for unrelated carers but rather should be offered training, reimbursement and support in the same way and at the same level.

The argument about the government's responsibility towards kin carers is taking place both in a context of fiscal restraint and in relation to another controversy: whether the focus on family preservation, now over a decade old, is threatening the safety of children and should be discontinued. An article in *McCall's* magazine titled 'The Little Boy who Didn't Have to Die' told of the death of a child returned to his parents by the foster-care system. It said:

> Gregory appears to have been doomed by a decade-old national policy determined to patch up troubled parents and preserve families. Despite mounting evidence that family preservation programs aren't working, child welfare policy remains so focused on reuniting families that its original aim – keeping children safe – has become almost secondary.
>
> (Spake, 1994, p. 146)

Although it may seem that an article in a women's magazine should not determine the state of the nation, family-preservation proponents cannot afford to dismiss popular coverage as ill-informed, because public attention does influence policy formation and political controversy (see Sanders, 1999). Moreover, considerable divergence of opinion also exists between better informed researchers and practitioners. For example, Gelles (1993) calls for abandonment of the family reunification/family preservation model as both official and unofficial child-welfare policy. He writes:

> We are not sure under what circumstances family preservation is a penicillin and under what circumstances it is a poison. My most important argument is that family reunification and family preservation should not be the sole or even main means of treating and preventing child maltreatment.   (pp. 558–9)

Gelles points out that it is unpopular to argue against family preservation because it draws support both from the Right, who want limited intervention into the private sphere, and from the Left, who think it consistent with their tradition of supporting disadvantaged families and children. Nevertheless, the unpopularity of an argument should not stop that argument from being made.

From a feminist perspective, the American writer Bernard (1992) examines the 'dark side' of family preservation, noting that the American family is one of the country's most violent institutions and a cornerstone of women's oppression. She cautions readers to:

> consider carefully the full implications of the family-preservation policy without buying into the nostalgia for and mythology of families that are presented by an administration that has consistently undercut the goals of equality and social justice.   (p. 159)

Dore (1993) reminds social workers that family-preservation intervention is less effective with maltreating families characterised by extreme poverty, single-parent status, low educational attainment and mental health problems. She concludes that 'family preservation' can only (truly)

> occur when many families with children no longer struggle to exist at less than subsistence level, when poor parents are freed from anxiety and depression generated by raising children in hostile environments, and when it is widely acknowledged that the real cause of family breakdown is the failure of our society to value and support the parenting role.
> (p. 553)

Seader and Nelson (in Gambrill and Stein, 1993) argue that defining the treatment goal as 'family preservation' rather than 'the best interests of the child' necessarily changes the intervention. In many cases these goals conflict and it is the child who always seems to lose. Seider claims that there is no empirical evidence that family-preservation programmes are working and expresses concern that families may re-abuse their children when intensive 24-hour service is withdrawn.

On the other side of the debate, Seader also argues that it is not the family-preservation philosophy which is at fault but the way that services are provided. 'Services are limited because of agency biases, worker competencies, available community resources and so forth' (Gambrill and Stein, 1993, pp. 60–1). Also in Gambrill and Stein (1993, p. 65), Nelson argues that family preservation is not indiscriminately applied to all families entering the child-welfare system and that family-preservation workers themselves typically recommend placement outside the family in from 5 per cent to 50 per cent of their cases. Where family-preservation efforts are made, improvement in family functioning is an essential criterion for allowing the child to remain in the home.

Maluccio, Pine and Warsh (1994) acknowledge that family preservation is viewed as competing with child protection and in particular cases it may be incompatible. However, in its defence, they state, 'At the philosophical and policy levels, family preservation and child protection are complementary rather than competing values. In essence, the best way to protect children is to preserve as much of their families as possible' (p. 295).

Kinship care satisfies both camps in that it preserves the extended family if not the nuclear family and, at the same time, it is a placement which can ensure the safety of the child. However, the major issues associated with it, particularly standards and resourcing in comparison with those of non-related carers, remain to be addressed.

Before leaving kinship care, it is as well to say a few words about informal kinship care where the child-welfare system is not involved at all and the child merely goes to live with a relative. In these cases, the child may receive excellent care without the stigma that child-welfare involvement still seems to convey despite our best efforts to create a non-stigmatising system. On the other hand, no formal supports are available to the carer and the child may face the same risks that child-welfare legislation was designed to avoid: lack of permanency planning; lack of services to the child and family; and lack of pre-placement screening and post-placement supervision.

Informal care by kin is an integral part of many cultures and we do not know how many children are diverted from the formal system in this way, nor what befalls them. For some parents and kin, escape from state intervention and control may well outweigh the benefits, often meagre, which kin would receive were they part of the formal system. If we believe that the advantages of informal kinship care are greater than the risks, then we need do nothing to change this attitude. If, on the other hand, we believe that the risks are greater than the advantages, then it behoves us to offer more emotional and material support to formal kinship carers than we do at present.

Foster care

One type of foster care – kinship care – has been discussed above. However, when we speak of foster care, we tend to think of care by parent figures who are unrelated to the child, and indeed, most children looked after by local authorities are fostered by people unrelated to them.

Fostering is as old as human history in the sense that, through time, lost and abandoned children have been brought up by people who were not their birth parents. However, the origins of formal fostering have been traced to the wet-nursing system that developed in France around the fifteenth century. Formal fostering – that is, fostering sanctioned by law – came to Britain with the foundling hospitals of the eighteenth century but, as the name suggests, the children placed in foster homes under that system were babies. In the nineteenth century, a number of philanthropic organisations began to develop in response to the Poor Law and its perceived shortcomings in relation to the provision for children: there has always been a close association between poverty and the numbers of children requiring substitute care outside their families (Triseliotis, 1997). However, it was feared that the fostering of older children would undermine the deterrent element of the Poor Law, and thus, unlike in Scotland, older children were not fostered in England until after 1860. Indeed, mainstream fostering as it is currently understood was not introduced until the Children Act 1948. Prior to this, fostering was mainly a long-term arrangement, but the 1948 Act extended it to include fostering as a temporary service to children and families.

In the United Kingdom and Ireland, the vast majority of children placed away from home are living in foster care. In these countries, residential institutions have largely – and many believe, wrongly – become places of last resort, reserved for children whose severe difficulties make them unsuitable for foster care or whose foster-care placements have broken down. However, the balance between foster and residential care varies markedly across the European Union. In the southern states of the EU – Greece, Portugal, Spain – children living away from home are overwhelmingly placed in residential care. In Belgium, Germany and Italy, residential facilities also accommodate the majority of children in care. In Denmark, France and the Netherlands, roughly equal proportions of children are placed in foster care and residential care (Ruxton, 1996). It is thus apparent that the choice between foster and residential care is more a matter of philosophy than a reasoned decision about which setting would most benefit a particular child in his or her particular situation.

Wagner (1988) argues that residential and foster care are most fruitfully conceived as complementary approaches for children and families. There should be no question of which is 'better', but only of which is better for this particular child. For some young people, residential care is a positive choice rather than a last resort. For example, Triseliotis (1997) reports that an unresolved issue concerns the role foster care should play in the placement of adolescents. Some have claimed that the majority of teenagers prefer residential care. Others have argued that very difficult teenagers can be successfully fostered. Recent studies carried out by Triseliotis suggest that roughly half of young people and their parents prefer foster homes and half favour residential care. The same study indicates that teenagers' needs are responsive to a combination of care measures rather than 'either/or' solutions (Triseliotis, 1997).

Children come into foster care for a variety of reasons. One half (50.2 per cent) of the children who entered foster care in New York in 1990 were placed because of neglect and abuse. Another 20.9 per cent entered care because of parental conditions such as illness, death, handicap or financial hardship. A further 11.3 per cent entered because of offences such as running away, truancy or delinquent behaviour, while 12.5 per cent entered for other reasons such as parent–child relationship problems, a plan for adoption, or deinstitutionalisation. Only 1.9 per cent entered because of the child's physical, mental or emotional handicap (Tatara, 1993). While these figures are drawn from one American study, there can be little doubt that the major problems bringing children into foster care, in Britain as well, are not their own disorders but are related to parental dysfunction exacerbated by lack of social supports and severe environmental pressures.

There is also evidence which suggests that children entering foster care are tending to be older, less healthy, and more troubled than was formerly the case. In Ireland, for example, there is strong anecdotal evidence of increasingly challenging behaviour among children placed in foster care, and a growing risk of disrupted placements; there is also growing recognition of the implications of providing for a population of children who may have experienced abuse (see Colton and Williams, 1997).

In sum, foster care is no longer a system in which well-meaning and largely untrained women volunteer to take in babies and young children in difficult circumstances. It is fast becoming a set of systems in which trained professional carers supported by other trained professionals try to deal with children whose difficult circumstances have led to them becoming emotionally or behaviourally disturbed. The trend towards professionalisation in foster care parallels our general tendency to turn to 'experts' to 'fix' all that may be problematic in our lives, including our children and our family relationships; and we expect that such expert services will have to be paid for. The age of volunteerism is far from dead – many charitable organisations, for example, rely almost entirely on volunteers – but an increasing proportion of women in the workforce has meant that fewer are available to care for children in their homes unless they receive as much for foster care as they would for other work.

With professionalisation has come an increasing diversity in the types and functions of foster homes. No longer is a foster home just a foster home. It may be short-term or long-term, ordinary, or treatment/special. In so-called ordinary foster homes, the carer is responsible for providing a nurturing environment for the child but is not responsible for the child's progress towards treatment goals. Responsibility for therapeutic progress lies with the child's social worker or therapist. Conversely, in treatment or special foster homes, the carer is considered part of the treatment team and accepts her share of responsibility for mutual goal-setting, implementing agreed interventions and measuring goal achievement. Short-term foster homes typically offer emergency care, respite care, assessment, and placement prior to rehabilitation, while long-term foster homes, as the name suggests, offer more permanent placements, sometimes until the child is reunited with parents, is adopted, or enters independent living.

Specialist foster carers may have particular skills in dealing with particular types of children or problems: for example, sexually abused children or children who are HIV positive. In general, they are more highly trained, better paid and better supported than ordinary carers, and their role is to work with the child until specialist care is no longer needed and the child is ready to move on to a more permanent placement. The distinction between 'specialist' and 'ordinary' has been the subject of much controversy. On the one hand, it is argued that specialist carers deal with more troubled children and more is required of them: they may, for example, be required to attend meetings and write progress reports in addition to day-to-day behaviour management and implementation of the child's treatment plan. It is only fair, therefore, that they should be trained, paid and supported at a higher level.

On the other hand, 'ordinary' foster carers also deal with highly troubled children and they too must work not only with the child but with the child's social worker and family, and often with a number of other professionals involved with the child. The traditional definition of fostering as 'looking after other people's children as if they were one's own' no longer applies in any sphere of foster care. The children are not the foster carer's own, even though a relationship with a foster carer may be one of the most significant in the child's life. Nor is the looking after a matter restricted to the carer and the child. 'Ordinary' as well as 'specialist' carers must work as members of a team, whose goal is achievement of the child's permanency plan and whose activities include sharing information, planning collaboratively, addressing issues of power and control, establishing specific plans with time frames, negotiating who will do what, managing conflict, making decisions and evaluating team effort. 'Ordinary' as well as 'specialist' carers should be regarded as professional partners who deserve to be adequately trained, reimbursed and supported.

The argument here – and many would argue differently – is that separating foster carers into categories and treating the categories differently is unwarranted and divisive. Indeed, certain districts in Canada have abandoned the 'specialist' model after a period when bed shortage necessitated the placement of children wherever a bed was available rather than according to the best fit between carer and child. This unplanned 'experiment' revealed that, of children who would normally have been assigned to specialist care, those who were actually receiving specialist care did no better than those in ordinary – and much cheaper – foster homes. Of course, such after-the-fact results cannot be generalised to other settings and certainly do not indicate that specialist foster care has no benefits in comparison with non-specialist care. They do indicate, however, that more planned research needs to be done both with respect to process (What actually occurs in specialist as compared with ordinary foster care?) and outcomes (Do high-needs children do better in specialist homes?).

Separation issues

Children entering foster care have experienced a variety of situations but most have in common a background of insufficient parental nurturing, exposure to intra-familial or extra-familial violence, and a separation from attachment figures.

Our current focus is on the other side of the same coin: not on deprivation or separation but on the child's *attachment* to parenting figures. As previously mentioned, attachment commonly refers to a close emotional bond that endures over time. By the age of eighteen months, children are usually attached to more than one individual, with fathers and siblings sharing the attachment with mothers, who are usually the primary attachment figures. Preserving the attachment to parents, siblings and other kin is an important goal of contemporary child-welfare practice. Fahlberg (1991) has described the critical role of foster parents in nurturing the child's ability to attach, preserving the child's attachment to parents, and helping to build attachment with members of the biological family or with adoptive parents.

Closely akin to attachment is the concept of identity. Children's ideas about who they are and where and with whom they belong have a major impact on their adjustment in placement and on the success of efforts at reunification. To understand more about the identity issues of children in foster care, Weinstein (1960) interviewed 61 children five years old or older who had been in placement for at least one year. He found that continuing contact with biological parents is important for the child's adjustment in placement and tends to have an ameliorative effect on the otherwise detrimental consequences of long-term foster care. It was also found that the child's predominant family identification is an important factor in his or her well-being in placement. On average, children who identified primarily with their biological parents had the highest ratings of well-being of any group in the study. Children who identified primarily with the foster carer or who had mixed identifications came significantly lower. Interestingly, the two most problematic groups were those children with mixed identification (who could not decide where they belonged) and those with foster-carer identification whose biological parents did not visit them.

Varieties of residential care

Some children are not able to tolerate the intimacy of family life and do better in a residential facility. Residential centres vary considerably in size, from large barrack-like institutions to small-group homes accommodating no more than three or four adolescents. Because of the trend towards strengthening foster care and maintaining birth families, the number of children placed in residential care has been declining. However, the needs of that number are greater than was the case, say, ten or twenty years ago because the young people now admitted to residential care are often those with serious difficulties, for whom foster care is not an appropriate placement, or for whom foster care has failed to produce the desired effect. Indeed, in the United Kingdom, one of the main tasks of the residential sector is to help deal with the aftermath of fostering breakdown. Even in the days when fostering was reserved for younger and non-problematic children, breakdowns sometimes reached 50 per cent (Triseliotis, 1997).

The historical antecedents of residential care in western Europe can be traced back as far as the Middle Ages. The roots of current approaches, however, are more readily found in the nineteenth century when very large residential institutions were erected in many countries. These institutions were usually administered by churches and charities and were characterised by regimented regimes founded on discipline, training and religion. Their purpose was twofold: to care for the destitute and abandoned, whilst protecting society from the perceived threat to social order posed by 'dangerous' children (Ruxton, 1996). As Hendrick (1994) observes, children play a dual role, both then and now: as 'victims' but also as 'threats'.

After a long period of stagnation, following the Second World War, there was renewed interest in residential care across Europe. Experiments were undertaken with democratic forms of communal living, with 'children's republics' and 'children's communities'. Yet by the close of the 1960s, residential institutions were attacked for having repressive regimes and failing to provide individualised care. The following three decades saw the progressive decline of residential care in all European Countries. This trend has been fuelled by a corresponding growth in foster-family care. (Ruxton, 1996).

The decline of residential care across the European Union has been accompanied by an increasing movement away from large-scale residential provision towards smaller-scale units. However, although castles and other large structures are no longer fitted out for the purpose of accommodating separated children, the development of smaller living units in some EU countries has been slow (Colton and Hellinckx, 1993). Nor has the move towards a smaller scale resulted in the complete abolition of large institutions. Often, the older, large-scale structures have been split up into smaller units. Thus, several small-group homes may be located on one site. In addition, a large institution may serve as the operational centre for a network of smaller units dispersed throughout the locality. Whilst operating on a small scale does not by itself ensure successful outcomes, research suggests that small-scale homes are more conducive to child-oriented care practice than are large establishments.

In addition to size, residential provisions can be classified in terms of the age of the youngsters accommodated or the particular type of service offered. One of the major types of residential care throughout Europe is 'children's homes', which look after children who do not have behaviour problems, or whose problems in this respect are not severe. Children's homes range from relatively large, multi-purpose, facilities to smaller hostel and family-group provisions.

A few years ago, a key function of residential institutions was to act as 'assessment centres'. Such centres used to accommodate children of all ages for short periods of time, usually with the aim of observing the child's behaviour to ascertain what sort of help was required. Over the last fifteen years or so, this form of residential care has been severely criticised. It is argued that, rather than being undertaken in 'artificial' residential environments, assessment should take place in the family unit. Further, it is difficult in practice to separate care and treatment from assessment, and many children remained in assessment centres for lengthy periods. Although a number of countries, including Denmark, have retained assessment centres, they have been closed in the UK.

Group care

Group homes are small residential units in which five or six children, usually adolescents, are cared for by house parents who work in shifts. A group setting has a number of advantages. It can allow greater variation in behaviour than a family unit and the impact of difficult behaviour – acting out – is reduced because it is diffused among a series of adults, who do shift work rather than being on duty 24 hours a day. The young person has an opportunity for a variety of interpersonal relationships with different adults and with peers who share the same experiences day by day. A broad range of remedial and therapeutic programmes and group activities can be brought together in the home and made available for planning positive daily-living experiences. The accessibility of the child to the staff facilitates his or her diagnosis, observation and treatment. Therapy for emotional problems, remedial programmes for learning problems and controls for behavioural problems can be integrated and related directly to the young person's daily life. The consistent routine of group care can contribute to a sense of continuity, regularity and stability for a disturbed youth. Many young people requiring group care come from very disorganised home environments and need structure to help them learn impulse control.

Specific approaches used in a planned, therapeutic, group environment include individual psychotherapy, behaviour modification, play therapy, art therapy, group work and a positive peer culture. Although individual psychotherapy was dominant in earlier times, it has largely been replaced by various forms of group work and behaviour modification as preferred models of treatment. In all such approaches, an attempt is made to use the everyday living environment as a therapeutic tool. Staff have the task of making desired behaviours and consequences explicit to residents and of managing the system of rewards and punishments necessary to reinforce expectations. Common techniques include token economies, in which young people work for points or tokens to attain various levels of privilege.

Group-work approaches have emphasised social and peer supports and sanctions as a means of establishing new patterns of behaviour. Youths are given selected responsibilities for the day-to-day running of the house and for governing their own and each other's behaviour. In some cases, recreational challenges such as camps and nature trips are used to strengthen young people's perceptions of responsibility to the peer-group goals.

Despite the many advantages, certain problems are common to most group homes. One is resistance from individuals and groups in the neighbourhood. Neighbours may be afraid that the presence of the group home will threaten the peace, safety or property values of the neighbourhood. In addition, group homes are open systems and must function in cooperation with a number of constituencies such as schools, police, and community recreational and other facilities. Thus, community relations are of prime importance and must be proactively built and maintained. Useful strategies include efforts to involve the community in every stage of planning before the home is established, through advisory groups led by key community members, and ongoing consultation when the home is in place. Involvement of the young people in the local community, individually or collectively, can also have benefits.

A second problem has to do with the difficulties inherent in group living. There is always a lack of privacy. Because of the number of people involved, opportunities to make personal choices may be compromised. If appropriate supervision and controls are not provided, acting-out behaviours by some residents may jeopardise the welfare of others. It may also be more difficult to involve young people's families in their care and treatment since there is no one foster carer to provide the personal touch and assume the leading role. A variety of approaches have been developed in this regard in the United States.

Before leaving residential care, it is as well to say something about the problem of abuse of children in care, since much controversy has centred around the abuse of children in residential facilities.

Abuse of children in care

Over the past 10 years the public care system has been rocked by numerous highly publicised controversies surrounding the abuse of children, particularly those living in residential institutions. The report of the National Commission of Inquiry into the Prevention of Child Abuse (1996, p. 19) notes:

> the catalogue of abuse in residential institutions is appalling. It includes physical assault and sexual abuse; emotional abuse; unacceptable deprivation of rights and privileges; inhumane treatment; poor health and education.

The abuse of children in residential institutions is particularly disturbing, given that many such children have already been deeply harmed prior to being placed away from home. It is estimated that between a third and two-thirds of those in residential institutions have been abused before entry (National Commission of Inquiry into the Prevention of Child Abuse, 1996).

One of the most publicised cases of abuse of looked-after children was 'Pindown'. This term was coined by the senior manager directly responsible, to denote the regime he established in children's homes administered by Staffordshire County Council. Increasing public and media interest was reflected by a Granada Television *World in Action* programme shown nationally on 25 June 1990. Four days later, an independent inquiry was set up by the besieged local authority (Levy and Kahan, 1991).

In the conclusion to their report, the members of the inquiry, Alan Levy QC and Barbara Kahan, relate:

> the vast majority of children who underwent the regime perceived Pindown as a narrow, punitive and harshly restrictive experience. We think their perceptions were correct. ... The children who were in Pindown ... suffered in varying degrees the despair and the potentially damaging effects of isolation, the humiliation of having to wear night clothes, knock on the door to 'impart information' as it was termed, and of having all their personal possessions removed; and the intense frustration and boredom from the lack of communication, companionship with others and recreation. ... Pindown contained the worst elements of institutional control: baths on admission, special clothing, strict routine, segregation and isolation, humiliation and inappropriate bed-times.
>
> (Levy and Kahan, 1991, p. 167)

The official response to the Pindown scandal included a special review of residential care in England by the then Chief Inspector of the Social Services Inspectorate, Sir William Utting (Utting, 1991; see also, CCETSW, 1992; Department of Health, 1992; Howe, 1992). His report identified the lack of qualified staff as a central problem underlying the poor quality of children's homes. Only 22 per cent of non-supervisory staff had any relevant qualifications. Further, many officers-in-charge were found to be unqualified. Essentially, what emerged from the report was a picture of a system in which children with the most severe personal and social problems were being looked after by staff who had the least experience and training in child-care matters. Young, inexperienced, isolated and untrained staff were often left to tend, and work with, the most problematic clients.

Since Pindown, an attempt has been made to improve care, training, management, and inspection and complaints procedures. But it is highly questionable whether the scale of this effort is sufficient. Moreover, of late, confidence in the public care system has been further eroded by repeated revelations concerning the sexual abuse of children in the system.

While extra-familial sexual abuse is by no means limited to the public care system, much controversy has centred on the threat posed to children in residential care. The care system has repeatedly been shown to have failed to protect youngsters in children's homes from sexual abuse by paedophiles operating alone or in semi-organised 'rings' associated with a number of residential homes. Many of the perpetrators have sexually abused children and young people in their care and, in so doing, have betrayed positions of special trust. It appears, therefore, that rather than being protected by their special status, children living away from home are often exposed to greater risk (Colton and Vanstone, 1996).

Major child-abuse inquiries have been undertaken involving clusters of children's homes in North Wales and Cheshire (House of Commons, 2000). It has been estimated that over 350 children were sexually abused while in care in these areas. Most of the victims are now young adults. It is anticipated that the compensation bill paid by the Criminal Injuries Compensation Board will ultimately exceed £40 million.

Of course, the cost in human terms is incalculable. Child sexual abuse can have far-reaching adverse consequences for victims, and has been linked with short- and long-term emotional and behavioural problems, such as general psychopathology, anxiety, depression, aggression, low self-esteem, sexual problems, physical symptoms, cognitive disability, developmental delay, poor school performance, 'acting out' disorders, and suicide (Colton and Vanstone, 1996). Significantly, at least 12 suicides of former residents in children's homes in North Wales have been linked to the abuse they suffered as children in care (NCH Action for Children, 1996).

Sir William Utting recently prepared a second report for the Department of Health, based on a review established in 1996 in response to ongoing disclosure of abuse suffered by children living away from home (Utting, 1997). The report confirms that Britain is failing to provide adequately for children living away from home. Far fewer children are now placed in residential care than was the case 20 years ago. Moreover, residential homes are much smaller today, with an average of 10 child-care places per home. Nevertheless, Sir William argues that the danger of child abuse remains an ever-present threat. The report finds that over a third of children in residential care are not receiving an education; it also condemns inadequate staffing and the placement of vulnerable children alongside other youngsters who are likely to bully them. Whilst acknowledging that the care of children looked after by local authorities has improved, the report contends that progress is unsatisfactory and greater regulation is necessary.

The quality of foster care is also criticised. This includes the inadequate regulation of foster carers, whose difficulties in coping with complex and stressful tasks can result in abuse or bullying.

Sir William's main criticisms on the quality of care for children placed away from home were: inappropriate residential-care placements, poor standards of health and education in residential care, inadequate regulation of foster carers, no inspection of residential special schools, and children in prison sharing accommodation with adult offenders.

To ameliorate these problems, Sir William recommended a comprehensive strategy for residential care, legislation to regulate private foster care, extending the Children Act 1989 to include regulation of all boarding schools, linking residential and foster care to facilitate more choice of placements, giving greater attention to the educational and health needs of children placed away from home, and improving the regulation of the recruitment of staff working with children.

Maggie Charnock (1998, p. 2), a member of the steering group for the feasbility study by the National Voice for Young People, argues that many people are unconcerned about the abuse of children and young people in care, including professionals, members of the public, the police, insurance companies and even a number of local authorities. She believes that this attitude is born out of 'careism' – a term which denotes prejudice against young people on the grounds of their care status. To tackle the abuse of children and young people in care, she recommends that 'careism' should be recognised and abolished. She also recommends that a national organisation should be set up to give a voice for young people in care and that those responsible for abuse, including local authorities, should face criminal prosecution.

Alternative forms of residential care

Recently, attempts have been made to develop new, creative forms of residential care. These include 'communes' in Germany, which offer shelter to young people who volunteer to live together, and attend school for vocational training. Similarly, in many EU countries, houses located in residential communities provide accommodation for groups of young people. Although adult care workers facilitate some of these groups, in many cases the group is exclusively comprised of young people, who receive a minimum of adult supervision.

In Germany, small autonomous units have formed networks with one another to provide a wider range of programmes and activities, which can be shared by youngsters from all the units within the network. This pooling of resources makes for economies of scale, and helps to overcome the high costs which otherwise discourage the development of smaller units.

In view of the evidence that residential care is increasingly reserved for more challenging children and young people, there is an obvious need for small-scale facilities which offer effective help to such youngsters. In Germany and Ireland, small-scale, specialised facilities have been set up for children and adolescents with severe behavioural difficulties. A number of projects have been developed in Germany for young drug addicts and runaways. Residential workers in Germany have given increasing attention to the problems experienced by girls and young women, in particular those who have been sexually abused. In the UK, attempts have been made to improve practice in relation to overcoming the special difficulties encountered by children and young people from different ethnic backgrounds (Colton and Hellinckx, 1993).

Alternatives to residential and foster care

Recognition of the heterogeneous nature of children in the care system, in terms both of their needs and of possible ways of meeting them, together with the high costs of residential care and the criticisms levelled against it, have fuelled the development of community-oriented alternatives. The key objectives of such provision are twofold: first, to prevent entry into residential or foster care; and secondly, to maintain the young person in his or her own social environment. The most common alternatives to residential and foster care in the European Union are: day centres, centres for independent living under supervision, and home-based treatment schemes. All three approaches are widely used in the Netherlands (Colton and Hellinckx, 1993).

Day centres are places where children and young people in need can go after school. The child, family and school are all involved in the intervention programme. Day centres focus help on young people who are at risk of being placed away from home. Parents gain respite and support, whilst maintaining the care of their children.

Centres for independent living under supervision typically involve young people living in apartments, either by themselves or in small groups. They are usually supervised by care workers based at larger residential establishments, or by workers specialising in this form of care. The goal is to provide young people with the opportunity to develop the skills essential for an independent life, including practical household skills. This type of care tends to focus on the young people themselves, and parents are often left out. However, the involvement of young people's families is important in the transition to independent living. Such a finding is not surprising when we consider the difficulties often experienced by young people from supportive homes who have never been in care, when they first venture into independent living. Many cannot manage at first without help from parents in cash or kind and some return home several times before they are finally able to establish independence. For youngsters leaving care, the situation is fraught with additional practical and emotional difficulties. At a practical level, they may have educational deficits which contribute to a lack of readiness for employment, as well as scant survival skills in such areas as finding accommodation, budgeting, cooking and general household management. At an emotional level, the separation from the child-welfare system, which did offer some support and protection, may cause the child to re-experience the original loss of parenting figures and the subsequent losses inherent in changing placements. Before the move to independence, there was the social worker and perhaps a foster carer or child-care worker. Now, unless the child has a supportive relative or friend or has maintained contact with a former foster carer, there is no-one at all.

A third alternative to foster and residential settings is *centres for home-based treatment,* which offer intensive help in the child's family home. Several times each week, family members receive training in relation to the practical and social aspects of family life. This intervention addresses the parenting process as a whole rather than focusing on specific, isolated problems; on family relationships, rather than on individual family members.

Secure accommodation

Secure accommodation is the most restrictive placement option available and there are strict criteria governing its use. A local authority may only restrict the liberty of a child that they are looking after if it can be shown:

(a) that –
  (i) he has a history of absconding and is likely to abscond from any other description of accommodation; and
  (ii) if he absconds he is likely to suffer significant harm;

(b) that if he is kept in any other description of accommodation he is likely to injure himself or any other persons.

(Children Act 1989, Section 25(1))

Where these criteria are met, a child may be kept in secure accommodation for a maximum of 72 hours without a court order, although the direct authority of the Secretary of State is required before children under the age of 13 can be placed in secure accommodation. If the local authority wishes to restrict liberty for more than 72 hours, or more than a total of 72 hours over a period of 28 days, they must obtain a court order.

The restrictions on the use of secure accommodation do not apply to children detained under mental-health legislation. However, they do apply to all children in residential care, nursing or mental nursing homes. Further, children in voluntary and registered children's homes cannot be kept in secure accommodation. It is important to note that any person with parental responsibility may at any time remove a child in accommodation whose liberty is being restricted.

Except for those remanded into accommodation as a consequence of committing criminal offences, applications for secure accommodation are made to the family proceedings court (or the County Court or the High Court). If made, the order may be for up to three months. This may be renewed on application to the court for periods of up to six months.

Applications for children on remand are made to the youth or other magistrate's court, and, if granted, last for the duration of the remand or for a maximum of 28 days.

Where an order for secure accommodation is granted, the local authority must hold a review within a month, and thereafter at intervals not exceeding three months, to (a) establish that the criteria for placing the child in secure accommodation still apply, and (b) determine whether an alternative form of accommodation would be appropriate.

The child must be legally represented in all secure-accommodation proceedings, unless he or she has refused such representation. A guardian *ad litem* must be appointed in non-criminal proceedings to keep a child in secure accommodation, except where the court considers that this is not necessary in the interests of the child (Ball, 1996).

The report of the National Commission of Inquiry into the Prevention of Child Abuse (1996, p. 20) reports that children placed in secure units may be at 'increased risk of bullying and violence'. It further notes the lack of 'comprehensive annual statistics on what *behaviour* has caused children to be placed in secure accommodation' and cites recent research indicating that a third of children placed in secure accommodation are 'locked up unnecessarily'. The report also makes reference to other research which showed that over 90 per cent of those sentenced to long-term detention had suffered abuse and/or loss as children. Unfortunately, 'most had not received effective help to enable them to come to terms with their experiences'.

Adoption

The adoption of children dates back to antiquity. References to adoption can be found in the Bible and in the legal codes of the Chinese, Hindus, Babylonians, Romans and Egyptians. Its purpose has varied considerably by country and era: for example, to cement relationships with foreign powers; to make possible the continuance of religious traditions; to overcome difficulties in recognising an out-of-wedlock child; and, more recently, to provide permanent homes for children in need of them.

Modern adoption has it roots in the Victorian foster-care system where babies, often illegitimate, whose mothers could not care for them were found homes with other families. However, adoption legislation was not passed until as late as 1926 in England and 1930 in Scotland. The delay in developing a legal framework around a common practice partly resulted from attitudes concerning the possible inheritance by adopted children of 'bad blood' and criminal tendencies from their biological parents (Triseliotis, 1997). Not only might 'the apple not fall far from the tree', but this rotten apple might then stand to inherit the worldly goods that decent adoptive parents had worked so hard for. Attitudes have changed since then and in 1993 the total number of adoptions in England and Wales was 6,859 (811 in Scotland), with step-parent and relative adoptions comprising roughly half the total. However, these figures are less than half the total for 1977: a fact which might be explained by improved contraceptive techniques, policies which encourage single mothers to keep their babies, and an emphasis on maintaining links with biological families.

The evolution of adoption in the United Kingdom

According to Triseliotis (1997), there have been three distinct periods in the evolution of adoption in the United Kingdom since the introduction of adoption legislation a little over seventy years ago. The first period occurred in the 1920s and 1930s, between the two world wars, when adoption was mainly practised by working-class people who were relatively unconcerned about heredity and inheritance. Adoption concentrated on older children, rather than infants, and sometimes included children with disabilities. Triseliotis argues that, except for the post-1970s, this period was the closest that adoption policy and practice have come to their modern purpose of 'providing a home for a child' (Triseliotis, 1997).

The second period, after the Second World War, ran from the early 1950s to the early 1970s. For various reasons, adoption became popular among the middle classes, and was seen as a way of offering children to childless couples and as a solution to the problem of out-of-wedlock births. Thus, adoption during this period focused less on 'providing a home for a child' than on 'providing a child for a home'. Bowlby's research on the adverse effects of separation and institutionalisation on children had a strong influence on adoption policy and practice. His claim that children over two years of age should not be adopted appeared to support the view that placement of children with disabilities or 'dubious' social backgrounds should be avoided (Triseliotis, 1997). The inescapable inference here is that, if a child is to be provided for a home, it should be a child worthy of the honour, not a child who has been damaged in some way by unfortunate previous experiences.

The third period in the evolution of adoption began towards the end of the 1960s. Between 1969 and the beginning of the 1990s the number of infants and very young children adopted by non-relatives fell from around 21,000 to about 4,500. For example, the 1993 figure (6,859 children adopted in England and Wales) is less than half of the figure for 1977. This fall in the number of children adopted reflected factors such as the wider availability of contraception, increased access to abortion services, and a reduction of the stigma associated with births outside marriage, which meant that more single mothers kept their children. Ruxton (1996, p. 347) reports:

> Statistics from several northern European countries from the end of World War II onwards ... show how the fall in the number of babies available for adoption went hand in hand with improvements in the standard of living and, in particular, with improved welfare provision to single parent families. ... Experience in today's Europe shows a progressive and sustained decline in the number of healthy babies offered for adoption in each country.

Consequently, adoption agencies in Britain turned their attention to the placement of children with 'special needs'; that is, older children with emotional and behavioural problems or with mental and physical disabilities (Triseliotis, 1997).

This shift in perspective back to 'a home for a child' drew on research suggesting two things: first, that there were large numbers of children in care who required new permanent homes since they had little chance of being reunited with their birth parents; and, secondly, that with an enabling family environment, older children could overcome earlier psychological adversities and do well. At the same time, the idea of psychological or social parenthood was becoming accepted: proponents of social parenthood argue that effective parenting depends not on a biological connection with the child but on positive psychological and social interactions day by day. All these factors encouraged people to adopt. It might also be noted that transferring children from the care system to adoptive homes was financially attractive to local authorities, 'who otherwise would have faced many years of funding residential or foster care placements' (Triseliotis, 1997, p. 334).

The outcome of the drive to place children with special needs in adoptive homes appears to be mixed. On the plus side, thousands of children have gained permanent families. New knowledge and skills have been developed with regard to the preparation, matching and post-placement support of adoptive families and children. On the debit side, however, this new knowledge has not been applied by all agencies. Further, some adoptive families have been unable to cope with the level of emotional and behavioural problems manifested by the children adopted. As a result, some children have experienced yet more disruption and unhappiness (Triseliotis, 1997).

Research indicates that the stability of adoptive placements can be as high as 85–90 per cent, especially for children placed with their adoptive families before the age of nine. However, the breakdown rates for older children are sometimes as high as 50 per cent, and there is a close association between increasing age and higher breakdown rates. Because it is felt that many older children who might require adoptive families are more psychologically damaged than was previously the case, agencies are now more cautious about their placement. They are tending to place such youngsters with permanent foster carers, or with foster carers with a view to adoption later on if things work out (Triseliotis, 1997).

An essential condition for the adoption of any child is the consent of the biological parents or a legal termination of parental rights so that the child is free for adoption. Termination of rights may occur either by the consent of the biological parents or involuntarily, following a finding that they have failed to exercise their parental responsibility. A number of areas of uncertainty exist regarding parental consent which may call into question whether a particular child is in fact free for adoption. For example, if the birth mother consents but the birth father does not, should the birth father's rights prevail even if he has had no contact with the child at all? Once consent has been given, should it be irrevocable and, if not, how long should the birth parents be given to change their minds before the adoption becomes final? Further, since consent must be given by children of a certain age to their own adoption, should the child's wishes override those of the parents if there is a difference of opinion? Another area of uncertainty in modern times concerns which of the parents has the right to consent to or block the child's adoption when the child has been created through artificial insemination or surrogate parenting.

An adoption is not made final until the child has lived in the adoptive home under the guidance of a social-welfare agency for a certain period of time, usually a year. Waiver provisions give flexibility so that courts can shorten the time if doing so is in the best interests of the child. Once the adoption is finalised, it is 'for keeps' and cannot be abrogated because the birth parents wish to withdraw their consent or the adoptive parents decide they do not want the child. Adoptive parents may lose their children in exactly the same ways as biological parents: they may relinquish their right to the child or the child may be removed if allegations of neglect or abuse are upheld. With the increase of adoption of children with special needs, more adoptions are dissolving, causing some people to advocate more humane ways to undo these placements legally so that children can move on to more appropriate placements without feelings of failure.

Open adoption

Triseliotis (1997, p. 335) argues that mistakes were made in the past when placing children with special needs, including the revivalist approach with which the policy was pursued, the introduction of time limits, the use of the law to assume parental rights and thus stop parental access before placing the children with new families, and the severance of important emotional links between older children and their birth families.

Two of the 'mistakes' identified by Triseliotis (1997) included lack of parental input before the child was placed with an adoptive family, and severance of ties with the child afterwards. The notion that confidentiality is preferable for all three members of the adoptive triad – birth parents, adoptive parents and children – is termed closed or confidential adoption. It rests on the 'fresh start' principle whereby it is deemed better for the child to start again with a fresh family and without the emotional 'baggage' that continued contact with the family of origin might compel the child to carry. However, in recent years, this closed model is increasingly giving way to an open or cooperative adoption model. As fewer infants have become available for adoption, birth mothers have found more leverage in the process of relinquishment and preferences about adoptive parents. Agencies have learned that mothers are less concerned about confidentiality than with helping to select the adoptive parents and with maintaining some kind of connection with the child after the adoption. Adults who were adopted as infants, for their part, have begun assertively to seek to have their sealed records opened and have demanded the right to know about their biological origins.

The movement to place for adoption children with special needs (those children hitherto considered 'unadoptable') has also changed adoption practice dramatically. These children are often older, have memories of their birth parents and siblings, and have ideas of their own about maintaining ties. Adoptive parents of such children have often thoughtfully considered their motives in seeking adoption before approaching the agency: they know what kind of child they might be able to help and they want full information about potential adoptees, sometimes including a meeting with the birth family. Since it is difficult to recruit parents who are willing to face the difficulties inherent in adopting a special-needs child, agencies' attitudes towards such parents focus less on 'screening out' (the common attitude towards people who want to adopt infants) than on helping parents in every possible way to achieve satisfaction in their adoptive parenthood. Many adoption agencies today have revised traditional 'closed' practices towards varying degrees of openness. These changes may include planned communication between the adoptive and birth parents prior to the placement. In the case of a baby, all the parents may have face-to-face meetings before the birth, at the time of the agreement for placement and at various times after the birth. At such meetings, the birth mother and the adopting parents may share first names, photographs, addresses and telephone numbers. The information exchanged may include ethnic and religious backgrounds, level of education, aspects of personality and interests, physical and medical characteristics, and other matters of common interest. These options are agreed when birth and adoptive parents, with the help of an agency social worker, discuss the extent of 'openness' in the present and future. Such arrangements are usually entirely voluntary on the part of both parents and adopters, as courts would be very reluctant to attach contact requirements as part of an adoption order.

Inter-country adoption

By contrast with their counterparts in northern and western European countries, British adoption agencies and practitioners took a stance against inter-country (and transracial) adoption, preferring to concentrate their efforts on the placement of own-country special-needs children (Triseliotis, 1997). Until 1990 only about 50 adoption orders a year in England and Wales concerned children from other countries, and many of those children were related to the adopting parents. However, the number has increased since 1992. This owes much to increased public awareness of the appalling conditions suffered by children in residential institutions in Romania and other eastern European countries. There is ongoing interest in adopting from Central and South America, India, South-East Asia, and China (Ruxton, 1996).

However, some argue that inter-country adoption, which is driven by the demand of childless couples in the West, has created an unregulated market involving the one-way movement of children from poor to rich countries. Proponents of this view say that much more should be done to provide support for such children in their own countries. Some cases entail 'child trafficking', with babies smuggled illegally and large profits made by 'go-betweens'. It is further held that these adoptions occur at the expense of domestic placements for older children and those with disabilities. Evidence is also cited of high placement breakdowns, resulting in admission to the public care system (Ruxton, 1996).

Conversely, others insist that inter-country adoption is successful in that children are saved from poverty, institutionalisation, and a life on the streets; they experience loving family life and significantly improved life chances. It is pointed out that many of the children concerned are rejected in the country of their birth, and that inter-country adoption is encouraged by the governments of many so-called 'donor' countries. In addition, child trafficking and badly prepared placements are consequences of lack of regulation, which can be rectified through cooperation between countries (Ruxton, 1996).

Such an approach is reflected in the principles underpinning the Hague Convention on Intercountry Adoption (29 May 1993), which prescribes that inter-country adoptions should only take place after the best interests of the child have been properly assessed and in circumstances which protect his/her fundamental rights. Birth parents or others responsible for consenting to adoptions should understand what they are consenting to and its implications. They should be objectively counselled and should not be offered financial or other inducements. Agencies acting in inter-country adoptions should be suitably staffed and supervised. No-one should derive improper financial gain from adoption. Finally, adoptive parents should be carefully and objectively assessed for their suitability (Ruxton, 1996, p. 352).

The Convention will establish a framework whereby the sending country is responsible for the assessment of the child's circumstances, needs and interests, and for transmitting to the receiving country the information that shows this has been done. Receiving countries are responsible for arranging the assessment of the adoptive parents and transmitting the results to the sending country. Adoptions carried out between each ratifying country, in accord with the Articles of the Convention, are known as 'Convention Adoptions' (Ruxton, 1996). The Draft Adoption Bill, published by the British government in March 1996, contains provisions that would enable the United Kingdom to ratify the Hague Convention on Intercountry Adoption.

Same-race placements

Within the EU, few children from ethnic minority groups are placed in adoptive families of the same ethnic origin, despite the fact that in some countries such children comprise a majority of those entering care and requiring adoption. Agencies in the UK appear to have done more than their counterparts in other EU countries to place a child within his or her own culture. However, even here progress has been slow. The reason usually given for not placing ethnic minority children with same-race adoptive parents is that insufficient numbers of ethnic minority families come forward to adopt (James, 1986). However, Ruxton (1996) argues that this is partly because inadequate emphasis is given by many agencies to proactive recruitment of such families (see also, Gambe et al., 1992).

Adoption by single people

Another issue which has attracted much debate in recent years is whether single people should be allowed to adopt. Whilst such adoptions are not possible in all EU member states, a recent review of adoption law in the UK pointed to highly successful adoptions by single people, with particular reference to those involving older children and those with disabilities. It is argued that abused children often experience difficulty coping with one close relationship at a time, let alone the several relationships involved in joining a family with a mother, father and perhaps other children. The single parent is able to focus exclusively on the child because there are no competing demands from a spouse, and thus, may provide a more appropriate placement than a couple could. Studies show that single adoptive parents are more likely to be women who have occupations and skills that lend themselves to understanding children's special issues. For example, nurses, social workers and teachers are highly represented among single adoptive applicants. They usually have extended family back-up and a high percentage were themselves brought up in single-parent homes (Feigelman and Silverman, 1983).

Adoption by gays and lesbians

If adoption by single people is controversial, adoption by homosexuals is far more so. Although it has been argued that lesbian households may be safer for a child than heterosexual ones because no men are present, public opinion in the EU – as measured by a survey in 1993 – seems to be against such placements. To be sure, the great majority of people in countries like Denmark, the Netherlands and Spain do believe that gay and lesbian people should enjoy equal rights to those of heterosexual couples in relation to marriage and inheritance. However, only in the Netherlands did the proportion in favour of homosexuals having the right to adopt children (47 per cent) exceed the proportion against (40 per cent) (Ruxton, 1996).

Adoption by foster parents

Foster carers are another relatively recent group of adoptive applicants. Although there have always been some foster carers who have adopted their foster children, the practice has not been encouraged. In the 1960s and 1970s, adoption by foster carers was termed 'the back door to adoption', a route whereby carers could 'try on' children until they found the one they wanted to adopt. Social workers tended to feel in general that this was harmful to children since the carers' prime purpose was not to do the best for the child in the context of a temporary placement but to evaluate the child as a candidate for adoption. It was felt that people who wanted to adopt should apply for adoption, people who wanted to foster should apply to foster, and there should be no overlap between the two, particularly since children whom their foster carers wished to adopt might not be free for adoption. This attitude has recently been seen as unrealistic since foster carers grow fond of their charges, the affection may be reciprocated and, in cases where the child is free to be adopted, the continuance of an established and positive relationship may be the best option for the child. Difficulties may arise with respect to changed relationships with the child's natural family: permanent adoption is a very different proposition from temporary fostering. However, the recent trend towards open adoption may go some way to alleviate these difficulties, as may supportive pre- and post-placement work by the adoption agency.

Inter-country adoptions, same-race placements, and the placement of children with homosexual, single, or foster-care adopters are all issues which seem likely to represent an ongoing challenge for adoption agencies and professionals. Triseliotis (1997) considers that other challenges include: recruiting new families for some 'very "damaged" and problematic' youngsters against a background of increasing numbers of reconstituted families which are themselves having to care for children from more than one relationship; developing more uniform and better informed preparatory and matching methods; improving training of adoptive (and foster) parents in relation to managing problematic behaviours; organising more uniform post-placement services; and developing skills to manage open adoptions.

The legal framework

Now that we have considered some of the practice issues related to adoption, it is time to consider the legal framework. Local authority social workers may be involved in adoption in three ways: first, because adoption is being considered for children on their caseload; secondly, because they may have to prepare the detailed report required by the court in an adoption case under Schedule 2 of the Adoption Rules 1984; and thirdly, because the Adoption Act 1976 places on all local authorities a statutory duty to:

> establish and maintain within their area a service designed to meet the needs in relation to adoption of:
>
> (a) children who have been or may be adopted,
> (b) parents and guardians of such children, and
> (c) persons who have adopted or may adopt a child, and for that purpose to provide the requisite facilities, or secure that they are provided by approved adoption societies.
>
> (Ball, 1996, p. 98)

Besides local authorities, a number of other adoption agencies are approved by the Secretary of State for Health (Ruxton, 1996, p. 362).

Because the making of an adoption order has such a profound impact on the child's legal status, strict requirements are laid down for all stages of the adoption process. An adoption order can only be made by an authorised court; that is, the magistrates' family proceedings court, the County Court or, in certain circumstances, the High Court. The statutory provisions and procedural rules are contained in the Adoption Act 1976, the Adoption Rules 1984, the Adoption Agencies Regulations 1983, and the Adoption (Amendment) Rules 1991 (Ball, 1996).

As previously mentioned, applications by single people are allowed, but there is a strong presumption in favour of married couples. Moreover, unmarried couples are not permitted to apply jointly. The birth parents' agreement to the adoption is necessary. However, if this cannot be obtained, either because their whereabouts are unknown or because they will not agree to adoption, an application may be made for the court to dispense with the parents' agreement. Usually, the grounds for such a course are that the parents are withholding consent 'unreasonably' – for example, because there is no reasonable prospect of them being able to resume care of the child (Ruxton, 1996).

Before the court considers the application, a comprehensive report must be compiled which provides detailed information about the child, the birth parents, prospective adoptive parents, and the role and involvement of the agency concerned. The court may appoint a 'guardian *ad litem*' to represent the child's interests.

The welfare of the child is the first consideration of the court. Section 6 of the Adoption Act 1976 requires that:

> the court or adoption agency shall have regard to all the circumstances, the first consideration being given to the need to safeguard and promote the welfare of the child throughout his childhood; and shall so far as is practicable ascertain the wishes and feelings of the child regarding the decision and give due consideration to them, having regard to his age and understanding.

It may be that the child's welfare can be safeguarded by a less drastic change in his or her legal status than that effected by adoption. Under the Children Act 1989, the court may make orders other than those applied for – such as a residence order instead of an adoption order. Residence orders may be made by courts hearing adoption applications irrespective of whether or not the parents have agreed to adoption. In addition to determining who the child lives with, the residence order gives the person in whose favour the order is made parental responsibility for the duration of the order. The court can also add any conditions it considers necessary to the order. By contrast with adoption, residence orders generally cease to have effect when the child is 16, but may not do so if the court considers the case exceptional; the child's name can only be changed with the consent of all those with parental responsibility, or on the direction of the court; moreover, those with a residence order cannot appoint a guardian for the child in the event of their death, or indeed, consent to the child's adoption (Ball, 1996).

Where either the child is already in the care of the agency and the question of parental consent is in doubt, or the mother wishes the child to be adopted before any specific application is ready, the agency may apply to the court for an order freeing the child for adoption. The parents must consent to the order, or their consent must be dispensed with. Such an order removes existing parental responsibility and vests it in the agency, which will hold it until an adoption order is made. Unless they have signed a declaration that they do not wish to be further involved, after a year the birth parents will be informed if an adoption order has been made, or the child has been placed for adoption. If they have not signed the declaration and the child has not been placed, the birth parents may apply for revocation of the freeing order. Applications for freeing orders have been subject to long delays; further, once freed, the children concerned are, in effect, placed in a legal limbo until adopted (Ball, 1996).

The publication in March 1996 of the Department of Health and Welsh Office's paper *Adoption – A Service for Children,* with a Draft Adoption Bill for consultation, represented the culmination of a lengthy review of adoption law. The Draft Bill seeks to bring adoption legislation in line with the Children Act 1989, in particular by providing that the child's welfare must be the court's and the adoption agency's paramount consideration. It would also replace the process of 'freeing for adoption' by an entirely new framework for placement for adoption, with or without parental agreement, and involving the court before placement in cases of dispute. In addition, the Draft Bill would make it possible for step-parents to obtain parental responsibility without making an adoption application, and includes provisions which would allow the United Kingdom to ratify the Hague Convention on Intercountry Adoption – discussed earlier in the chapter (Collier, 1996). This Draft Bill has so far not been taken forward by the Labour government.

In this chapter, we have discussed the placement options available to children who are being looked after. We will go on now to look at anti-discriminatory and anti-oppressive practice, in the next chapter.

Case example

Case example 6.1   John

John (aged 12 years, 5 months)

John comes from a family of five children. He has an older brother (14) and an older sister (13), and two younger sisters (10 and 9). He is the only child in the family who is of mixed parentage. The three oldest children have had a number of care episodes, in all three cases beginning when they were twelve years old. The older brother and sister no longer live at home, but live with different relatives in the rather large extended family surrounding John. His mother comes from a family of eight children. There are lots of aunts, uncles and cousins in the family.

John's parents (Mike and Mary) are married to each other, but the relationship has been very turbulent. Mike frequently comes home drunk on payday, and gives the remainder of his salary to Mary, which is usually insufficient for the family to buy food, clothing and other necessities. When Mary confronts him about this, he becomes violent and on two occasions has caused her to have broken limbs. She has been in the local refuge on two occasions, but after each she has gone back after about six weeks away.

Another source of tension in the relationship is that Mike suspects that Mary is having relationships with other men. He had no suspicions about this until John was born. John, who was conspicuously not Mike's son, is aware that he is not Mike's child, but has no knowledge of who his biological father might be. He has never discussed this with his mother, nor has she broached the issue with him.

John's difficulties appeared to begin after a very turbulent first year in secondary school. He has always had racial taunts from children at school, but when he went to secondary school, it seemed to become much worse. He was assaulted on his way home from school in his second week, by a group of about five or six older children at the school. Since then, he has been very reluctant to go to school, but managed to attend with cajoling and persuading. In his second year this has been much more difficult, and he has only attended school about 40 per cent of the time.

Since the beginning of the second school year, John's behaviour at home has become much more difficult as well. There are frequent rows with his mother. When things calm down, he is unable to explain to his mother why he is so angry with her. She is finding it very difficult. Finally, she approached the social services saying that she was not able to have him at home anymore.

Although reluctant to provide accommodation for John at first, the social worker agreed to try a plan of respite, in view of the very severe difficulties at home. John was admitted to the local children's home for the first time for a two-week period, a week last Friday. The plan is to use the experience to work out how to improve the relationship between John and his mother. The social worker, however, is concerned that given the experience of the older children in the family, John's respite arrangement might drift into something more permanent. From the social services' perspective, this is something to avoid.

Questions

1. We know that children of mixed heritage are placed away from home in disproportionate numbers. What effect might John's mixed heritage have on the social worker's thinking?
2. A continuing controversy centres around whether the focus on family preservation is threatening the safety of children and should be discontinued. Bearing this controversy in mind, do you think that the social worker's initial reluctance to provide accommodation for John was justified under the circumstances?
3. If John's respite arrangement does become more permanent, this might be something to avoid from the perspective of social services. Is it something to avoid from the perspectives of John and his family? Why, or why not?
4. If John is placed away from home, what kind of placement might be most appropriate for him? Keep in mind the restrictiveness continuum and all you have learned about the advantages and disadvantages of different types of placement for different types of children.
5. Preserving the attachment to parents, siblings and other kin is an important goal of contemporary child-welfare practice. Do you agree that this should be an important goal? Why, or why not? What steps might be taken to preserve John's attachment to his family if he were to be placed away from home? What would be the probable result if these steps were not taken?

CHAPTER 7

Anti-discriminatory and anti-oppressive practice with children and families

Objectives

After reading this chapter you should have a clearer understanding of the difference between anti-discriminatory practice and anti-oppressive practice as they apply to work with children and families. You will be introduced to a number of factors that may select certain children and young people for social disadvantage (for example, race, disability, use of drugs, HIV status, homelessness, sexual orientation). These will then be considered in relation to looked-after children, before a discussion of the issue of children's rights.

Anti-discriminatory and anti-oppressive practice

Issues of discrimination and oppression began to receive serious attention in social work from the mid-1980s (Ahmed, 1986, 1994; Dalrymple and

Burke, 1995; Owusu-Bempah, 1997; Thompson, 1997). According to Thompson (1997, p. 238), we are now 'much more aware of the need to see the individual in his or her social context', and 'to see that context in a fuller and richer sense than is traditionally the case in the social work literature'.

The term 'anti-discriminatory practice' is widely used in social-work training and practice to refer to attempts to reduce both 'individual and institutional discrimination, particularly on the grounds of race, gender, disability, social class and sexual orientation' (Thomas and Pierson, 1995, cited in Thompson, 1997, p. 238). Thompson (1997, p. 239) argues that a basic feature of anti-discriminatory practice is the ability/willingness to see that discrimination and oppression are so often central to the situations that social workers encounter. In his view, social workers must develop a sensitivity to the existence of discrimination and oppression all around them and recognise that there is no middle ground; they are either part of the solution or a part of the problem. The three 'key imperatives' of justice, equality and participation must be addressed, and traditional forms of social-work practice must be revisited and amended to ensure they are anti-discriminatory. The achievement of such practice begins with non-discriminatory practice and anti-oppressive assessment.

Dalrymple and Burke (1995, p. 3) argue that it is important to distinguish between anti-oppressive and anti-discriminatory practice, 'as all too often the terms are used interchangeably without thought being given to the impact of both terms'. For these authors, anti-oppressive practice is concerned with minimising the power differences in society. They quote Phillipson (1992) who considers that anti-oppressive practice 'works with a model of empowerment and liberation and requires a fundamental rethinking of values, institutions and relationships'. By contrast, 'legislation which deals with issues of discrimination – such as the Race Relations Act or the Sex Discrimination Act – is *specific* and aimed at addressing unfair treatment faced, for example, by black people or women. Anti-discriminatory practice uses particular legislation to *challenge* the discrimination faced by some groups of people' (Dalrymple and Burke, 1995, p. 3).

Whilst not denying the usefulness of anti-discriminatory practice, Dalrymple and Burke (1995, p. 3) feel it is limited in its 'potential to challenge power differentials'. Moreover, they believe that it is 'important for us to develop a practice which ultimately addresses structural inequalities'.

In what follows, we examine categories of children who have emerged as major concerns for child-welfare agencies. Some of these children belong to communities or groups who are victims of discrimination and oppression; some are the focus of moral panics, and are perceived as threats to moral and social order; others are variously perceived as both victims and threats.

Changing populations in child welfare

Black children

Children from black and ethnic minority communities in Britain are victims of the racism which permeates all levels of British society (Ahmed, 1994; Owusu-Bempah, 1997). Ahmed (1994) states: 'it is a fact that racism operates at an ideological, structural, systemic and interpersonal level within contemporary British society'. Ruxton (1996, p. 13) notes that an increase in xenophobia and racism has been widely reported across the European Union, 'leading to far greater fear and uncertainty among ethnic minority populations. In many cases children and their families have been repeatedly subjected to harassment and attacks.'

Although the proportion of people under 16 in the general population is comparatively low, the age structure of the various UK ethnic minorities varies considerably from the average. Around 3.2 million people, or roughly 6 per cent of the population, belong to an ethnic minority group, of whom 36 per cent are under 16 (NCH Action for Children, 1996, pp. 24–5). Table 7.1 shows the proportion of children under 16 belonging to each of the major ethnic groups. It can be seen that Pakistani or Bangladeshi families contain a particularly high proportion (45 per cent) of dependent children. This compares with 29 per cent for black and 21 per cent for white households.

Mean size of household also varies considerably between ethnic groups. As Table 7.2 shows, the mean size of households headed by someone of Pakistani or Bangladeshi origin is larger than in Indian households and twice that of white-headed households.

The incomes of some ethnic minority groups fall far below the national average and much of their population live in deprived areas. Black people in Britain experience disadvantage and deprivation through racism and

Table 7.1 *Children under 16 by ethnic group (per cent)*

Ethnic group	Per cent
White	21
Indian	30
Pakistani/Bangladeshi	45
Black	29
Remaining groups	42
All ethnic minorities	36
All	22

Source: NCH Action For Children (1996), p. 28.

Table 7.2 *Average household size by ethnic group of head of household*

Ethnic group	Number of persons
White	2.40
Indian	3.63
Pakistani/Bangladeshi	4.76
Black	2.59
Remaining groups	2.64
All ethnic minorities	3.22
All	2.44

Source: NCH Action For Children (1996), p. 27.

discrimination that permeate many areas of life. They are more likely than white people to be unemployed or low paid; their housing is likely to be overcrowded and lacking amenities. Access to public services, even access to schools in some areas, is more difficult for them. Infant mortality is much higher in certain ethnic groups than in the rest of the population, and some ethnic groups have their own special health problems such as sickle-cell anaemia and thalassaemia (Bradshaw, 1990).

In addition, disproportionate numbers of black children are looked after by local authorities, with less chance than white children of being reunited with their parents, and disproportionate numbers of black adolescents are in custodial establishments (Ahmed, 1994).

Traveller children

According to Dalrymple and Burke (1995, p. 110), the level of discrimination faced by travellers is so severe that 'they face insecurity and harsh living conditions and are denied access to social, educational and health services'. The Northern Gypsy Council views this as a consequence of 'the criminalisation of Gypsies through institutionalised racism'. Prior to the Children Act, travellers' contact with Social Services led to children being separated from their families and culture through the care system. The 1989 Act, however, 'offers the opportunity for practitioners to consider the context of the lives of travellers and to work with them from an anti-oppressive perspective to promote change and lessen the inequalities of their lives' (Dalrymple and Burke, 1995, p. 110).

Children with disabilities

Children with disabilities form another major group of children subjected to discrimination. The World Health Organisation defines disability as a restriction or lack of ability to perform normal activities, resulting from an impairment to the structure or function of the body or mind (NCH Action for Children, 1996).

In the UK, the notion of social justice for people with disabilities has gained ground over recent years. In large part this reflects the growing influence of the Disability Rights Movement, which is increasingly led by disabled people themselves. Although it does not by any means go as far as many would have liked, NCH Action for Children views the Disability Discrimination Act 1995 as an important milestone in the recognition of rights for disabled people. Most of the provisions impact on adults, but those to improve access to transport and buildings will also benefit children. In addition, the Carers (Recognition and Services) Act 1995 gives carers the right to ask social services for an individual assessment of the caregiver's needs and their willingness and ability to continue providing care. The intention is that carers' needs should be recognised and that carers are not left to cope alone in very difficult and demanding circumstances. 'Carers' include those caring for a child with disabilities, and young people under 18 who provide care on a regular basis (NCH Action for Children, 1996).

Nevertheless, battles remain to be fought to ensure that the public resources required to make reality out of public rhetoric are forthcoming. While the inclusion of children with disabilities as 'children in need' under the Children Act may have helped to stimulate better provision, it is clear that service remains patchy and that families still routinely have to fight for help (Department of Health, 1994). Moreover, many disabled children are denied the educational services which are appropriate to their needs (NCH Action for Children, 1996). Ruxton (1996, pp. 10–11) reports that such children face 'considerable discrimination in all European Societies....[This includes] ... lack of access to buildings, transport, health and social care, restrictive opportunities in relation to education, training and work, and stigma and abuse.'

Remarkably, Ruxton (1996) reports that it is not known how many disabled children there are in the EU population. The NCH Action for Children *Factfile 1996/97* reports that there are some 365,500 disabled children in the UK, which represents about 3 per cent of the population of children under the age of 16. Boys are more likely than girls to have a disability, and the most common form is a behavioural disability. Children over five are more likely than children under five to have a disability; this may in part be due to the identification of disabilities once a child starts school. Most children with disabilities are able to live in their communities; it was estimated that only 1.5 per cent were living in communal establishments.

Several studies have highlighted some of the problems and issues confronting children with disabilities and their families. These include a national survey carried out by the Social Policy Research Unit of over 1,000 parents (Beresford, 1995). The survey explored the needs and circumstances of families caring for a severely disabled child. It found that severely disabled children of all ages are highly dependent on their parents to meet their basic care needs; older disabled children are likely to have social, communication and behavioural difficulties. One in two of the children studied were dependent on medical equipment. On average, household incomes are lower among families of children with disabilities; 90 per cent of lone parents in the study and over a third of two-parent families had no income other than benefits. Four out of ten of the families lived in unsuitable housing. Only half of those who took part in the survey described their relationships with professionals as positive and supportive. For parents, the most common unmet needs were for financial resources, help in planning for the child's future, and knowledge about available services. For the children, the most common unmet needs concerned their physical needs, learning skills, and someone to discuss their problems with. Families from ethnic minority groups, lone parents, and those caring for the most severely impaired children had particularly high levels of unmet need. They also tended to live in the poorest circumstances.

Children and HIV/AIDS

Notified cases of AIDS are increasing in all countries of the European Union. Annual rates of new cases are highest in France, Italy and Spain. At the end of 1994, the total number of AIDS cases diagnosed for the whole EU exceeded 120,000. Yet, because of the long incubation period, these figures reflect only a small part of the problem. Moreover, an estimated 560,000 people have been infected with HIV in the World Health Organisation European Region (which includes the EU and Central and Eastern Europe), 58,808 of whom have died (Ruxton, 1996).

By January 1996, there were 455 reports of HIV infection in children aged 14 or under in the United Kingdom. Some 94 per cent of these children were born to mothers infected with HIV, the majority of whom (75 per cent) were living in the Thames region of England. It has been estimated that, since 1979, a minimum of 857 children have been born to mothers with HIV infection, of whom 188 have developed AIDS (NCH Action for Children, 1996).

Roughly 85 per cent of children infected with HIV or AIDS have acquired the virus through vertical transmission from mother to child. It has been estimated that in around one in seven cases, transmission is from mother to baby during pregnancy. Some older children have been infected through blood products, others through unprotected sex and/or the sharing of needles for injected drugs. There are also children who are not HIV positive, but live with family members who are infected (Ruxton, 1996).

Current policy and practice focuses on, first, the need to provide family-based rather than institutional care; secondly, developing a child-centred approach that recognises children's rights in relation to future care and treatment, and the right to attend school without disclosure of their HIV status. In addition, preventative measures in schools attempt to dispel myths and educate teachers, pupils and parents. Efforts are also being made to ensure that HIV prevention is a key part of health-education programmes (Ruxton, 1996).

Children and drugs

Illegal drugs are a growing problem across Europe. As many as 1 million people are estimated to use illegal drugs in the European Union. Seizures of heroin in the EU increased from 1.9 tonnes in 1987 to 5.2 tonnes in 1992, with cocaine seizures rising from 3.5 to 17 tonnes (Ruxton, 1996). Over a ten-year period from 1984 to 1994, the number of drug seizures in the United Kingdom rose from 28,560 to 108,000. Cannabis was involved in the majority of such seizures, accounting for 82 per cent in 1994 (NCH Action for Children, 1996). Alongside established drugs such as cannabis and amphetamines, there has been a recent rise in the use of Ecstasy and LSD in Britain.

Crime, including burglary and prostitution, may be a means to meet the cost of addiction. For example, Ruxton (1996) reported that property crime in Amsterdam was two or three times higher than in cities which did not share the increase in problematic opiate users. In Italy, there has been a significant increase in the numbers committed to institutions for drug-related offences. In cities such as Palermo and Naples, many children and their families are deeply embroiled in the drugs trade.

There is a paucity of reliable data on drug misuse by children. In part, this is because drug research among children frequently depends on self-reporting with all its associated problems. Despite such difficulties with data-collection methods, we do have some idea about drug misuse in children and young people in the United Kingdom. Current patterns of drug misuse in children include the use of a wide range of drugs in the younger age group, the narrowing of the gender gap, the emergence of polydrug use (the use of more than one drug at the same time) as the norm, and a decrease in the age of initiation.

In 1994, around 2 per cent of school pupils aged 11 to 12 reported taking illegal drugs or misusing solvents. The figure increases with age to 6 per cent of 12–13-year-olds, 13 per cent of 13–14-year-olds, 25 per cent of

14–15-year-olds, and 33 per cent of youngsters aged 15–16 years (NCH Action For Children, 1996).

An international comparative study appears to show that England and Wales have relatively more drug use among young people than the Netherlands, Spain and Portugal. Around one in four young people aged 14–21 in England and Wales admitted taking and/or selling drugs (Junger-Tas et al., 1994). The campaign to legalise cannabis in the UK, in line with the more liberal approach adopted in the Netherlands, has failed to find favour with any of the major political parties.

The rise in the use of illegal drugs such as cannabis, amphetamines, opiates, cocaine, and hallucinogens has been paralleled by an increase in volatile-substance abuse (VSA). 'Glue-sniffing' became popular among some young people in the mid-1970s. Since then, there has been a rise in the number of different substances inhaled to produce a 'high'. These include glues, gas-fuels, aerosols and other volatile substances. Estimates of the numbers of those involved in VSA vary between 3 per cent and 11 per cent. Between 1971 and 1993, some 921 young people died as a result of VSA (NCH Action For Children, 1996).

Teenage parents

The fertility rate among women under 20 in the United Kingdom has increased slightly over the 1990s, whereas in other European countries it has fallen. Indeed, the UK has the highest fertility rate among young women in the EU, followed by Austria, Portugal and Greece. In 1992, some 3 per cent of all 15–19-year-olds in the UK gave birth, which was five times as many as in the Netherlands (Ruxton, 1996).

The main factors contributing to the low birth rate among young women in the Netherlands are cultural openness about sexuality, successful campaigns in the popular media, widespread sex education, free contraceptive services and contraceptives, and easy access to confidential family-planning services, all of which have been underpinned by strong government support. This approach has not led to earlier sexual activity, as evidenced by the fact that the median age at first experience of intercourse is 17 in both the UK and the Netherlands. Rather, the difference between the two countries in pregnancy rates for 15–19-year-olds seems to reflect that in the Netherlands sex education is more effective and social attitudes are more open towards sexual behaviour than in the UK (Ruxton, 1996). An additional factor may be that services, such as housing, provided in the UK to single mothers with children, make pregnancy attractive to young women who see no other way to access desired services.

Runaway and homeless young people

Although homelessness among young people became a prominent issue for child-welfare agencies during the 1980s and 1990s, there is no reliable comparative data on the numbers affected across the EU. However, it seems that the problem is increasing both in the poorer regions of southern states such as Italy and Portugal, and in the large cities of northern states such as Germany and the UK (Ruxton, 1996).

In the absence of official statistics, our understanding of youth homelessness in the UK is based on research undertaken by voluntary agencies and academics. This research was summarised by NCH Action for Children (1996), who found that in 1994, it was estimated that there were over 100,000 single homeless people aged 16–24. Also, over 2,000 young people, some as young as nine, called Childline in 1994/5 because they had nowhere to stay: 34 per cent had fled from sexual or physical abuse and 33 per cent had been thrown out by their parents; 8 per cent of youngsters who rang Childline in one month because they had nowhere to stay had fled from foster or residential care. Many had done so to escape violence and bullying. Giddens (1989) reports that many runaway children turn to prostitution to live.

As mentioned earlier, local authorities in England and Wales have a duty under the Children Act 1989 to provide appropriate services for 'children in need'. Whilst the 1989 Act offers no definition as to who should be considered as children in need, campaigners against homelessness argue that homeless 16- and 17-year-olds are children in need and, as such, should be entitled to housing. However, research shows that social services departments are generally failing to fully implement the 1989 Act for homeless 16- and 17-year-olds, owing, in large part, to a lack of the requisite financial resources (NCH Action for Children, 1996).

Young lesbians and gay men

Recent years have seen the growth of knowledge about issues relating to sexuality and social work. The impetus for this has been twofold: first, recognition that sexuality is a defining characteristic for any person and, as such, has significance for social-work practice; secondly, the raising of the profile of child protection, particularly the 'discovery' of the sexual abuse of children both within families and in the care system itself (Lloyd, 1997).

In addition, there is increasing awareness of the difficulties faced by young lesbians and gay men looked after by social care agencies. Dalrymple and Burke (1995, p. 111) note that the reality of life for such young people is that it is thought that:

- being lesbian or gay is wrong and they should be referred for treatment;
- they have to prove that they are 'really gay';
- those adults who are sympathetic find it difficult to support young lesbian or gay people as they are afraid of being labelled themselves.

Although the problem is most acute in faith-based voluntary agencies, both statutory and voluntary societies have so far failed to address the problem. Dalrymple and Burke (1995) argue that the task of service providers is hindered by discriminatory legislation. However, the guidance accompanying the Children Act 1989 does recognise that 'gay young men and women may require very sympathetic carers to enable them to accept their sexuality and to develop their own self esteem' (Department of Health, 1991c, para. 9.53). Dalrymple and Burke (1995, p. 111) consider that practitioners and carers must make use of such positive elements of legislation to combat discrimination against young lesbians and gay men. They must 'discuss sexuality with young people, ensure that their wishes and feelings are heard and that decisions are made in their best interests'.

Anti-discriminatory and anti-oppressive practice with looked-after children

In contemplating current challenges in looking after children, the ongoing struggle to forge anti-discriminatory and anti-oppressive approaches to practice should be high on everybody's list. Ahmed (1994) acknowledges that the Children Act 1989 marked a significant political shift in child-care legislation in that Section 22(5) places a new duty on local authorities to give due consideration to three important factors: a child's race, ethnic and linguistic background. A fourth factor, religion, had been part of child-care law for many years. However, Ahmed (1994, pp. 123–4) argues that the multiculturalism which underpins Section 22(5) of the 1989 Act presents the following three 'theoretical and practice challenges which have to be confronted'. First, multiculturalism lacks a power analysis; other cultures are seen as valuable and interesting but, crucially, racism is either ignored or minimised as the personal prejudices of an ignorant, misguided and intolerant few. Secondly, multiculturalism has been 'perverted by the arguments of the new right into a new form of racism, by converting cultural diversity into a deterministic theory of race'. Thirdly, it defines minority ethnic groups as being internally unified homogeneous entities with no class or gender differences or conflicts. Thus, it has done a disservice to black women's interests because black women must often deal with a number of factors: for example, to counter the traditionalism which often lowers their status, they must deal with traditionalists within black communities as well as the racism of the dominant group, which permeates all spectrums of British society, Right and Left.

A central issue of concern for anti-racist social work is the number of black children in care. In their large-scale survey of over 9,000 placement starts and endings in six authorities, Rowe et al. (1989) found children of colour were over-represented in admissions to care; but the extent to which this occurred varied considerably between black and ethnic minority groups. For example, Asian children were under-represented in all age groups. By contrast, African and Afro-Caribbean children were over-represented. This applied with particular force in relation to the pre-school and 5 to 10 age groups, where admission rates were more than double those of white children. Yet the most striking finding on the numbers of black and ethnic minority children looked after by local authorities concerns children of mixed racial parentage. Bebbington and Miles (1989) estimated that such children were two and a half times as likely to be looked after than white children. They found a very high admission rate for children of mixed parentage in all age groups, but particularly among pre-schoolers. The latter were also the most likely to have multiple admissions.

However, it should be noted that other research studies cited in *Patterns and Outcomes* have found black boys are less likely to be fostered than whites. Studies also found that being of mixed parentage is more likely to be associated with placement breakdown (Department of Health, 1991d). In other European countries, it has been reported that one in ten children in residential care in Germany are 'foreign', and that the figure for the Netherlands is around 20 per cent (Ruxton, 1996).

Patterns and Outcomes also highlighted the need for ethnic record keeping:

> If departments do not even know how many children from black and minority ethnic groups they are looking after, or their cultural and linguistic background, it is most unlikely that they will be able to provide appropriately for them. ... There are still no national and few local authority figures on ethnicity. (Department of Health, 1991d, p. 14)

Ahmed (1986, p. 100) acknowledges that establishing systems of 'record keeping that includes ethnic origins of the clients arouses misgivings and confusion in many people'. However, he argues that such systems are essential because

> guesswork needs to be replaced with more reliable data. These data are needed to formulate policies that reflect equal opportunities for all

groups regardless of their ethnic origins. Data are also needed to monitor the implementation of equal opportunities policies.

Patterns and Outcomes laments that none of the research studies summarised 'offers data on the dominant issue of whether children must always be placed with families of the same racial background' (Department of Health, 1991d, p. 14). The question of same-race placements has also been prominent with regard to residential care. Coombe (1986) looks at how the special needs of black children could be met within a white establishment, but notes that discussion is required as to where and by whom their needs are best met. It is the belief of many in the black community that black children are best catered for by their own communities. Coombe (1986, p. 147) further argues that:

> It is imperative that social workers, when working with black clients, take note of the position in which black people find themselves. In a society where they are treated as second-class citizens, black youngsters more than ever need the support of their parents and peers. The personal conflict a black child may have about being in a white-run establishment or foster home is often denied; but such children need help to come to terms with their position, and this area of work needs to be developed.

Some progress has been made in recruiting black foster parents and residential staff during the 1990s. However, greater commitment to such recruitment efforts is required across the European Union. A survey of European organisations by the European Forum for Child Welfare in 1993 showed that relatively few children from ethnic minority groups are placed in families of the same ethnic origin. This is despite the fact that in some countries such children constitute the largest part of those entering the care system (Gambe et al., 1992; Ruxton, 1996).

Ruxton (1996, p. 343) calls for research to be undertaken in all member states of the European Union into the extent of, and reasons for, 'differential rates of admission to care from different minority ethnic groups'. He further suggests that 'residential and foster care staff should be deliberately recruited from all ethnic and religious groups represented within the [EU] and training be provided on the implications of a child's cultural background for planning and provision of services'.

More recently, Owusu-Bempah (1997, pp. 50–5) questions programmes designed to improve the self-identity of black children in care. It is argued, somewhat controversially that such programmes are inherently racist and characterised as 'sheer victim blaming'. It is ironic that some advocate them as 'a necessary anti-racist strategy for social work'. Owusu-Bempah accepts that 'black social service users suffer discrimination on the grounds of "race"', but argues that racism damages black children's life chances rather than their self-worth. Whilst acknowledging that this 'is likely to affect their psychological functioning', the author argues that 'our efforts should be directed towards improving [black] children's life chances rather than their self-concept'.

If nothing else, this is sufficient to indicate that, as with most areas of theory and practice, anti-racist social work is a contested perspective.

Children's rights

We have examined aspects of childhood that might make children and their families vulnerable to discrimination, but we have not yet considered the extent to which children face discrimination simply by virtue of being young. In recent years much greater emphasis has been placed on the rights of children. A watershed decision in children's rights in the UK was the well-known Gillick case (*Gillick* v. *West Norfolk AHA* [1985] All ER 402). As a result of a challenge by a mother (Victoria Gillick) of her child's hypothetical ability to seek medical treatment without parental consent, the case went ultimately to the House of Lords, the highest appeal court in Britain. Although specifically about the issue of doctors prescribing contraception to under-16-year-olds without parental consent, the judgment had profound implications for consent to treatment more generally and for children's rights in relation to their parents. As a result of the judgment, several principles were firmly established. For example, Lord Fraser observed that it was not realistic to consider that a child or young person 'remains in fact under the complete control of his parents until he attains the definite age of majority, now 18 in the United Kingdom, and that on attaining that age he suddenly acquires independence'. He noted as well that the child's understanding and intelligence were important considerations. Lord Scarman noted that

> parental rights are derived from parental duty and exist only so long as they are needed for the protection of the person and property of the child. ... The underlying principle of the law ... is that parental right yields to the child's right to make his own decisions when he reaches a sufficient understanding and intelligence to be capable of making up his own mind on the matter requiring decision.

Lord Denning described the rights of parents in relation to their children as a 'dwindling right', which 'starts with a right of control and ends with little more than advice'. These principles played an important role in the thinking behind the Children Act 1989.

Hendrick (1994, p. 283) observes that the question of 'family regulation in the liberal state only occasionally attends to children's rights *within* the family'. He argues that Parliament's decision to shift child-care legislation towards 'the family' endangers children's rights because it removes the child from the centre of child-protection policy and places it within a rather spurious domesticity. We have seen a similar shifting of focus in the education reforms, where views of the parents as consumers of the service, with increased rights of choice, and access to information about school performances ('league tables'), were taken on board as part of the political ideology. In the debates, however, there was little consideration given to the children and young people as the ultimate consumers of the education service provided. Whether of Left or Right, family-autonomy theorists of the 1980s reformulated children's rights in terms of a parental right to freedom from state supervision, based on the view that children have a right to develop and maintain unrestricted psychological ties with their parents. This is more a political theory about the correct relationship between families and the state rather than a genuine theory of children's rights. Hendrick (1994) quotes Dingwall and Eekelaar, who argue that it is impossible to 'escape from the fact that the recognition of children's interests necessarily entails the abridgement of family autonomy'. Hendrick concludes that because the 1989 Act 'rarely falls in this direction, it has little interest in furthering children's rights'.

Eekelaar and Dingwall (1990, p. 23) report that the official documents leading up to the 1989 Act said little about children's rights, despite the fact that this was a major issue among those seeking reform. The concept of children's rights was used in two ways. First, it connoted 'a general aspiration to improve the conditions of children not just in this country but throughout the world'. This aspiration is reflected in the movement that resulted in the United Nations Convention on the Rights of the Child 1989 (see Franklin, 1995; Ruxton, 1996; Newell, 1991). The UN Convention and European Charter on children's rights catalogue entitlements that represent political programmes expressing certain ideals of social justice.

The second, narrower, interpretation of the concept of children's rights distinguished by Eekelaar and Dingwall (1990, p. 23) concerns the degree to which children are recognised as having some degree of personal autonomy. For example, 'How far can a child resist a course of action that an adult (usually a parent) wishes to impose, and determine for him or herself what should happen?' According to Eekelaar and Dingwall (1990, p. 23), the 1989 Act virtually ignores such questions. To be sure, it does state that, in certain contexts, courts or welfare agencies must consider the wishes and feelings of the children concerned. Further, special provisions have been enacted allowing children 'in some circumstances to refuse to undergo medical examination'. Aside from that, however, it would appear that the decision-makers' views will usually outweigh those of the child if there is a disagreement.

Lyon and Parton (1995, p. 53) acknowledge that the 1989 Act does seem to take children's rights more seriously than previous legislation, and provides 'new opportunities for advancing the wishes, autonomy and independent actions of children and young people'. However, they argue that the Act does this in a very qualified way. The Act is highly legalistic both in the way it is framed and in the way mechanisms for addressing the central balances are operationalised. In addition, developments and legal cases since the Act came into force in October 1991 show how this is played out in practice:

> The articulation of children's rights, rather than constituting children and young persons as subjects has provided a new set of strategies and mechanisms for using the voices of children as elements in the newly constituted government of families. Rather than subjects in their own right, children have become reconstituted as legal – as opposed to welfare – objects for the purpose of governing families at a distance.
>
> (Lyon and Parton, 1995, p. 53)

The UN Convention on the Rights of the Child was formally adopted in November 1989 and has been ratified by 186 countries. By ratifying, a government signifies its intention to comply with the provisions in the Convention, and must make regular reports on its progress towards implementation to the UN Committee on the Rights of the Child. All member states of the European Union have ratified the Convention. Thus, the Convention forms a common framework of commitment to children's rights which can and should underpin the development of law, policy and practice throughout EU states.

The Convention makes it clear that children should no longer be viewed as the property of their parents, nor as objects of concern to be seen but not heard. Under the Convention, the 'best interests' of the child should be a primary consideration in all legislation and policy concerning children. The Convention sets minimum standards regarding children's civil, political, economic, social and cultural rights. These standards can be grouped into the following three major categories:

1. **Provision** – children's rights to minimum standards of health, education, social security, physical care, family life, play, recreation, culture and leisure, and adequate standards of living.

2. **Protection** – children's rights to be safe from discrimination, physical abuse, exploitation, substance abuse, injustice, and conflict.
3. **Participation** – children's rights to a name and identity, to be consulted and taken account of, to access to information, to freedom of speech and opinion, and to challenge decisions made on their behalf.

Key articles of the UN Convention include rights to freedom from discrimination (Article 2), to express views freely on all matters affecting the child (Article 12), to freedom of expression (Article 13), thought (Article 14) and association (Article 15).

Ruxton (1996, p. 22) considers that the Convention is 'a highly significant document in that it provides a comprehensive framework within which to examine the impact of all legislation, policy and practice relating to children's rights'. However, he adds that a 'key challenge for the UN Committee is ... to establish clear interpretations of each of the articles in the Convention so that legislation and policy develop coherently'.

The European Union Charter on the Rights of the Child 1990 seeks to promote the adoption of the UN Convention in a way that is appropriate to Europe's legal, economic and demographic situation (see Ruxton, 1996). In January 1996, the Council of Europe's Parliamentary Assembly adopted a Strategy for Children 1996, which advocates measures to make children's rights a political priority in member states of the Council of Europe.

In practice, it seems that greater attempts have been made in Scandinavia than in other parts of the EU, including not least the United Kingdom, to address children's rights. However, the appointment of a Children's Commissioner for Wales, an action so far resisted in England, is likely to be a major step forward in the development of children's rights. Ruxton (1996, p. 18) argues that to meet the challenges of today's Europe – which include the single market and the removal of border controls – there needs to be 'competence' on children at the level of the European Union. This would accord the lives of children greater priority by allowing for improved information collecting about their circumstances, and wider consideration of the legislation, policies and practices that affect their lives. As a result, action could be taken based on the framework recommended in the Council of Europe's Strategy for Children. Thus, the rights and interests of children could be effectively represented throughout Europe in line with the UN Convention on the Rights of the Child.

The UN Convention on the Rights of the Child attempts to address the problem of discrimination against children simply on the grounds that they are young. In this chapter we have also looked at some specific groups of children who suffer from discrimination and oppression: black children; traveller children; children with disabilities; children who live with HIV/AIDS; children who misuse drugs or whose families are involved in the drug trade; teenage parents; runaway and homeless children; and lesbian and gay children. We have seen that anti-racist social work is strewn about with thorns: interventions intended to be helpful such as trying to raise the self-esteem of black children may be seen as a denial of the reality that if black children were not discriminated against, their self-esteem would not be low. It is sometimes difficult for social workers trying to improve the lot of individual children and families to keep in mind that discrimination against the individual occurs in the context of institutionalised oppression. Power differences in society – the fuel driving the engine of oppression – occur because some groups of people are valued more highly than others: whites over blacks, men over women, heterosexuals over homosexuals, and so forth. Social workers cannot change this – or not immediately at any rate – but they can be aware of it, they can examine their own values in the light of it, and they can view their clients in a social context which includes organised oppression.

Now that we have examined some of the issues relating to discrimination and oppression and seen how those issues affect looked-after children, the next, and last, chapter will consider some final thoughts.

Case examples

Case example 7.1   Rifat's story

Rifat is the 32-year-old mother of three children: Amina (12), Ahmed (10) and Rashid (8). She is Muslim and her family originated from Pakistan. She was born in Britain, and grew up in a relatively well-to-do part of Cardiff. When she was 13 she was sent back to Pakistan in order for her adolescence not to be undermined by Western living, and a marriage was subsequently arranged. Although academically able, she was consequently not able to extend her education into secondary schooling. She and her husband returned to Cardiff before the birth of her first child. Soon after the birth, he began to be violent towards her. She never told anyone, either within the community (because of the stigma she felt she would attract) or outside the community, because she was afraid the children would be removed from her.

When her husband began to turn his aggression towards the youngest child, Rashid, she decided to leave him. Despite considerable community and family pressure to return to her husband, she maintained her separation. Because of an injury inflicted on Rashid, which was observed at school, a child-protection conference was arranged. Between the time of the injury being reported, and the conference, the mother had left the family home, taking the three children with her.

Questions

1. Consider how racism may contribute to the difficulties being faced by the family at the point of referral to the social services department.

2. Consider how racist assumptions and/or practices may underlie an assessment of the family.

3. How can the social worker integrate anti-discriminatory practice into her intervention? Be specific. Consider what barriers or obstacles there might be.

Case example 7.2 Sharon's story

Sharon Jones (25), originally from the Welsh valleys, lives in Swansea with her husband Lee, and their two sons, Tyrone (20 months) and Kyle (10 months). It is a 'traditional' marriage; Lee controls the family finances, and gives Sharon some money every week to buy the food. She considers the amount insufficient, but he says that she needs to manage it better. He works in a furniture warehouse. He provides virtually no support to Sharon with the care of the children. He will not get up when Kyle is having a disturbed night, as he maintains he needs his sleep because of his work. Kyle had severe colic during his first thirteen weeks, and with the older child also making demands, Sharon felt almost unable to cope. Lee considers that she was making too much of it. On Saturdays Lee spends the whole of the day in the betting shop, and on Sunday he is in the pub until dinner. He takes little interest in how the children are developing. He expects Sharon to keep them quiet in the evenings so that his television viewing is not disturbed.

At a routine developmental check, Sharon raised her concern with the health visitor that Tyrone had an unusual gait ever since he had broken his leg and was admitted to hospital some months previously. She maintained that he had fallen from an armchair. The health visitor was also concerned about Kyle, whose pattern of weight gain and loss since birth, fluctuating at or below the third centile, suggested 'failure to thrive'. The health visitor referred both children to the paediatrician, who ascertained that Tyrone had a healed spiral fracture of the femur (causing his unusual gait). Because of the nature of the injury, both children were referred to the social services with a suggestion that a child-protection conference be convened.

Questions

1. Consider how the operation of sexism may contribute to Sharon's difficulties up until, and including, the point of referral to the social services department.
2. Consider how sexist assumptions may underlie an assessment of the family.
3. How can the social worker integrate anti-discriminatory practice into her intervention? Be specific. Consider what barriers or obstacles there might be.

Case example 7.3   Lorna's story

Lorna (14) is the last of three children born to Mr and Mrs Wates. Her older brother (Tim, 20) and sister Jane (19) have since left the home and live locally. Tim is working (as a trainee manager for a local supermarket) and Jane is at university studying psychology. Mr Wates left the family eight years ago when Lorna was 6 years old and emigrated to Canada, having virtually no contact with the three children other than cards at Christmas and birthdays. The divorce was finalised four years ago. A year after the divorce, Mrs Wates met Mr Hunt, and after a period of six months they were married. He moved in to live with Mrs Wates and the two girls. Tim was already living away from home.

Lorna was born with a congenital hearing difficulty (resulting in a severe degree of hearing impairment) and attends a special school for deaf pupils. It is a boarding school and she attends as a weekly boarder, coming home every weekend and during holidays. The school originally had a policy of teaching lip-reading, but recently began teaching Sign Supported English. Lorna has become quite proficient using it.

After a year of consultations and hospital outpatient appointments, Mrs Wates has been diagnosed as having multiple sclerosis. This has placed a great strain on the couple and on the family, but they are beginning to adjust to it.

Recently, as a school holiday period approached, Lorna confided in a school teacher that her stepfather had been doing things to her that she did not like, which to the teacher sounded sexual in nature. Lorna indicated that she had tried to tell people before, but either they did not understand or they did not believe her; she was not sure which. The teacher did not probe further, but referred the matter to the head, and the head referred it to social services. Arrangements were made for Lorna to go and stay with her grandmother during the school holiday period, whilst the matter was investigated further.

Questions

1. Consider how the operation of 'disablism' might influence the events leading up to the referral, either in relation to information above or more generally.
2. Consider the practical difficulties the social worker might encounter in undertaking a child-protection investigation.

Final thoughts

In the first chapter of this book, we looked at the origins and key elements of the Children Act 1989. We learned that the Act gives paramount consideration to the rights of children to be protected against abuse and to be brought up in a safe environment where their physical, psychological, social, spiritual and cultural needs can be met. Parents have responsibilities rather than rights: indeed, their major right under the Act is to be given assistance by the local authority to meet the needs of their children. Similarly, local authorities have a responsibility to facilitate parents bringing up their children, according to the philosophy that children are best looked after within the family. The local authority has the right to intervene with the family only in so far as is necessary to safeguard the welfare of the child, and even then the authority has a duty to enhance and support parental responsibility as far as possible.

This sounds appropriately child-centred. However, in practice, the emphasis still seems to be very much on child protection (protecting the child from abuse) rather than on family support (enhancing the child's welfare in a family context). Despite the fact that support for vulnerable families lies at the core of the Act, it is evident that much more work remains to be done to create an effective system of family support in England and Wales. Insufficient resources are devoted to the kind of preventive work with families that would avert the need for more serious and more costly interventions.

The pressures on vulnerable families have significantly increased over the last two decades. During that period, the extent of child poverty was allowed to increase threefold, despite the fact that it is a key factor precipitating crises within families. We have discussed poverty at some length in this book, noting that a proactive approach to child welfare is undermined in a society where there is an increasing gap between rich and poor. Poverty exists not just at an individual level but also across communities and entire regions. Many poor areas include large numbers of people from ethnic minority communities for whom the barriers of racism preclude an adequate education and well-paid work. Other communities have been marginalised because the industries that provided them with employment have been relocated, cut in size, or closed. In the valleys of South Wales, for example, many young people depend on income support as their parents did before them. They have no work, few prospects, minimal education, and a great deal of 'leisure' time. Thus, it is hardly surprising that some of them smash things, assault each other; and bear children whose prospects are not much better and whose involvement with child-welfare agencies tends to be high.

Those who leave in search of work may then find themselves cut off from the support systems of family, friends and familiar neighbours, and thus obliged to try to bring up their children essentially alone. Increasingly, the network of extended family is too far flung to be of any practical assistance in the day-to-day tasks of child rearing and household management. As we learned in Chapter 1, there has been a dramatic rise in the proportion of lone-parent households over the last 30 years. More women (many of whom are lone parents) are working and in need of affordable, good quality child care. They are also often in need of emotional and practical support, which they will probably not get from their communities because the type of close-knit community where neighbours routinely support each is other fast disappearing. Overburdened and unsupported parents are among those most often seen on child-welfare caseloads.

As we have seen, the Children Act 1989 substantially enlarged local authorities' duties towards children in need and their families, but the necessary corresponding increase in resources was not provided. An effective family-support system requires a comprehensive approach embracing primary, secondary and tertiary prevention. With regard to the first of these, there is no substitute for action on the part of central government to combat social exclusion. Equally, action by government is essential to ensure that social-welfare personnel have the attitudes, skills and resources to enable them to carry out their duties in relation to the second and third levels of prevention. The organisation, structure and delivery of services must be conducive to the full implementation of Part III of the Children Act. Policy and practice must reflect the provisions contained in the Act, and the linguistic, cultural and ethnic diversity of England and Wales.

The current emphasis on protection on the part of local authorities owes a good deal to the fact that local authorities have been obliged to prioritise against a background of severe resource constraint, coupled with relentless, and often unfair, criticism in relation to child-abuse tragedies. From the point of view of individual social workers, the fact that they adopt a reactive rather than a proactive approach may be related to the increasing number and complexity of their cases. The natural response of an overburdened worker is to deal reactively with the crises first (child protection) rather than proactively working with other families to prevent their crises from occurring (family support). Whatever the cause, studies (Gibbons et al., 1995; Farmer and Owen, 1995) have suggested that large numbers of children in need are inappropriately drawn into the child-protection system, and even then do not receive the services they require.

In effect, local authorities are undertaking a 'social policing' role, which tends to create antagonism between child-welfare workers and the families they serve. A formidable task confronting child-welfare workers, therefore, is to find ways to reduce this discord by positively redefining their relationships with vulnerable families and communities. One way is to develop practical intervention methods that draw on the strengths of communities, and identify the social-support systems of clients or service users from the latter's own perspective. In Chapter 4, for example, we mentioned network analysis and the now seemingly forgotten Barclay Report, which urged social workers to create, stimulate and support social networks among people in the community, and proposed the establishment of a 'community social-worker' role. Child-welfare workers cannot take on the task of building networks within communities at the meso- and macro-levels, but it might be possible for them, at the micro-level, to bring together service users with similar experiences into informal support groups, to link users with volunteers who have the necessary skills to help them solve problems, or even to focus on building and strengthening the user's existing social networks.

Child-welfare workers also face significant challenges in relation to children placed away from home. Indeed, at the time of writing, provision for such children is the greatest source of concern. Extensive research undertaken in the 1980s showed that the child-care system was failing badly when judged against the outcomes for children and young people. All aspects of their development were found to be more problematic than those of children cared for by their own families or adopted at a young age.

In response, the Department of Health sponsored the development of the Looking After Children (LAC) materials (see Chapter 6), which are designed to promote good parental care by identifying the experiences, concerns and expectations of children at different ages and stages together with the likely impact of different actions. In a nutshell, they introduce ideas about outcomes in social-work practice. The LAC materials have been widely acclaimed and now appear to represent the mainstream of child-care practice. However, the Assessment and Action Records are very long: on average, they take between two and four hours to complete and range from 35 pages for a child under a year old to a 58-page document with 375 questions (Garrett, 1999) for a child over 15 years. If they are properly used, to promote dialogue and sharing of information with the child and family, the time associated with their use grows even longer. Jackson (1998) points out that the length and complexity of the Records reflect the complexity of children's lives and do not stem from a bureaucratic desire to create paperwork. And of course, dialogue and information-sharing should be part of any routine social-work interaction.

Nevertheless, research into the implementation of the materials (Bell, 1999; Jones et al., 1998) indicates that local authorities have failed to allow for the time, management and organisational requirements of filling in the forms. One might allow that the Records are a good idea, having taken into account the common arguments against the LAC materials: that they are based on and reflect white, middle-class aspirations and expectations; they reflect a Eurocentric concept of parenting; they fail to acknowledge the influence of culture, race, class and gender on child development; they fail to acknowledge economic constraints; and they represent state interference in local authority social work, resulting in the de-professionalisation of social workers, whose performance can now be more readily regulated, monitored and appraised. Given all this, it is still noteworthy that a system, which is generally accepted as fruitful, should have been launched with insufficient attention to the resources required to maintain it.

Public confidence in the care system in the United Kingdom has been profoundly shaken by numerous highly publicised controversies surrounding the abuse of children and young people, particularly those in residential institutions. A succession of official reports over a fifteen-year period chronicle how the residential-care system in all parts of the UK has failed to protect vulnerable youngsters (Colton, 2000). Most recently, the inquiry into child abuse in North Wales, chaired by Sir Ronald Waterhouse, revealed a quite shocking pattern of sexual abuse by paedophiles operating alone or in semi-organised 'rings' (House of Commons, 2000).

Wolmar (2000) argues that the abuse scandals described in the Waterhouse report are 'like the tumor which warns of a widespread cancer'. This view is supported by the fact that police forces have launched investigations into historical cases of child abuse in children's homes in every part of the country. At the time of writing, 47 of 49 mainland forces have either completed or are working on such inquiries (Wolmar, 2000).

Abuse of children and young people in residential institutions is particularly disturbing given that many such young people had already been deeply harmed prior to being placed away from home. It is estimated that between one-third and two-thirds of children in residential care homes have been abused before entry (National Commission of Inquiry into the Prevention of Child Abuse, 1996). This includes a large proportion of young people who have been sexually abused prior to placement in residential care. Thus, it appears that rather than being afforded additional care and protection, young people removed from their families – supposedly in their 'best interest' – are frequently exposed to greater risk.

The long-standing concern about the quality of our public care system is often attributed, in large part, to the lack of appropriately qualified staff. Many local authorities have discovered that it is not easy to recruit, far less to retain, suitably trained and psychologically stalwart child-welfare workers who can manage the demands of the work without growing insensitive to the needs of clients on the one hand, or burning out from an intense response to clients' pain on the other. The recent overall decline in applications to social-work qualifying programmes suggests that decreasing numbers of people are prepared to take on the challenge of professional social work.

The dilemma is perhaps most apparent in the area of residential work. Residential child and youth work in the United Kingdom might be viewed as a poor relation. Historically, the training and salaries of residential workers have been less than those accorded other social workers. The result is that the residential child-care system in the United Kingdom is one in which young people with the most severe personal and social problems are being looked after by adults with the least experience and training in child-care matters. Young, inexperienced, isolated and untrained workers are often left to tend and work with the most problematic young people. To be sure, periodic attempts have been made to improve the training, supervision, management, selection and inspection of residential social workers, but it is clear that the scale of such efforts has been inadequate to date.

The foregoing tends to paint a very dismal picture, but there is hope on the horizon. There are signs that the welfare of vulnerable children is at long last beginning to receive something approaching the priority it deserves. The present government has, by contrast with previous administrations since 1979, demonstrated a commitment to combating social exclusion, and has introduced a range of practical measures for which it deserves credit. Moreover, following the publication of Sir William Utting's review of safeguards for children living away from home (Utting, 1997), the government introduced an initiative called 'Quality Protects'. This is a major three-year programme designed to transform the management and delivery of social services for children in England. A similar programme, entitled 'Children First', was introduced in Wales. Local authorities are required to demonstrate steady improvement in the management of services and outcomes for children and young people, including those placed away from home. The government has committed itself to a series of national objectives. These include ensuring that the life chances of children looked after by local authorities are maximised by educational opportunities, health care and social care. The 'Quality Protects' initiative is accompanied by the injection of additional financial resources to help local authorities improve the quality of child-welfare services (Department of Health, 1998, 1999).

Many consider that professional registration for social workers also represents a vital safeguard for vulnerable children and young people. It is encouraging to note, therefore, that the government – as part of its attempt to improve the regulation of the personal social services – plans to establish a General Social Care Council (GSCC). This body will be responsible for setting standards for services and for individual social workers, and for the registration of all those working in the services. Welcome developments are also taking place in relation to post-qualifying training for child-welfare workers, which are designed to enhance professional competence in relation to complex child-care cases.

However, whilst improved education and training, supervision, selection systems and registration can all contribute to raising the standards in child welfare, professionalism is not a panacea for the challenges inherent in the child-welfare system. Indeed, certain aspects of professionalism can be problematic in themselves. For example, the professional ability to make decisions in the 'best interests' of the child may override any concept of children's rights or natural justice. It is, therefore, evident that efforts to ensure a better deal for vulnerable children require an increased emphasis on children's rights. The much heralded Children Act 1989 for England and Wales did seem to take children's rights more seriously than previous legislation, and provided new opportunities for advancing the wishes, autonomy and independent actions of children and young people. Nevertheless, the Act does this in a very qualified way. A broader, more creative approach is required. As a useful first step, local authorities, voluntary and private agencies should ensure that they adhere fully to the 1989 United Nations Convention on the Rights of the Child. This recognises that children are holders of a specific body of rights, which includes participation as well as the more traditional areas of prevention, protection and provision.

The quality of provision that a community makes for its vulnerable and dependent members stands as a testimony to what that community holds dear and what it rejects. Thus, the quality of child-welfare services in England and Wales, including, it must be said, the appalling abuse suffered by children in residential care homes, and the conspicuous failure to develop proactive family-support services, ultimately mirrors deeply embedded social attitudes and associated structures of social injustice and inequality. Historically, social-work clients have been drawn from the poorest strata of society. Today, right-wing commentators cruelly refer to this social group as the 'underclass' (see Murray, 1994). In the nineteenth century, welfare provision took the form of a stigmatising, deterrent, Poor Law, predicated on a mean-spirited distinction between the 'deserving' and 'undeserving' poor (Gregg, 1973; Holman, 1988). Notwithstanding over 150 years of quite awesome social, economic, political and technological transformation, the Poor Law legacy can still be discerned in attitudes towards the dependent and powerless. With regard to children and young people placed away from home, for example, the public attitude tends toward indifference or, at best, ambivalence. Whilst people are, on the whole, sympathetic towards child victims of abuse, there is long-standing anxiety about the threat to social order represented by troubled and troublesome young people. Ambivalence is reinforced by the social class background of vulnerable children and families. Also, given the disproportionately large numbers of black children, and children with disabilities, placed away from home, ambivalence is further reinforced by factors such as racism and negative attitudes towards disability.

Given the challenges that we have highlighted, a number of rather obvious questions arise. First, why would anyone want to become a child-welfare worker? Secondly, what does it take to be a child-welfare worker? Finally, what needs to be done to ensure that we can attract and retain professionals who wish to work with children and families?

For years it has been recognised that social work with children and families is more stressful than social work with other client groups. Bennett et al. (1993) reported higher levels of job-related stress, general anxiety and depression for workers involved with children and families than for workers with other client groups. Likewise, Marshall and Barnett (1993), who looked specifically at child-protection work, found significantly greater job strain and psychological distress amongst child-protection social workers, compared with other occupational groups in both nursing and social work. Morrison (1990) explored two dimensions of the emotional impact of child-protection work on workers: the effect of clients on workers; and the response of the agency to worker distress. Morrison found that some workers react to continued exposure to clients' traumatic material by growing a sort of protective skin. They become insensitive to clients' needs because they can no longer bear to listen properly to what the client has to say. Other workers burn out and leave. Some are able to cope because they have mastered the art of self-care and have solid support systems in place for themselves both within and outside the agency. Similarly some agencies seem oblivious to the possible effects of the job on their workers: they neither take preventative measures nor provide assistance to those in distress. Other agencies facilitate peer-support systems, allow sufficient time for workers to de-brief after distressing encounters with clients, and provide counselling for workers to allow them to cope more immediately. Lack of attention to possible worker distress has obvious consequences for child-protection services: difficulty in recruiting workers (Fryer et al., 1989), difficulty in retaining them when the agency has already paid for their training, and reduced performance among workers who have 'burnt out'

(McGee, 1989) but not left. The incidence of long-term sick leave and unfilled posts in agencies tends to be high, putting additional strains on the workers who remain.

It comes as no surprise, therefore, that in recent years it has become more common to hear social-work students speaking in terms of going into child and family work for a short while, a year or two (because that's where the jobs are and because it is a good stepping stone to other work), rather than intending to specialise in child and family work over an entire career. The longer-term consequence of this trend is very worrying because, quite shortly, we will have a body of child-care social workers who are largely inexperienced, lacking the necessary skills to work with children and families, described in Chapter 3. It takes time to develop skills, and a skilled workforce requires both workers committed to children and families, and agencies committed to those workers.

So what are the rewards of working with children and families? To begin with, work with children is inherently rewarding for anyone who has an interest in children and childhood. In contact with younger children, one cannot help but be impressed by their spontaneity, their current engagement in a world of discovery, their way of seeing, which is not veiled by artificial social responses one tends to acquire with maturity. Perhaps, even, one is reminded of the best bits of one's own childhood or the pleasures of bringing up one's own children. This is essentially an approach that views childhood, not as a precursor to adulthood, but as a stage of life with a value all its own. The danger, of course, is that the worker will over-romanticise notions of childhood and see the child client through a nostalgic haze: but there is still no doubt that work with children is its own reward, bringing pleasure merely through the interaction with the child – and bringing also perhaps a determination that *this* life will be a little better because of whatever the worker can do to help.

Working with older children is more challenging but it, too, can be rewarding. Adolescence is a process of becoming, often turbulent, when the young person challenges adult values while still trying to fit into the adult world. Many adolescents coming to the attention of a child-welfare worker have been hurt in one way or another; they are frustrated and angry, and tend to reject well-meant offers of assistance because they have seen so much of the negative part of life that they have lost faith in the positive. Here is an opportunity. Here is a life on the brink that can be positively influenced by a worker who is armed not only with good intentions (remember the road to hell) but with the necessary skills developed over time. There are fascinating opportunities as well to track developments in a rapidly changing society. What is different about teenagers today compared with when you yourself were a teenager? What has changed with respect to clothes, music, preferred foods, values, attitudes, opinions and aspirations? What do these changes mean in relation to where we are going as a society? The opportunities to learn from one's teenaged clients are endless and infinitely exciting, if one will only make the effort to engage them.

The same may be said of parents. We have seen that family forms are becoming more diverse. Gender roles within families are changing. The patterns of support networks are at the same time shrinking and becoming more far-flung. Expectations about what a marriage should be, what a 'good' parent is, what a child should do and not do, how parents and children should relate to each other, how families should relate to their communities and to the larger society – all these, the entire warp and weft of our society, are in a state of flux. No one is in a better position to watch the patterns in the fabric shift than those who are in daily contact with parents and their children.

Of course, social work with families and children is not just a learning opportunity for the worker, attractive though that is, nor is it a casual social contact. It is a planned, purposeful encounter with the aim of promoting the welfare of the child, ideally through promoting the welfare of the family system. Social workers with developed skills in this area can take immense satisfaction in using those skills and watching the results of their labours come to fruition. You may be working directly with children or parents, or you may be working with other professionals towards the provision of services, but whatever your role, you will know that a skill you have learned and taken the trouble to develop has been of use in making a positive change in someone's life. That is why evaluation (or quality-assurance strategies, or evidenced-based practice, or whatever terminology we care to use) is so important. Without some indicator or measured evidence of change, this satisfaction will be denied to workers, as it may be to families in whose lives the change has occurred.

Social workers may take pleasure from the knowledge that they have been effective, but we must never forget that social work is not really about the worker's effectiveness: it is about empowering disadvantaged people and groups so that *they* can be effective, so that they can take control over making the needed changes in their own communities and their own lives. In child protection, it is easy to see the need for empowering children – unless one views rebellious teens as threats to society whose power to destroy needs to be curtailed. It is sometimes less easy to see the need for empowering abusive parents. However, destructive and abusive behaviour both often stem from a perceived lack of power, so that the individual must compensate by demonstrating whatever power he has in whatever arena is available. You might have no other power in your life but you can make yourself powerful by hitting your child or robbing a shop. Empowerment is therefore a basic element of social work and a fundamental skill for all those involved in work with families and children.

We seem to have moved from the rewards of working with children and families to the skills needed to do so. And, indeed, the question we asked after 'Why would anyone want to become a child-welfare worker?' was 'What does it take to be a child-welfare worker?' It is difficult to identify the qualities needed to be a child-welfare worker without implying that what we really need is superman, supermother, and the bionic person all rolled into one. Perhaps we do. However, let us try to identify some qualities which an ordinary person might possess or be able to develop.

The first is undoubtedly the capacity for self-care. Repeatedly, in this book, we have mentioned the need to take care of yourself and it will not hurt at all to mention it again. You must have a means of unwinding. You must have a private life and personal friends who are essentially separate from your work life and with whom you can engage in activities that are pleasurable and rewarding. Then, you must have a support system at work – people to laugh and cry with, to discuss cases with, to offer non-judgemental advice and support, people to feel safe with. Anderson (2000, p. 846) suggests:

> Child Protection Service workers have the same needs for emotional debriefing as law enforcement officers, fire fighters, Emergency Medical Service workers, emergency room personnel, and rape/crisis workers, many of whom would say that the hardest part of their job is working with maltreated or injured children. (Anderson, 2000, p. 846)

Interestingly, Anderson's recent study in the US (Anderson, 2000) found that child-protection service workers there are using social-support coping strategies less than did a similar group ten years earlier, as reported by Parry (1989). This points to the need for workers to actively seek out supportive peers, but it also points to the need for agencies to pay greater attention to the health of their workers.

A second necessary attribute for a child-welfare worker is the ability to work as a member of a team. Teamwork is often frustrating because other members of your team may have different perspectives and different priorities – particularly if they come from other disciplines – and they might seem to be holding up the work rather than facilitating it. The strategy here is probably a few deep breaths, a real effort to understand the other's point of view, and willingness to compromise.

Third comes assertiveness – which is different, of course, from aggression. Workers must often be assertive with clients when it is necessary to obtain compliance or to confront them with the consequences of their behaviours. Workers must be assertive with other professionals when advocating on behalf of a client or expressing an opinion about a case. Assertiveness may be necessary too in dealing with the worker's own agency. Sometimes the policies, practices and structures of agencies do not seem to be designed with the welfare of the client in mind, and it may take a combination of assertiveness, diplomacy and patience for any change at all to be put in hand. An example here is a request for training. Farmer and Pollock's recent book (1998) gives some vivid examples of bad practice in relation to working with looked-after sexually abused children. Some of these examples are very clearly related to the lack of staff qualifications and the lack of in-service training either sought or provided. It may seem that it is not up to the worker to seek training: it is up to the agency to determine what training is needed and to provide it. In one way, this is true enough, but on the other hand, workers are in an excellent position to know what additional knowledge and skills would help them with their task, and they have a duty to their clients to be sufficiently assertive to request the necessary training.

A fourth attribute is the capacity to work while being interrupted, and a fifth related attribute is the ability to prioritise. Child-welfare workers work on a number of cases simultaneously, with situations precipitately arising, and children and co-workers in various stages of crisis. It is necessary to be able to quickly size up situations and plan appropriately, deciding at the same time what needs to be done now, what can be left until later today, and what can wait until tomorrow or even until next week. Some people thrive naturally on this kind of supercharged activity. Others wilt. Most learn to cope after practice.

Finally, you should know your limitations! There will always be things you can do well, things you can do less well, and times when you should yell for help. It is particularly important to be self-aware in the 'yell for help' scenarios, but it is also necessary in general to be able to appraise your strengths and weaknesses objectively. The strengths can be used for your clients' benefit, the weaknesses can be remedied through training, supervision and experience – but only if you know which is which.

We come now to look at what can be done to recruit and retain staff in the area of child-care work. Broadly, there are two strategies that need to be developed. First, we must think in terms of raising the profile and status of social work as a profession. Secondly, we need to consider how to reverse the trend within social work of people viewing child-welfare practice as the first rung of the ladder towards something else.

Let us consider the status of social work as a profession first. In comparison both with other professions in the UK and with social work in other European countries, social work in the UK is in decline. Concerns about the low morale within other large groups of public-service-sector workers (teachers, nurses, and most recently the police) have brought government responses aimed at redressing the situation. With respect to teachers, the government announced policies aimed at reducing the administrative workloads of teachers, so that they could focus more of their energies on what they were trained for – teaching. With respect to nurses, the difficulty of recruiting new entrants into the occupation (seen in part as being related to the higher-level requirements introduced by the Nursing 2000 strategy) brought a swift government response – higher salary gradings for nursing staff. Most recently, measures were announced by the government to address staffing difficulties within the police service. However, despite the overall decline in applications to social work programmes in recent years, there appears to be no concerted effort on the part of the government to redress this. One might be forgiven for noting that the services of teachers, nurses and the police are used by the public in general, whereas social-work services are still largely (though not exclusively) used by the most disadvantaged sectors of society. Perhaps the degree of government attention to the respective sectors reflects the degree to which society values their users.

The engagement of social-work programmes in the ERASMUS and SOCRATES networks has provided opportunities to come together with European counterparts for the purpose of mutual learning. In comparison with social work in Europe, social work in the UK has clearly lost its therapeutic orientation over the last quarter-century. Twenty-five years ago, for example, a person qualifying as a social worker would have been assumed to be qualified as a counsellor as well. However, in recent years, counselling has become cut off from mainstream social-work practice, and given much less emphasis in training than it used to receive in the UK. In most European countries, social-work training is a three-year programme; the debate about three-year social-work training in the UK has continued for over a decade. In most European countries, working therapeutically with people in dire circumstances is an essential part of the training to become a social worker. We described the need for counselling skills in working with families and children in Chapter 3, and indeed such skills remain an important part of the child-welfare worker's repertoire. However, if one wanted to conduct therapy with people in the UK as social workers do in Europe, it would probably be necessary to think of top-up training after qualifying. The fact that social workers do not conduct therapy and are no longer adequately trained to do so certainly adds nothing to the status of the social-work profession.

The media also have a role in the way that social work is perceived by the general public. It is almost impossible to overestimate the impact that the series of inquiries into child-abuse fatalities has had on the status of social work as a profession. We can see this more clearly when we compare the British approach to child protection with that in European countries, where the vilification of professionals, by comparison, is unheard of. As described by Hetherington et al. (1997, p. 25), in a dialogue between French, Flemish, German and English social workers, for the former three, the question of child-abuse fatalities

> did not resonate with any of them in the way it does in England, because measures of serious incidents do not function as primary indicators of professional, public or political evaluations of the efficacy of their child protection systems. However, child death in the context of delivery of public child welfare services is by no means unknown or unrecognised in these countries.

So what is required to redress the balance? First, social-work practitioners must always be prepared to advocate for the profession. It is imperative in the face of the small number of cases that go disastrously wrong to remind people of the overwhelmingly large number of cases that go right. Secondly, it is important to ensure that social-work education programmes produce critically reflective practitioners whose practice is soundly based on theory and evidence from empirical research. Thirdly, it is vital to develop more positive relations with the media. This is a challenging area because social workers themselves do not speak with a single voice but have different perspectives on issues and different agendas. One thing they do seem to have in common is that they adopt a primarily defensive stance, reacting to criticism, and this is a less than helpful approach. It is important to be able to engage the media proactively on issues of common concern. For example, consider a recent article about the role of the media in the development and implementation of a national child-abuse secondary prevention programme, coming from the Netherlands (Hoefnagels and Mudde, 2000). There is no reason why similar initiatives could not be undertaken in the United Kingdom.

Let us make one final point. In order to rise to the challenges we have highlighted, it is essential that child-welfare workers maintain a clear sense of mission. Social work with children in need and their families requires those who undertake it to see their task as one of service to the cause of social justice. Hence, the child-welfare worker is so much more than a mere functionary within a welfare bureaucracy. This sense of mission is a prerequisite if we want to develop an integrated and coherent system of child welfare, characterised by pro-active, preventive, help for vulnerable children and families; if we want highly skilled, intelligently targeted protection for children at risk of abuse and neglect; and if we want competent, imaginative, child-centred care and after-care for children and young people.

Nothing that we have said concerning the challenges confronting child-welfare workers should detract from their achievements. Much important and successful work is accomplished in extremely testing circumstances. Despite the impression conveyed by an often hostile mass media, child-welfare workers invariably strive with sensitivity, integrity and courage to provide high standards of service for vulnerable children, young people and their families. Their work makes a vital contribution to the well-being of the whole society.

References

Ahmed, S. (1986), 'Ethnic Record Keeping: Questions and Answers', in V. Coombe and A. Little (eds) (1986), *Race and Social Work: A Guide to Training* (London: Tavistock).

Ahmed, S. (1994), 'Anti-racist Social Work: a Black Perspective', in C. Hanvey and T. Philpot (eds) (1994), *Practising Social Work* (London: Routledge).

Ainsworth, M., Blehar, M., Waters, E. and Wall, S. (1978), *Patterns of Attachment: A Psychological Study of the Strange Situation* (Hillsdale, NJ: Lawrence Erlbaum).

Aldgate, J. and Tunstill, J. (1995), *Making Sense of Section 17: Implementing Services for Children in Need within the 1989 Children Act* (London: HMSO).

Aldgate, J., Bradley, M. and Hawley, D. (1996), 'Respite Accommodation: a Case Study of Partnership under the Children Act 1989', in M. Hill and J. Aldgate (eds) (1996), *Child Welfare Services: Developments in Law, Policy, Practice and Research* (London: Jessica Kingsley).

Allan, G. (1997), 'Family', in M. Davies (ed.) (1997), *The Blackwell Companion to Social Work* (Oxford: Blackwell).

Anderson, D. (2000), 'Coping Strategies and Burnout among Veteran Child Protection Workers', *Child Abuse and Neglect*, 24 (6): 839–48.

Ariès, P. (1962), *Centuries of Childhood* (London: Jonathan Cape).

Ball, C. (1996), *Law for Social Workers*, 3rd edition (Aldershot: Arena).

Bandura, D. (1965), *Principles of Behaviour Modification* (New York: Holt, Rinehart and Winston).

Banyard, P. and Grayson, A. (1996), *Introducing Psychological Research: Sixty Studies that Shaped Psychology* (Basingstoke: Macmillan – now Palgrave).

Barnes, P. (1995), *Personal, Social and Emotional Development of Children* (Oxford/Milton Keynes: Blackwell/Open University).

Barrett, J. (1998), 'New Knowledge and Research in Child Development', *Child and Family Social Work*, 3 (4): 267–76.

Bebbington, A. and Miles, J. (1989), 'The Background of Children who Enter Local Authority Care', *British Journal of Social Work*, 19 (5).

Bell, M. (1999), 'The Looking After Children Materials: a Critical Analysis of their Use in Practice', *Adoption and Fostering*, 22 (4): 15–23.

Belsky, J. and Vondra, J. (1989), 'Lessons from Child Abuse: the Determinants of Parenting', chapter 6 (pp. 153–202) in D. Cicchetti and V. Carlsson (eds), *Child Maltreatment: Theory and Research on the Causes and Consequences of Child Abuse and Neglect* (Cambridge, UK: Cambridge University Press).

Bennett, P., Evans, R. and Tattersall, A. (1993), 'Stress and Coping in Social Workers: a Preliminary Investigation', *British Journal of Social Work*, 23 (1): 31–44.

Beresford, B. (1995), *Expert Opinions: A National Survey of Parents Caring for a Severely Disabled Child* (London: Social Policy Research Unit).

Bernard, L. D. (1992), 'The Dark Side of Family Preservation', *Affilia*, 7 (2): 156–9.

Berrick, J., Barth, R., and Needell, B. (1993), 'A Comparison of Kinship Foster Homes and Family Foster Homes', in R. P. Barth, J. D. Berrick and N. Gilbert (eds), *Child Welfare Research Review* (New York: Columbia University Press).

Besharov, D. J. (1985), 'Right versus Rights: the Dilemma of Child Protection', *Public Welfare*, 43 (Spring): 19–27.

Besharov, D. J. (1990), *Recognizing Child Abuse: A Guide for the Concerned* (New York: Free Press).

Birchall, E. and Hallett, C. (1995), *Working Together in Child Protection* (London: HMSO).

Blackburn, C. (1991), *Poverty and Health: Working with Families* (Milton Keynes: Open University Press).

Blackburn, C. (1993), *Improving Health and Welfare Work with Families in Poverty: A Handbook* (Milton Keynes: Open University Press).

Bowlby, J. (1952), *Maternal Care and Mental Health* (Geneva: World Health Organisation).

Bowlby, J. (1953), *Child Care and the Growth of Love* (Harmondsworth: Penguin).

Bowlby, J. (1969, 1973), *Attachment and Loss*, 2 vols (London: Hogarth Press).

Bowlby, J. (1977), 'The Making and Breaking of Affectional Bonds', *British Journal of Psychiatry*, 130: 201–10.

Bowlby, J. (1985), *Attachment and Loss*, vol. 3 (Harmondsworth: Penguin).

Bowlby, J. (1988), *A Secure Base: Clinical Applications of Attachment Theory* (London: Routledge).

Bradshaw, J. (1990), *Child Poverty and Deprivation in the UK* (York: Joseph Rowntree Report).

Bray, M. (1991), *Poppies on the Rubbish Heap – Sexual Abuse: The Child's Voice* (Edinburgh: Canongate).

Bronfenbrenner, U. (1970), *Two Worlds of Childhood* (New York: Russell Sage Foundation).

Bronfenbrenner, U. (1977), 'Towards an Experimental Ecology of Human Development', *American Psychologist*, 32: 513–31.

Bronfenbrenner, U. (1979), *The Ecology of Human Development* (Cambridge, MA: Harvard University Press).

Bronfenbrenner, U. (1986), 'Ecology of the Family as a Context for Human Development', *Developmental Psychology*, 22: 723–42.

Bronfenbrenner, U. (1989), 'Ecological Systems Theories', *Annals of Child Development*, 6: 187–249.

Brown, J. (1990), 'The Focus on Single Mothers', in C. Murray (1990), *The Emerging British Underclass* (London: Institute of Economic Affairs).

Burman, E. (1994), *Deconstructing Developmental Psychology* (London: Routledge).

Butler-Sloss, E. (1988), *Report of the Inquiry into Child Abuse in Cleveland 1987*, DHSS, Cm 412 (London: HMSO).

Candappa, M. et al. (1996), *Policy into Practice: Day Care Services for Children under Eight: An Evaluation of the Implementation of the Children Act* (executive summary) (London: HMSO).

CCETSW (1992), *Setting Quality Standards for Residential Child Care: A Practical Way Forward* (London: Central Council for Education and Training in Social Work).

CCETSW (1996), *Assuring Quality in the Diploma of Social Work – 1: Rules and Requirements for the DipSW*, second revision (London: CCETSW).

Charnock, M. (1998), 'Abuse of Children and Young People in Care', *Children's Residential Care Unit Newsletter* (London: National Children's Bureau).

Child Abuse Prevention and Treatment Act of 1974, codified as amended at 5102(1) 42 USC (Supp. 1989).

Child Poverty Action Group (1996), *Poverty: The Facts* (London: Child Poverty Action Group).

Cleaver, H. and Freeman, P. (1995), *Parental Perspectives in Cases of Suspected Child Abuse* (London: HMSO).

Cleaver, H., Wattam, C., Cawson, P. and Gordon, R. (1998), 'Children Living at Home: the Initial Child Protection Enquiry – Ten Pitfalls and How to Avoid Them', in H. Cleaver, C. Wattam and P. Cawson (1998), *Assessing Risk in Child Protection* (London: NSPCC).

Collier, F. (1996), 'Foreward', in D. Cullen (1996), *Adoption: A Service for Children – Response to the Draft Bill* (London: British Agencies for Adoption and Fostering).

Colton, M. (2000), 'Professionalization and Residential Child and Youth Care in the United Kingdom', *International Journal of Child and Family Welfare* (forthcoming).

Colton, M. and Hellinckx, W. (eds) (1993), *Child Care in the EC: A Country-specific Guide to Foster and Residential Care* (Aldershot: Arena).

Colton, M. and Vanstone, M. (1996), *Betrayal of Trust: Sexual Abuse by Men who Work with Children* (London: Free Association Books).

Colton, M. and Williams, M. (eds) (1997), *The World of Foster Care* (Aldershot: Arena).

Colton, M., Drury, C. and Williams, M. (1995a), *Children in Need* (Aldershot: Avebury).

Colton, M., Drury, C. and Williams, M. (1995b), *Staying Together: Supporting Families under the Children Act* (Aldershot: Arena).

Colton, M., Roberts, S. and Sanders, R. (1996), *An Analysis of Area Child Deaths and Other Cases of Public Concern in Wales: A Report for Welsh Office* (Swansea, Wales: University of Wales, Swansea).

Coombe, V. (1986), 'Black Children in Residential Care', in V. Coombe and A. Little (eds) (1986), *Race and Social Work: A Guide to Training* (London: Tavistock).

Corby, B. (1989), 'Alternative Theory Bases in Child Abuse', in W. Stainton Rogers, D. Hevey and E. Ash (eds) (1989), *Child Abuse and Neglect: Facing the Challenge* (Milton Keynes: Open University Press).

Corby, B. (1993), *Child Abuse: Towards a Knowledge Base* (Milton Keynes: Open University Press).

Coulborn Faller, K. (1988), *Child Sexual Abuse: An Interdisciplinary Manual for Diagnosis, Case Management and Treatment* (New York: Columbia University Press).

Crain, W. (1992), *Theories of Development: Concepts and Applications* (Englewood Cliffs, NJ: Prentice-Hall).

Cunningham, H. (1995), *Children and Childhood in Western Society since 1500* (Harlow, Essex: Longman).

Dalrymple, J. and Burke, B. (1995), *Anti-Oppressive Practice: Social Care and the Law* (Milton Keynes: Open University Press).

Davies, J., Berger, B. and Carlson, A. (1993), *The Family: Is it Just Another Lifestyle Choice?* (London: Institute of Economic Affairs).

Davies, M. (ed.) (1997), *The Blackwell Companion to Social Work* (Oxford: Blackwell).

Dennis, N. and Erdos, G. (1992), *Families without Fatherhood* (London: Institute of Economic Affairs).

Department of Health (1989a), *An Introduction to the Children Act 1989* (London: HMSO).

Department of Health (1989b), *The Care of Children: Principles and Practice in Regulations and Guidance* (London: HMSO).

Department of Health (1991a), *Child Abuse: A Study of Inquiry Reports* (London: HMSO).

Department of Health (1991b), *Children Act 1989, Guidance and Regulations,* Vol. 3: *Family Placements* (London: HMSO).

Department of Health (1991c), *Children Act 1989, Guidance and Regulations,* Vol. 4: *Residential Care* (London: HMSO).

Department of Health (1991d), *Patterns and Outcomes in Child Placement: Messages from Current Research and their Implications* (London: HMSO).

Department of Health (1992), *Choosing with Care* (The Warner Report) (London: HMSO).

Department of Health (1994), *The Children Act Report 1994* (London: HMSO).

Department of Health (1995), *Child Protection: Messages from Research* (London: HMSO).

Department of Health (1998), *The Quality Protects Programme: Transforming Children's Services,* LAC (98) 28.

Department of Health (1999), *The Quality Protects Programme: Transforming Children's Services,* 2000–01, LAC (99) 33.

Department of Health and Social Security (1974), *Report of the Committee of Inquiry into the Care and Supervision Provided in Relation to Maria Colwell* (London: HMSO).

Department of Health and Social Security (1982), *Child Abuse: A Study of Inquiry Reports* (London: HMSO).

Department of Health and Social Security (1985a), *Social Work Decisions in Child Care: Recent Research Findings and their Implications* (London: HMSO).

Department of Health and Social Security (1985b), *Review of Child Care Law* (London: HMSO).

Department of Health, Department for Education and Employment and Home Office (2000), *Framework for the Assessment of Children in Need and their Families* (London: HMSO).

Department of Health, Home Office, Department for Education and Employment (1999), *Working Together to Safeguard Children* (London: HMSO).

Dominelli, L. (1986), 'Father–Daughter Incest: Patriarchy's Shameful Secret', *Critical Social Policy*, 16: 8–22.

Dore, M. M. (1993), 'Family Preservation and Poor Families: When 'Home-building' is Not Enough', *Families in Society*, 74 (8): 545–54.

Driver, E. and Droisen, A. (1989), *Child Sexual Abuse: Feminist Perspectives* (Basingstoke: Macmillan – now Palgrave).

Dunn, J. (1988), *The Beginnings of Social Understanding* (Oxford: Blackwell).

Dunn, J. (1993), *Young Children's Close Relationships Beyond Attachment* (London: Sage).

Duquette, D. N. (1988), 'Legal Interventions', in K. Coulbourn Faller, *Child Sexual Abuse: An Interdisciplinary Manual for Diagnosis, Case Management and Treatment* (New York: Columbia University Press).

Durkin, K. (1996), *Developmental Social Psychology* (Oxford: Blackwell).

Eekelaar, J. and Dingwall, R. (1990), *The Reform of Child Care Law: A Practical Guide to the Children Act 1989* (London: Routledge).

Erikson, E. (1963), *Childhood and Society* (New York: Norton).

Evans, D. (1997), 'Demonstrating Competence in Social Work', in M. Davies (ed.) (1997), *The Blackwell Companion to Social Work* (Oxford: Blackwell).

Fahlberg, V. (1988), *Fitting the Pieces Together* (London: British Agencies for Adoption and Fostering (BAAF)).

Fahlberg, V. (1991), *A Child's Journey through Placement* (Indianapolis, IN: Perspectives Press).

Farmer, E. and Owen, M. (1995), *Child Protection Practice: Private Risks and Public Remedies – Decision Making, Intervention and Outcome in Child Protection Work* (London: HMSO).

Farmer, E. and Pollock, S. (1998), *Sexually Abused and Abusing Children* (Chichester: Wiley & Sons).

Feigelman, W. and Silverman, A. (1983), *Chosen Children: New Patterns of Adoptive Relationships* (New York: Praeger).

Finkelhor, D. (1984), *Child Sexual Abuse: New Theory and Research* (New York: Free Press).

Finkelhor, D. (ed.) (1986), *A Sourcebook on Child Sexual Abuse* (Newbury Park, CA: Sage).

Finkelhor, D. (1993), 'Epidemiological Factors in the Clinical Identification of Child Sexual Abuse', *Child Abuse and Neglect*, 17: 67–70.

Fisher, D., Marsh, P., Phillips, D. and Sainsbury, E. (1986), *Children In and Out of Care* (London: Batsford).

Fisher, R. and Ury, W. (1991), *Getting to Yes: Negotiating an Agreement without Giving In* (London: Business Books).

Fox Harding, L. (1991), *Perspectives in Child Care Policy* (Harlow: Longman).

Franklin, B. (ed.) (1995), *The Handbook of Children's Rights: Comparative Policy and Practice* (London: Routledge).

Fryer, G. E., Miyoshi, T. J. and Thomas, P. J. (1989), 'The Relationship of Child Protection Worker Attitudes to Attrition from the Field', *Child Abuse and Neglect*, 13 (3): 345–50.

Gambe, D., Gomes, J., Kapur, V., Rangel, M. and Stubbs, P. (1992), *Anti-Racist Social Work Education: Improving Practice with Children and Families – A Training Manual* (London: Central Council for Education and Training in Social Work (CCETSW)).

Gambrill, E. D. and Stein, T. J. (eds) (1993), *Controversial Issues in Child Welfare* (Boston: Allyn & Bacon).

Garbarino, J. and Gilliam, G. (1980), *Understanding Abusive Families* (Cambridge, MA: Lexington Books).

Garrett, P. M. (1999), 'Mapping Child-Care Social Work in the Final Years of the Twentieth Century: a Critical Response to the "Looking After Children" System', *British Journal of Social Work*, 29: 27–47.

Gelles, R. and Cornell, C. (1985), *Intimate Violence in Families* (Beverly Hills, CA: Sage).

Gelles, R. J. (1993), 'Family Reunification/Family Preservation: Are Children Really Being Protected?', *Journal of Interpersonal Violence*, 8 (4): 557–62.

Gibbons, J., Conroy, S. and Bell, C. (1995), *Operating the Child Protection System* (London: HMSO).

Giddens, A. (1989), *Sociology* (Cambridge: Polity Press).

Gil, D. G. (1978), 'Violence against Children', in C. M. Lee (ed.) (1978), *Child Abuse: A Reader and Sourcebook* (Milton Keynes: Open University Press).

Goldstein, J., Freud, A. and Solnit, A. (1973), *Beyond the Best Interests of the Child* (New York: Free Press).

Goldstein, J., Freud, A. and Solnit, A. (1979), *Before the Best Interests of the Child* (New York: Free Press).

Gregg, P. (1973), *A Social and Economic History of Britain, 1760–1972* (London: Harrap).

Griffiths Report (1988), *Community Care: Agenda for Action* (London: HMSO).

Hallett, C. (1995), *Inter-agency Coordination in Child Protection* (London: HMSO).

Hallett, C. and Birchall, E. (1992), *Coordination and Child Protection: A Review of the Literature* (London: HMSO).

Hallett, C. and Stevenson, O. (1980), *Aspects of Interprofessional Co-operation* (London: Allen & Unwin).

Hardyment, C. (1983), *Dream Babies* (Oxford: Oxford University Press).

Harlow, H. (1958), 'The Nature of Love', *American Journal of Psychology*, 13: 673–85.

Heath, A., Colton, M. and Aldgate, J. (1989), 'Educational Progress of Children In and Out of Care', *British Journal of Social Work*, 19 (6): 447–60.

Heath, A., Colton, M. and Aldgate, J. (1994), 'Failure to Escape: a Longitudinal Study of Foster Children's Educational Attainment', *British Journal of Social Work*.

Hendrick, H. (1994), *Child Welfare: England, 1872–1989* (London: Routledge).

Hetherington, R., Cooper, A., Smith, P. and Wilford, G. (1997), *Protecting Children: Messages from Europe* (Lyme Regis, Dorset: Russell House).

Hill, M. and Aldgate, J. (1996), 'The Children Act 1989 and Recent Developments in Research', in M. Hill and J. Aldgate (eds) (1996), *Child Welfare Services: Developments in Law, Policy, Practice and Research* (London: Jessica Kingsley).

Hills, J. (1995), *Joseph Rowntree Foundation Inquiry into Income and Wealth*, Vol. 2: *A Summary of the Evidence* (York: Joseph Rowntree Foundation).

Hoefnagels, C. and Mudde, A. (2000), 'Mass Media and Disclosures of Child Abuse in the Perspective of Secondary Prevention: Putting Ideas into Practice', *Child Abuse and Neglect*, 24 (8): 1091–101.

Holman, B. (1988), *Putting Families First: Prevention and Child Care – A Study of Prevention by Statutory and Voluntary Agencies* (Basingstoke: Macmillan – now Palgrave).

Home Office, Department of Health, Department of Education and Science and Welsh Office (1991), *Working Together under the Children Act 1989: A Guide to Arrangements for Inter-Agency Co-operation for the Protection of Children from Abuse* (London: HMSO).

House of Commons (1984), *Second Report from the Social Services Committee, Session 1983–84, Children in Care* (London: HMSO).

House of Commons (1987), *The Law on Child Care and Family Services* (London: HMSO).

House of Commons (2000), *Report of the Tribunal of Inquiry into the Abuse of Children in Care in the Former County Council Areas of Gwynedd and Clwyd since 1974* (London: HMSO).

Howe, D., Brandon, M., Hinings, D. and Schofield, G. (1999), *Attachment Theory, Child Maltreatment and Family Support* (Basingstoke: Macmillan – now Palgrave).

Howe, E. (1992), *The Quality of Care* (London: Local Government Management Board).

Jackson, S. (1998), 'Looking After Children: A New Approach or Just an Exercise in Form Filling? A Response to Knight and Caveney', *British Journal of Social Work*, 28: 45–56.

James, M. (1986), 'Finding and Working with Families of Caribbean Origin', in V. Coombe and A. Little (eds), *Race and Social Work: A Guide to Training* (London: Tavistock).

Janssens, J. M. A. M. and Kemper, A. A. M. (1996), 'Effects of Video Home Training on Parental Communication and a Child's Behavioural Problems', *International Journal of Child and Family Welfare*, 96 (2): 137–48.

Jenks, C. (ed.) (1982), *The Sociology of Childhood: Essential Readings* (London: Batsford).

Jones, D., Pickett, J., Oates, M. and Barbor, P. (1982) *Understanding Child Abuse* (Basingstoke: Macmillan – now Palgrave).

Jones, G. (1995), *Leaving Home* (Milton Keynes: Open University Press).

Jones, H., Clark, R., Kufeldt, K. and Norman, M. (1998), 'Looking after Children: Assessing Outcomes in Child Care – the Experience of Implementation', *Children and Society*, 12: 212–22.

Jones, L. (1993), 'Decision-making in Child Welfare: a Critical Review of the Literature', *Child and Adolescent Social Work Journal*, 10 (3): 241–62.

Jordan, B. (1997), 'Social Work and Society', in M. Davies (ed.) (1997), *The Blackwell Companion to Social Work* (Oxford: Blackwell).

Junger-Tas, J., Terlouw, G-J. and Klein, M. W. (eds) (1994), *Delinquent Behaviour among Young People in the Western World: First Results of the International Self-Report Delinquency Study* (Amsterdam: Kugler Publications).

Kellmer Pringle, M. (1975), *The Needs of Children* (London: Hutchinson Educational).

Kelly, G. and Pinkerton, J. (1996), 'The Children (Northern Ireland) Order 1995: Prospects for Progress?', in M. Hill and J. Aldgate (eds) (1996), *Child Welfare Services* (London: Jessica Kingsley).

Kempe, C. H. and Helfer, R. E. (eds) (1968), *The Battered Child* (Chicago: University of Chicago Press).

Kempe, R. S. and Kempe, C. H. (1978), *Child Abuse* (Milton Keynes: Open University Press).

Kenward, H. and Hevey, D. (1989), 'The Effects of Physical Abuse and Neglect', in W. Stainton Rogers, D. Hevey and E. Ash (eds) (1989), *Child Abuse and Neglect: Facing the Challenge* (Milton Keynes: Open University Press).

Kessen, W. (1993), 'Darwin and the Beginnings of Child Psychology', in M. Gauvain and M. Cole (eds), *Readings on the Development of Children* (Oxford: Scientific Americana Books/W. H. Freeman).

Kirschenbaum, H. and Henderson, V. (1990), *The Carl Rogers Reader* (London: Constable).

Knight, T. and Caveney, S. (1998), 'Assessment and Action Records: Will they Promote Good Parenting?', *British Journal of Social Work*, 28 (1): 29–43.

Kohlberg, L. (1981), *Essays on Moral Development* (New York: Harper & Row).

La Fontaine, J. (1990), *Child Sexual Abuse* (Cambridge: Polity Press).

Laird, J. (1979), 'An Ecological Approach to Child Welfare: Issues of Family Identity and Continuity', in C. Germain (ed.), *Social Work Practice: People and Environments* (pp. 174–209) (New York: Columbia University Press).

Lamb, M., Gaensbauer, T., Malkin, C. and Schultz, L. (1985), 'The Effects of Child Maltreatment on Security of Infant–Adult Attachment', *Infant Behavior and Development*, 8 (1): 35–45.

Lee, M. and O'Brien, A. (1995), *The Game's Up: Redefining Child Prostitution* (London: The Children's Society).

Levy, A. and Kahan, B. (1991), *The Pindown Experience and the Protection of Children: The Report of the Staffordshire Child Care Inquiry 1990* (Staffordshire County Council).

Lloyd, S. (1997), 'Sexuality and Sexual Relations', in M. Davies (ed.) (1997), *The Blackwell Companion to Social Work* (Oxford: Blackwell).

London Borough of Brent (1985), *A Child in Trust: Report on the Panel of Inquiry Investigating the Circumstances Surrounding the Death of Jasmine Beckford* (London Borough of Brent).

London Borough of Greenwich (1987), *A Child in Mind: Protection of Children in a Responsible Society: Report of the Commission of Inquiry into the Circumstances Surrounding the Death of Kimberley Carlile* (London Borough of Greenwich).

London Borough of Lambeth (1987), *Whose Child? The Report of the Panel Appointed to Inquire into the Death of Tyra Henry* (London Borough of Lambeth).

Lyon, C. and Parton, N. (1995), 'Children's Rights and the Children Act 1989', in B. Franklin (ed.) (1995), *The Handbook of Children's Rights: Comparative Policy and Practice* (London: Routledge).

Macaskill, C. (1991), *Adopting or Fostering a Sexually Abused Child* (London: Batsford).

Maluccio, A., Pine, B. and Warsh, R. (1994), 'Protecting Children by Preserving their Families', *Children and Youth Services Review*, 16 (5/6): 295–307.

Marsh, P. (1999), 'Leaving Care and Extended Families', *Adoption and Fostering*, 22 (4): 6–14.

Marshall, N. L. and Barnett, R. C. (1993), 'Variations in Job Strain across Nursing and Social Work Specialities', *Journal of Community and Applied Social Psychology*, 3: 261–71.

Marshall, W. and Barbaree, H. (1990), 'An Integrated Theory of the Etiology of Sexual Offending', in W. Marshall, D. Laws and H. Barbaree (eds) (1990), *Handbook of Sexual Assault* (London: Plenum Press).

Maslow, A. (1943), 'A Dynamic Theory of Human Motivation', *Psychological Review*, 50: 370–96.

Maslow, A. (1973), *The Further Reaches of Human Nature* (Harmondsworth: Penguin).

Mayer, J. and Timms, N. (1970), *The Client Speaks* (London: Routledge and Kegan Paul).

McCauley, R. (1977), *Child Behaviour Problems* (Basingstoke: Macmillan – now Palgrave).

McGee, R. A. (1989), 'Burnout and Professional Decision Making: an Analogue Study', *Journal of Counselling Psychology*, 36: 345–51.

Miller, A. (1992), *Breaking Down the Wall of Silence to Join the Waiting Child* (London: Virago).

Millham, S., Bullock, R., Hosie, K. and Haak, M. (1986), *Lost in Care: The Problems of Maintaining Links between Children in Care and their Families* (Aldershot: Gower).

Minuchin, S. (1974), *Families and Family Therapy* (Cambridge, MA: Harvard University Press).

Morrison, T. (1990), 'The Emotional Effects of Child Protection Work on the Worker', *Practice*, 4 (4): 253–71.

Mrazek, P. B. and Bentovim, A. (1981), 'Incest and the Dysfunctional Family System', in P. B. Mrazek and C. H. Kempe (eds) (1981), *Sexually Abused Children and their Families* (New York: Pergamon Press).

Murray, C. (1990), *The Emerging British Underclass* (London: Institute of Economic Affairs, Health and Welfare Unit).

Murray, C. (ed.) (1994), *Underclass: The Crisis Deepens* (London: Institute of Economic Affairs Health and Welfare Unit).

National Commission of Inquiry into the Prevention of Child Abuse (1996), *Childhood Matters* (London: HMSO).

National Institute of Social Work (1982), *Social Workers: Their Roles and Tasks* (London: Bedford Square Press).

NCH (1994), *The Hidden Victims: Children and Domestic Violence* (London: NCH).

NCH Action For Children (1996), *Factfile 96/97* (London: NCH, formerly known as NCH Action For Children).

Nelson, B. J. (1984), *Making an Issue of Child Abuse: Political Agenda Setting* (Chicago: University of Chicago Press).

Newell, P. (1989), *Children are People Too: The Case Against Physical Punishment* (London: Bedford Square Press).

Newell, P. (1991), *The UN Convention and Children's Rights in the UK* (London: National Children's Bureau).

Newson, J. and Newson, E. (1974), 'Cultural Aspects of Childrearing in the English-speaking World', in M. Richards (ed.), *The Integration of the Child into a Social World* (London: Cambridge University Press).

Open University (1990), *The Children Act: Putting it into Practice* (Milton Keynes: Open University Press).

Owusu-Bempah, J. (1997), 'Race', in M. Davies (ed.) (1997), *The Blackwell Companion to Social Work* (Oxford: Blackwell).

Packman, J. (1975), *The Child's Generation* (London: Blackwell and Robertson).

Packman, J. and Jordan, B. (1991), 'The Children Act: Looking Forward, Looking Back', *British Journal of Social Work*, 21 (4).

Parker, R. (ed.) (1980), *Caring for Separated Children* (Basingstoke: Macmillan – now Palgrave).

Parker, R., Ward, H., Jackson, S., Aldgate, J. and Wedge, P. (1991), *Looking After Children: Assessing Outcome in Child Care* (London: HMSO).

Parry, J. K. (1989), 'Mutual Support Groups: Do they Relieve Staff Stress?' *The Jewish Social Work Forum*, 25: 43–9.

Parten, M. (1932), 'Social Participation among Preschool Children', *Journal of Abnormal and Social Psychology*, 27: 243–69.

Parton, C. and Parton, N. (1989), 'Child Protection: the Law and Dangerousness', in O. Stevenson (ed.) (1989), *Child Abuse: Public Policy and Professional Practice* (Hemel Hempstead: Harvester Wheatsheaf).

Parton, N. (1985), *The Politics of Child Abuse* (Basingstoke: Macmillan – now Palgrave).

Parton, N. (1991), *Governing the Family: Child Care, Child Protection and the State* (London: Macmillan).

Pence, A. (1992), 'Quality Care: Thoughts on R/rulers', paper given at *Workshop on Defining and Assessing Quality*, Seville, 9–12 September.

Petrie, P., Poland, G. and Wayne, S. (1995), *After School and in the Holidays: A Survey of Provision* (London: Thomas Coram Research Unit).

Phillipson, J. (1992), *Practising Equality: Women, Men and Social Work* (London: Central Council for Education and Training in Social Work (CCETSW)).

Pine, B., Krieger, R. and Maluccio, A. (eds) (1993), *Together Again: Family Reunification in Foster Care* (Washington, DC: Child Welfare League of America).

Pollock, L. (1993), *Forgotten Children: Parent–Child Relations from 1500 to 1900* (Cambridge: Cambridge University Press).

Reder, P., Duncan, S. and Gray, M. (1993), *Beyond Blame: Child Abuse Tragedies Revisited* (London and New York: Routledge).

Reigate, N. (1996), 'Networking', in M. Davies (ed.) (1996), *The Blackwell Companion to Social Work* (Oxford: Blackwell).

Report of the Committee on Children and Young Persons (Ingleby Committee) (1960), Cmnd 1191 (London: HMSO).

Report of the Committee on Local Authority and Allied Services (Seebohm Committee) (1968), Cmnd 3703 (London: HMSO).

Robinson, C., Weston, C. and Minkes, J. (1995), *Making Progress: Change and Development in Services to Disabled Children under the Children Act 1989* (Bristol: Norah Fry Research Centre).

Rousseau, J. J. (1993; orig. 1762), *Emile* (London: J. M. Dent/Everyman Publications).

Rowe, J. and Lambert, L. (1973), *Children Who Wait* (London: Association of British Adoption and Fostering Agencies).

Rowe, J., Hundleby, M. and Garnett, L. (1989), *Child Care Now* (London: British Agencies for Fostering and Adoption (BAAF)).

Rush, F. (1980), *The Best Kept Secret* (Englewood Cliffs, NJ: Prentice-Hall).

Russell, D. E. H. (1984), *Sexual Exploitation: Rape, Child Sexual Abuse and Workplace Harassment* (California: Sage).

Rutter, M. (1972), *Maternal Deprivation Reassessed* (Harmondsworth: Penguin).

Ruxton, S. (1996), *Children in Europe* (London: NCH Action For Children).

Sampson, A. (1994), *Acts of Abuse: Sex Offenders and the Criminal Justice System* (London: Routledge).

Sanders, R. (1999), *The Management of Child Protection Services: Context and Change* (Aldershot: Arena).

Sanders, R. and Thomas, N. (1997), *Area Child Protection Committees* (Aldershot: Ashgate).

Sanders, R., Jackson, S. and Thomas, N. (1997), 'Degrees of Involvement: the Interaction of Focus and Commitment in Area Child Protection Committees', *British Journal of Social Work*, 27: 871–92.

Schaffer, H. R. and Emerson, P. E. (1964), 'The Development of Social Attachments in Infancy', *Monographs of the Society for Research in Child Development*, 29 (94).

Schorr, L. (1991), *Within Our Reach: Breaking the Cycle of Disadvantage* (New York: Doubleday/Anchor Press).

Smith, D. and Featherstone, T. (1991), 'Family Group Conferences – the Process', in *Family Decision Making* (Lower Hutt, New Zealand: Practitioners Publishing).

Smith, T. (1996), *Family Centres and Bringing Up Young Children* (London: Children's Society/HMSO).

Spake, A. (1994), 'The Little Boy who Didn't Have to Die', *McCall's* (November) pp. 142–51.

Spring, J. (1987), *Cry Hard and Swim: The Story of an Incest Survivor* (London: Sage).

Stainton Rogers, R. (1989), 'The Social Construction of Childhood' (Chapter 1, pp. 23–29), in W. Stainton Rogers, D. Hevey and E. Ash (eds), *Child Abuse and Neglect: Facing the Challenge* (London: Batsford/Open University Press).

Stainton Rogers, R. and Stainton Rogers, W. (1992), *Stories of Childhood: Shifting Agendas of Child Concern* (London: Harvester Wheatsheaf).

Stainton Rogers, W., Hevey, D. and Ash, E. (eds) (1989), *Child Abuse and Neglect: Facing the Challenge* (London: Batsford/Open University).

Stanley, J. and Goddard, C. (1993), 'The Effect of Child Abuse and Other Family Violence on the Child Protection Worker and Case Management', *Australian Social Work*, 46 (3): 3–10.

Statham, J. (1997), *Day Care Services for Children under Eight: An Evaluation of the Implementation of the Children Act in Wales* (London: Thomas Coram Research Unit).

Tatara, T. (1993), *Characteristics of Children in Substitute and Adoptive Care: A Statistical Summary of the VCIS National Child Welfare Database* (Washington, DC: American Public Welfare Association).

Thoburn, J. (1997), 'The Community Child Care Team', in M. Davies (ed.) (1996), *The Blackwell Companion to Social Work* (Oxford: Blackwell).

Thoburn, J., Lewis, A. and Shemmings, D. (1995), *Paternalism or Partnership? Family Involvement in the Child Protection Process* (London: HMSO).

Thoburn, J., Murdoch, A. and O'Brien, A. (1986), *Permanence in Child Care* (Oxford: Blackwell).

Thomas, M. and Pierson, J. (1995), *Dictionary of Social Work* (London: Collins Educational), cited in N. Thompson (1997), 'Anti-Discriminatory Practice', in M. Davies (ed.) (1997), *The Blackwell Companion to Social Work* (Oxford: Blackwell).

Thompson, N. (1997), 'Anti-Discriminatory Practice', in M. Davies (ed.) (1997), *The Blackwell Companion to Social Work* (Oxford: Blackwell).

Tisdall, K. (1996), 'From the Social Work (Scotland) Act 1968 to the Children (Scotland) Act 1995', in M. Hill and J. Aldgate (eds) (1996), *Child Welfare Services* (London: Jessica Kingsley).

Townsend, P. (1979), *Poverty in the United Kingdom* (London: Penguin).

Trawick-Smith, J. (1997), *Early Childhood Development: A Multicultural Perspective* (Englewood Cliffs, NJ: Merrill/Prentice-Hall).

Triseliotis, J. (1997), 'Foster Care and Adoption', in M. Davies (ed.) (1997), *The Blackwell Companion to Social Work* (Oxford: Blackwell).

Tunnard, J. and Ryan, M. (1991), 'What Does the Children Act Mean for Family Members?', *Children and Society*, 5 (1): 67–75.

Utting, W. (1991), *Children in the Public Care: A Review of Residential Care* (London: HMSO).

Utting, W. (1997), *People Like Us: The Report of the Review of the Safeguards for Children Living Away from Home* (London: HMSO).

van Pagee, R., Van Miltenberg, W. and Pasztor, E. (1991), 'The International Transfer of Foster Parents Selection and Preparation Technology: the Example of the Netherlands and the United States', *Child Welfare*, 70 (2): 219–27.

van IJzendoorn, M. and Kroonenberg, P. (1988), 'Cross-Cultural Patterns of Attachment: a Meta-analysis of the Strange Situation', *Child Development*, 59: 147–56.

Wagner, G. (1988), *Residential Care: A Positive Choice* (London: HMSO).

Walker, A. (1990), 'Blaming the Victims', in C. Murray (ed.) (1990), *The Emerging British Underclass* (London: Institute of Economic Affairs).

Ward, H. (1995), *Looking After Children: Research into Practice* (London: HMSO).

Waterhouse, L. (1997), 'Child Abuse', in M. Davies (ed.) (1997), *The Blackwell Companion to Social Work* (Oxford: Blackwell).

Watson, J. B. (1928), *Psychological Care of Infant and Child* (New York: Norton).

Weinstein, E. A. (1960), *The Self-Image of the Foster Child* (New York: Russell Sage Foundation).

Whittaker, J. (1996), 'Community-Based Prevention Programs: a Selective North American Perspective', *International Journal of Child and Family Welfare*, 96 (2): 114–26.

Wolmar, C. (2000), 'The Untold Story behind Child Abuse', *Guardian*, 16, February 2000, p. 18.

Woodhead, M. (1990), 'Psychology and the Cultural Construction of Children's Needs' (Chapter 3, pp. 60–77), in A. James, and A. Prout (eds), *Constructing and Reconstructing Childhood: Contemporary Issues in the Sociological Study of Childhood* (London: Falmer Press).

Woodhead, M. (1998), 'Quality in Early Childhood Programmes – a Contextually Appropriate Approach', *International Journal of Early Years Education*, 6 (1): 5–17.

Index